Tax Administration 2024

COMPARATIVE INFORMATION ON OECD AND OTHER ADVANCED AND EMERGING ECONOMIES

OECD
BETTER POLICIES FOR BETTER LIVES

This document, as well as any data and map included herein, are without prejudice to the status of or sovereignty over any territory, to the delimitation of international frontiers and boundaries and to the name of any territory, city or area.

The statistical data for Israel are supplied by and under the responsibility of the relevant Israeli authorities. The use of such data by the OECD is without prejudice to the status of the Golan Heights, East Jerusalem and Israeli settlements in the West Bank under the terms of international law.

Note by the Republic of Türkiye
The information in this document with reference to "Cyprus" relates to the southern part of the Island. There is no single authority representing both Turkish and Greek Cypriot people on the Island. Türkiye recognises the Turkish Republic of Northern Cyprus (TRNC). Until a lasting and equitable solution is found within the context of the United Nations, Türkiye shall preserve its position concerning the "Cyprus issue".

Note by all the European Union Member States of the OECD and the European Union
The Republic of Cyprus is recognised by all members of the United Nations with the exception of Türkiye. The information in this document relates to the area under the effective control of the Government of the Republic of Cyprus.

Please cite this publication as:
OECD (2024), *Tax Administration 2024: Comparative Information on OECD and other Advanced and Emerging Economies*, OECD Publishing, Paris, https://doi.org/10.1787/2d5fba9c-en.

ISBN 978-92-64-90088-2 (print)
ISBN 978-92-64-37185-9 (PDF)
ISBN 978-92-64-36069-3 (HTML)
ISBN 978-92-64-96384-9 (epub)

Tax Administration
ISSN 2308-7331 (print)
ISSN 2307-7727 (online)

Photo credits: Cover © Bruce Rolff/Shutterstock.com.

Corrigenda to OECD publications may be found at: https://www.oecd.org/en/publications/support/corrigenda.html.

Preface

The 2024 edition of the Tax Administration Series (TAS), like its predecessors, provides comparative information on advanced and emerging tax administrations globally and seeks to draw out some of the trends and challenges they face.

The purpose and value of the TAS, first published in 2004, is to assist administrations, governments, taxpayers and other stakeholders towards identifying improvements in the effectiveness of tax administration. This potential is unlocked through its data but also the more than one hundred examples of innovative initiatives and approaches implemented by tax administrations. I congratulate my fellow colleagues for the great work they are doing.

The past decade has seen significant changes in the operating models of tax administrations often driven through external factors such as the digitalisation of the wider economy, technological advancements, and the COVID-19 pandemic. This edition continues to observe the impacts of those developments. E-filing, e-payment, e-communication, the use of artificial intelligence and application programming interfaces have become mainstream in the past few years, and many administrations are now looking ahead and embarking on a wider digital transformation of their tax operations. Of course, we should not forget that as part of our journey we need to ensure that we provide accessible formats, multilingual support, and offline service options that can bridge gaps in communication and access, so that all citizens benefit from our services, including those with disabilities or those without internet access.

In addition, TAS 2024 also explores a variety of areas that have not been examined in such detail since 2019. A treasure trove of new data, the publication enables a closer look at tax administration operations, processes and arrangements covering not only the regular annual performance data but also information on compliance risk management, governance and human resource management, amongst other things.

I would like to express my appreciation to those involved in producing this engaging and informative report, and in particular Oliver Petzold as well as Paul Marsh and Fiona May of the OECD Secretariat. This edition of the TAS will continue to help us all understand more about the challenges that we face individually and collectively. Through this, not only can we consider what we might do in our own jurisdictions but also identify where tax administrations can collaborate to improve our services to taxpayers across the globe.

Bob Hamilton
Chair of the OECD Forum on Tax Administration
Commissioner of the Canada Revenue Agency

Foreword

Tax Administration 2024 is the twelfth edition of the OECD Centre for Tax Policy and Administration's comparative information series. First published in 2004, the primary purpose of the Tax Administration Series (TAS) is to share information that will facilitate analysis and dialogue on the design and administration of tax systems.

This edition of the TAS provides internationally comparative data on aspects of tax systems and their administration in 58 advanced and emerging economies. It includes performance-related data, ratios and trends up to the end of the 2022 fiscal year. For the first time since 2019, this edition also examines in more detail the administrative, operational and organisational practices of participating tax administrations.

The publication presents the results of the last four rounds of the International Survey on Revenue Administration (ISORA) that were launched between September 2020 and September 2023. The last survey iteration combined the annual and periodic parts of the ISORA survey, with the periodic part only being included every five years. The ISORA survey is a multi-organisation survey to collect information and data on tax administration. It is governed by four partner organisations: the Inter-American Center of Tax Administrations (CIAT), the International Monetary Fund (IMF), the Intra-European Organisation of Tax Administrations (IOTA) and the OECD. The Asian Development Bank (ADB) also participated in those ISORA surveys along with the four partner organisations.

To provide further insight into the ISORA data in certain places, TAS 2024 also uses data from the Inventory of Tax Technology Initiatives (ITTI). ITTI is an online database containing information on technology tools and digitalisation solutions implemented by tax administrations across the globe. It has been developed by the OECD's Forum on Tax Administration together with nine key partner organisations.

This report was approved by the Committee on Fiscal Affairs on 25 October 2024 and prepared for publication by the OECD Secretariat.

Acknowledgements

The OECD has produced the Tax Administration Series (TAS), its comparative information series on tax administration, since 2004. Since that time the publication has grown in terms of its coverage, influence and importance and is now widely recognised as an authoritative source of information on tax administration around the globe.

The 2024 Tax Administration publication presents the results of the third to sixth round of the International Survey on Revenue Administration (ISORA) which were launched between 2020 and 2023. It would not have been possible without the direct support and help of a large number of people, particularly the staff in the 58 tax administrations that provided data and jurisdiction examples, reviewed content and responded to feedback and questions on the data and text that form the basis of the publication.

The authors of the publication were Paul Marsh, Fiona May and Oliver Petzold all from the OECD's Forum on Tax Administration (FTA) Secretariat. Management and analysis of the ISORA data was undertaken by Oliver Petzold. The authors are thankful to Peter Green, Head of the FTA Secretariat, for his guidance and input during the drafting of this publication. They would also like to thank the work of the wider team at the FTA Secretariat, in particular Eunkyung Shin and Sonia Nicolas, and the OECD Centre for Tax Policy and Administration's Communications team.

This edition of the TAS also benefits from a chapter on how tax administrations are estimating tax gaps authored by Sun Jae Kim and Alla Sytnik both from the Canada Revenue Agency. They would like to thank the members of the FTA's Community of Interest on Tax Gaps for their input and valuable comments on this chapter.

Table of contents

FIGURES

TABLES

Reader's guide

Tax Administrations covered by the report

Tax Administration 2024 is the twelfth edition of the OECD Centre for Tax Policy and Administration's comparative Tax Administration Series (TAS). The primary purpose of the series, which commenced in 2004, is to share information that will facilitate dialogue among tax officials on important tax administration issues, and to identify opportunities to improve the design and administration of their systems.

This edition of the series provides internationally comparative data on various aspects of tax systems and their administration in 58 advanced and emerging economies. It covers 54 jurisdictions that are members of the OECD's Forum on Tax Administration (FTA). In addition, it includes information on the non-FTA jurisdictions that are members of the European Union as well as Morocco and Thailand (which increases the report's geographical coverage).

ISORA data gathering process and reporting

The publication presents the results of the last four rounds of the International Survey on Revenue Administration (ISORA) which were launched between September 2020 and September 2023. The ISORA survey is a multi-organisation international survey that collects national-level information and data on tax administration. The 2023 ISORA survey was completed by 166 jurisdictions.

The survey is governed by four partner organisations: the Inter-American Center of Tax Administrations (CIAT), the International Monetary Fund (IMF), the Intra-European Organisation of Tax Administrations (IOTA) and the OECD. Since the 2018 ISORA survey round, the Asian Development Bank (ADB) also participates in ISORA along with the four partner organisations.

The 2023 ISORA survey

The ISORA survey that was launched in September 2023, is the most comprehensive survey on tax administration since 2018. Following the completion of the 2018 ISORA survey, the ISORA partners engaged with participating administrations to gather feedback on the survey process, and they conducted a thorough review of the survey.

As a result of this process, the ISORA survey was split into parts:

1. ***An annual survey part***, collecting data mainly on the annual operational performance of tax administrations; and
2. ***A periodic survey part***, looking at the wider tax administration processes and arrangements which are less likely to change regularly, such as governance, human resource management and compliance risk management.

The 2023 ISORA survey combined both parts taking the first comprehensive look at tax administration in the past five years. The 2020, 2021 and 2022 ISORA surveys only contained the annual survey part. All survey iterations can be accessed via the IMF's Revenue Administration Fiscal Information Tool (RA-FIT; https://data.rafit.org/) under "Forms and Guides" in the section "Publications/Links".

The next comprehensive ISORA survey is expected to be conducted in 2028.

Survey management

The last four iterations of the ISORA survey collected data for fiscal years from 2018 to 2022. Survey information was gathered online using the RA-FIT tool. Participation was voluntary and 166 administrations completed the 2023 ISORA survey. Each partner organisation, and the ADB, supported participants by assisting them with the completion of the ISORA survey, based on an upfront agreed allocation key. The 58 administrations included in this publication corresponds to the group of administrations supported by the OECD.

While all data contained in the publication has been subject to a high-level review by the OECD, neither the OECD nor any other partner organisation formally validated the data. As a result, all data included in the publication should be considered as self-reported by the administrations concerned.

Publication of data

Starting with the data collected through the 2020 ISORA survey, all ISORA data is made available to the public on the RA-FIT data portal (https://data.rafit.org/). The data from the 2023 ISORA survey was made available in June 2024.

Historically, the OECD made all ISORA data for TAS participants also publicly available through the TAS and its data annex. This approach changes with the 2024 edition of the TAS. From now on, the TAS will not anymore have its own data annex. Instead, the TAS refers to the publicly available tables on the RA-FIT data portal. (For more information, see further below.)

As regards the other organisations, the ADB publishes jurisdiction-level ISORA data for its members. See, for example, its publication *A Comparative Analysis of Tax Administration in Asia and the Pacific: Seventh Edition* (Asian Development Bank, 2024[1]). The other ISORA partners, do the following:

- IMF publishes in aggregated form. See, for example, the IMF publication *ISORA 2018: Understanding Revenue Administration* (Crandall, Gavin and Masters, 2021[2]); and
- CIAT publishes selected data points. See, for example, the CIAT publication *Innovation, Digitalization and Technology Index (INDITEC): A tool for benchmarking Tax Administrations at the international level (Based on data from ISORA 2020 Survey)* (Díaz de Sarralde Miguez and Morán, 2022[3]).

Data comparability

TAS 2024 includes performance-related data, ratios and other information for the fiscal years from 2018 to 2022. The data for the fiscal years 2018 to 2021 data was collected through the 2020, 2021 and 2022 ISORA surveys and already included in previous editions of the TAS. However, several administrations updated some of their previously supplied data during the process of producing the 2024 edition of the TAS. For that reason, there might be some differences between this and previous editions of the TAS in figures and tables displaying 2018 to 2021 data.

In certain areas, TAS 2024 also uses data from the 2016 and 2018 ISORA rounds to show trends for the period between 2014 and 2022. However, over the past years a number of changes were made to ISORA questions to improve clarity and data quality. Therefore, care needs to be taken when comparing results from the different ISORA versions, and the wording of survey questions compared whenever relevant. The survey questions can be accessed on https://data.rafit.org/ under "Forms and Guides" in the section "Publications/Links".

Also, it should be noted that statistical data is often subject to revisions after publication. As a result, some data may not correspond to what has been published by administrations. For example, it may be that opening balances of a specific year (t) may not correspond to closing balances of the preceding year (t-1) that were published in earlier editions of this publication.

Even more care should be taken when comparing ISORA data with data gathered through pre-ISORA surveys, i.e. data included in the sixth and prior editions of the TAS. When the ISORA survey was initially created and at the request of survey participants, the four partner organisations made considerable effort to agree and document a range of words and terms used in the survey and their meaning. While this has improved data integrity and comparability between administrations, comparisons with pre-ISORA data may be limited as definitions may now exist for terms not previously defined, or in some instances, have changed.

Further, in relation to combined tax and customs administrations, it should be noted that the data in this publication refers to the tax administration activities of such administrations. The data may therefore not be directly comparable with key performance indicators published by them as these indicators may include both tax and customs related data.

Data from the Inventory of Tax Technology Initiatives

To complement the ISORA survey data, this edition of the TAS continues to draw on data from the Inventory of Tax Technology Initiatives (ITTI) which contains information on technology tools and digitalisation solutions implemented by tax administrations globally. ITTI has been put together with the assistance of the ISORA partners, the ADB, the African Tax Administration Forum, the Cercle de Reflexion et d'Echange des Dirigeants des Administrations Fiscale, the Commonwealth Association of Tax Administrators, the Pacific Islands Tax Administrators Association and the Study Group on Asia-Pacific Tax Administration and Research. (OECD et al., 2024[4])

The inventory data was collected in 2021 and 2022 through a global survey on digitalisation, and can offer further insight into the ISORA data in certain places. Therefore, where available, the TAS uses the ITTI data from 52 out of the 58 tax administrations that are covered in this report and that have completed the global survey on digitalisation.

The ITTI data is currently being updated and new data is expected to be available towards the end of 2024.

Publication structure

The tax administration series examines the fundamental elements of modern tax administration systems and uses data analysis and examples supplied by tax administrations to highlight key trends, recent innovations, and performance measures and indicators.

Structure

The main body of the publication is structured around eleven chapters: (i) an introduction followed by chapters on (ii) responsibilities and revenue collections; (iii) registration and identification; (iv) assessment; (v) services; (vi) compliance management; (vii) collection; (viii) disputes; (ix) governance; (x) budget and workforce, and a final chapter (xi) which takes a closer look at tax gap analysis.

The publication also contains two annexes:

- Annex A holds an overview of the ISORA data tables published on the RA-FIT data portal (https://data.rafit.org/).

  In previous editions, this annex replicated the ISORA data for the 58 tax administrations[1] covered in the TAS. Starting with TAS 2024, Annex A contains links to online tables that hold the annual and periodic ISORA data for fiscal years 2018 to 2022.

  The online tables show the data for the more than 175 jurisdictions that have completed at least one of the last four rounds of ISORA. They are grouped as follows:

  - The ***Annual Tables*** contain:
    - Six sets of tables with indicators derived from the data submitted via the ISORA survey (tables starting with "D"). The formulae and data points used for calculating the indicators are shown below each of these tables.
    - Thirteen sets of tables containing the raw ISORA survey data. Those are the tables starting with "A".
  - The ***Periodic Tables*** hold the data from the periodic part of the 2023 ISORA survey. Those tables start with "B" and they are grouped in seven table sets.
- Annex B has the details of the administrations that participated in this publication.

Tables and figures

The source notes below the tables and figures in the main body of the publication refer readers to the underlying ISORA data tables on the RA-FIT data portal. In some cases, they may refer to previous editions of the TAS or, where ITTI data is used, to the relevant MS Excel spreadsheets on ITTI.

The figures in the publication are also accompanied by hyperlinks (OECD StatLinks) that direct readers to corresponding MS Excel spreadsheets containing the underlying data. These links are stable and will remain unchanged over time.

Symbols and abbreviations that are used in the ISORA data tables are explained at the bottom of each table. The reader should note that where no data is shown for a specific jurisdiction in a table this is primarily due to the question not being applicable to a particular jurisdiction, or an opening question to a sub-section of the survey being answered in the negative and, therefore, the jurisdiction did not have to answer the follow-up questions.

Forum on Tax Administration

The FTA is a unique body bringing together tax commissioners and tax administration officials from over 50 OECD and non-OECD economies. The FTA is a forum through which tax administrators share knowledge, undertake research and develop new ideas to enhance tax administration around the world. Readers wishing to find out more about the FTA should go to: https://www.oecd.org/en/networks/oecd-forum-on-tax-administration.html. For more information on the OECD's work on tax administration, please visit: https://www.oecd.org/en/topics/tax-administration.html. (Both links accessed on 10 September 2024).

Caveat

Tax administrations operate in varied environments, and the way in which they each administer their taxation system differs in respect to their policy and legislative environment and their administrative practice and culture. As such, a standard approach to tax administration may be neither practical nor desirable in a particular instance. Therefore, this report and the observations it makes need to be interpreted with this in mind. Care should be taken when considering a jurisdiction's practices to fully appreciate the complex factors that have shaped a particular approach. Similarly, regard needs to be had to the distinct challenges and priorities each administration is managing.

Notes

[1] For Japan, given that it publishes its currency figures in millions the currency figures included in tables have had added a suffix of "000" in order to fit the survey requirements that currency figures needed to be provided in thousands. For Switzerland, in the context of the ISORA survey the term "tax administration" refers to the Swiss Federal Tax Administration. All duties performed by the Swiss cantonal or communal tax administrations are not attributed to the Federal Tax Administration and are therefore not included. This concerns in particular PIT and CIT, where the Federal Tax Administration merely performs a supervisory function. If a service is indicated as not performed by the "tax administration", this respective service may be rendered by the Swiss cantonal and/or communal tax administrations.

References

Asian Development Bank (2024), *A Comparative Analysis of Tax Administration in Asia and the Pacific: Seventh Edition*, Asian Development Bank, Manila, https://doi.org/10.22617/TCS240003-2. [1]

Crandall, W., E. Gavin and A. Masters (2021), *ISORA 2018: Understanding Revenue Administration*, International Monetary Fund, Washington, DC, https://doi.org/10.5089/9781513592930.087. [2]

Díaz de Sarralde Miguez, S. and D. Morán (2022), *Innovation, Digitalization and Technology Index (INDITEC): A tool for benchmarking Tax Administrations at the international level (Based on data from ISORA 2020 Survey)*, Inter-American Center of Tax Administrations (CIAT), Panama City, http://www.ciat.org/Biblioteca/DocumentosdeTrabajo/2022/WP-02-22-Sarralde-Moran.pdf (accessed on 10 September 2024). [3]

OECD et al. (2024), *Inventory of Tax Technology Initiatives*, https://web-archive.oecd.org/tax/forum-on-tax-administration/tax-technology-tools-and-digital-solutions/index.htm (accessed on 10 September 2024). [4]

Abbreviations and acronyms

ADB	Asian Development Bank
AEAT	Agencia Estatal de Administración Tributaria (Spain)
AI	Artificial Intelligence
ANGIE	Automated Network and Grouping Identification Engine
APA	Advance Pricing Agreement
API	Application Programming Interface
ATO	Australian Taxation Office
AUD	Australian Dollar
BAR	Board of Advance Rulings (India)
BAS	Business Activity Statement
BEPS	Base Erosion and Profit Shifting
CIAT	Inter-American Center of Tax Administrations
CIN	National Identity Card (Brazil)
CIT	Corporate Income Tax
COI	Community of Interest
COTS	Commercial-Off-The-Shelf
CoR	Certificate of Residence
CPFB	Central Provident Fund Board (Singapore)
CPC	Central Processing Centre
CRA	Canada Revenue Agency
CRS	Common Reporting Standard
CTC	Child Tax Credit
CVWMS	Collections Verification Workload Management System
DAC	Digital Access Code
DCE	Detection Controlled Estimation
DEPT	Digital Ecosystem and Partnership Team
DGFiP	General Directorate of Public Finances (France)

DID	Distributed Identifiers
DSP	Digital Service Provider
DTC	Disability Tax Credit
EITC	Earned Income Tax Credit
EU	European Union
EUR	Euro
FATCA	Foreign Account Tax Compliance Act
FAQs	Frequently Asked Questions
FSM	Foreign Source Matching
FTA	Forum on Tax Administration
FTE	Full Time Equivalent
GBP	Great Britain Pound
GDP	Gross Domestic Product
GST	Goods and Service Tax
GSTC	General Secretariat of Tax Committees (Saudi Arabia)
HMRC	HM Revenue and Customs (United Kingdom)
HNWI	High Net Wealth Individual
HR	Human Resources
HRR	High-Risk Refund
ICAP	International Compliance Assurance Programme
ICT	Information and Communication Technology
IMF	International Monetary Fund
IOTA	Intra-European Organisation of Tax Administrations
IRS	Internal Revenue Service (United States)
IRAS	Inland Revenue Authority of Singapore
ISORA	International Survey on Revenue Administration
ITR	Income Tax Return
ITTI	Inventory of Tax Technology Initiatives
KSA	Kingdom of Saudi Arabia
LTO/P	Large Taxpayer Office/Programme
MAP	Mutual Agreement Procedure
MNE	Multinational Enterprise
MOF	Ministry of Finance
MOM	Ministry of Manpower (Singapore)
MP	Medical Practicioner

MTF	Missing Trader Fraud
MTIC	Missing Trader Intra Community
NRA	National Revenue Agency (Bulgaria)
NTA	National Tax Agency (Japan)
NTCA	National Tax and Customs Administration (Hungary)
NTS	National Tax Service (Korea)
OCR	Optical Character Recognition
OECD	Organisation for Economic Co-operation and Development
OSP	One-Stop Payroll
OTP	One-Time Password
PAC	Payment Arrangement Calculator
PAYE	Pay-As-You-Earn
PAYGW	Pay As You Go Withholding
PIT	Personal Income Tax
RA-FIT	Revenue Administration Fiscal Information Tool
RFB	Receita Federal do Brasil
RPA	Robotic Process Automation
SDZ	Secure Drop Zone
SII	Servicio de Impuestos Internos (Chile)
SMS	Short Message Service
SPF	Stochastic Production Frontier
SSC	Social Security Contribution
SSTTP	Self-Serve Time to Pay
STA	State Taxation Administration (People’s Republic of China)
STA	Swedish Tax Administration
STI	State Tax Inspectorate (Lithuania)
STP	Single Touch Payroll
TAS	Tax Administration Series
TAS	Taxpayer Advocate Service (United States)
TF	Task Force
TFTC	Task Force on Tax Crimes and Other Crimes
TY	Tax Year
UHT	Underused Housing Tax
UK	United Kingdom
US	Unite States

VAT	Value Added Tax
VITARA	Virtual Training to Advance Revenue Administration
WHT	Withholding Tax
ZATCA	Zakat, Tax and Customs Authority (Saudi Arabia)

Executive summary

Tax Administration 2024 is the twelfth edition of the OECD's comparative information series on tax administration. Containing a wealth of data and other information, it is intended to be used by tax administration analysts allowing them to understand the design and administration of tax systems in other jurisdictions and to draw cross-border comparisons. While primarily aimed at analysts, it can also be a useful tool for senior tax administration managers or officials in ministries of finance when considering changes in tax system administration.

Using the data from the International Survey on Revenue Administration (ISORA), the 2024 edition of the Tax Administration Series (TAS) takes a closer look at national-level tax administrations in 58 jurisdictions, including performance-related data, ratios and trends up to the end of the 2022 fiscal year.

Broad tax administration developments continue to evolve

Past editions of the TAS have commented on the impact of a constantly changing environment on tax administration. These changes, driven by both internal as well as external factors such as the digitalisation of the wider economy, technological advancements, and the COVID-19 pandemic, are the key reasons behind tax administrations adapting their operating models. Some of these changes can take many years to implement, and the incremental progress that has been reflected in the previous editions of the TAS continues to be observed in this 2024 edition.

Tax administrations have increased and maintained their efficiency and effectiveness, in particular by looking at the opportunities to take more proactive approaches to influencing taxpayer compliance. This has frequently been driven by the increased use of technology and in response to the evolving expectations and needs of taxpayers. For example, tax administrations were rapid adopters of e-administration, enabling the online filing of tax returns as well as online payments and the full or partial prefilling of tax returns. This is evident when looking at the evolution of e-filing rates, which have increased significantly – between 17 and 23 percentage points – across the three main tax types since 2014, while e-payment rates have increased around 10 percentage points since 2018 and are now at about 90%.

Similarly, tax administrations have employed technological innovations for years now, and the number of administrations that are using virtual assistants, artificial intelligence and application programming interfaces continues to increase. For example, among those administrations covered by this publication, the uptake in the use of virtual assistants and artificial intelligence has almost doubled since 2018.

Tax Administration 2024 provides new insights and perspectives

While TAS 2024 illustrates that the broad tax administration developments continue to evolve, it also provides some unique insights into tax administration processes that have not been examined in such detail since the publication of the eighth edition in 2019.

This is due to the results of the 2023 ISORA survey which has proven to be a treasure of tax administration data as it was the most comprehensive international survey on tax administration since 2018. The survey results enable users to take a closer look at tax administration operations, processes and arrangements covering not only the regular annual performance data but also information as to how tax administrations:

- ***Are setup and the governance arrangements put in place:*** Tax administrations are subject to a range of checks and balances to ensure transparency in their operations and proper accountability for their overall management of the tax system. With the new data included in TAS 2024 it becomes apparent that tax administrations are subject to robust oversight and control, and they also prepare a significant number of strategic and operational documents. There may, though, be room for more transparency which may help further enhancing community confidence and trust in tax administration as not all of the administrations that prepare the strategic and operational documents also make them available to the public.
- ***Identify and meet taxpayer service preferences:*** Taxpayer contact volumes are very large scale. Tax administrations reported more than 3.5 billion incoming contacts via online taxpayer accounts, and there are more than 300 million incoming telephone contacts in addition to tens of millions of in-person visits, letters and emails. Meeting taxpayer preferences regarding contact and service channels is therefore an important aspect of tax administration work. TAS 2024 provides valuable insights into how they approach this issue by looking at the use of taxpayer satisfaction surveys, the existence of service delivery standards, the type of online services provided, as well as the availability of educational and business support initiatives.
- ***Manage compliance risk:*** Assessing the accuracy and completeness of taxpayer reported information is critical in ensuring the integrity of the tax system. While this often happens through audits, there is an increasing use of automated electronic checks, validations and cross-matching of taxpayer information. Tax administrations are also adapting their approaches to compliance risk management with increased availability of data and the use of new data science techniques. TAS 2024 examines in detail how tax administrations are organising their processes in this area. It does so by looking at tax administrations' approaches towards understanding and managing compliance risks, and some of the steps taken by administrations as regards preventing and addressing non-compliance.
- ***Approach debt collection***: The total amount of outstanding arrears at the end of fiscal year 2022 is large, in the region of EUR 2.7 trillion, and around EUR 810 billion are considered collectable. It is therefore important that the legislative framework includes provisions that enable tax officials to undertake certain actions as regards the management of debt, the collection of amounts overdue and the enforcement of actions that can be taken against delinquent debtors. TAS 2024 utilizes the new ISORA data to examine the debt collection powers and their use by tax administrations.
- ***Utilize dispute prevention tools:*** Dispute prevention and resolution are essential to help preserve trust in the tax system. As disputes can be resource intensive, many administrations are looking at strategies to prevent them. While this may include the provision of guidance and advice to taxpayers, TAS 2024 shows that many administrations offer specific dispute prevention mechanisms, including the provision of public and private rulings, the use of Advance Pricing Arrangements, and the use of co-operative compliance programmes.
- ***Manage their workforce:*** Effective people management in tax administration involves comprehensive recruitment, training, and retention strategies. By investing in continuous professional development, tax administrations can keep their staff informed of the latest laws, technologies, and working practices and methods. Moreover, a focus on employee well-being and engagement can lead to higher job satisfaction, lower attrition rates, and a more dedicated workforce. Exploring the wealth of data from the 2023 ISORA survey, TAS 2024 takes a detailed look at all those areas that can help cultivate a positive organisational culture that values integrity, accountability, and excellence, all of which are crucial for a well-functioning tax system.

Tax gap estimations

Finally, this edition of the TAS contains a special feature which looks at tax gap estimations. Over the past few years, an increasing number of jurisdictions have started analysing tax gaps as findings of these estimates can provide insights on the size and nature of non-compliance, emerging trends, and the general health of the tax system. Acknowledging that tax gap estimations are complex, the special feature provides an overview of key tax gap concepts and examples of international experiences in tax gap research.

1 Introduction

This chapter provides an overview of the content of the 2024 edition of the OECD's Tax Administration Series.

How tax administrations respond to a constantly changing environment has been a recurring theme of previous editions of the OECD's Tax Administration Series (TAS). These changes have frequently been driven by external factors such as responding to the digitalisation of the wider economy, technological innovation and the COVID-19 pandemic. As a result, tax administrations have been changing their operating models to address these challenges and to find new ways of meeting changing taxpayer expectations for services; all while supporting a workforce that is adapting to new operating models, technologies, and workplace arrangements.

These changes can take many years to implement, and the incremental progress has been reflected in the previous editions of the TAS as it has in this 2024 edition. This edition also considers a number of additional aspects based on numerous additional data points collected in the 2023 International Survey on Revenue Administration (ISORA) which have not been collected since 2018. With this periodic data, only captured every five years, TAS 2024 provides, amongst other things, more insight into how tax administrations:

- Are setup and the governance arrangements put in place;
- Understand and manage compliance risk;
- Prevent and address non-compliance;
- Identify and meet taxpayer service preferences; and
- Manage their workforce.

Alongside the ISORA 2023 survey, the tax administrations covered in the TAS were also invited to provide examples of innovative practices that they are undertaking to help achieve their objectives. They have provided a rich source of over 100 examples, covering a wide range of topics. While these examples do not form a basis for comparison across tax administrations in the same way as the ISORA data points can in some circumstances, they do add more colour to the data, and give pointers to the strategic direction of travel of tax administrations globally.

Furthermore, this edition of the TAS continues to use information from the Inventory of Tax Technology Initiatives (ITTI) (OECD et al., 2024[1]). ITTI collects data on the digital transformation and digitalisation work of tax administrations from across the globe, and this rich source of data can provide further insight into the developments taking place in tax administration, facilitating mutual learning and collaboration.

Regardless of the context that a tax administration operates in, the core objective remains the same, namely the timely and accurate collection of tax revenues to fund public services. ***Chapter 2*** explores this topic in more detail, and provides statistics on the range and value of taxes that administrations are responsible for. In addition, it also comments on other key responsibilities that go beyond tax collection.

Central to achieving their objective is the work of tax administrations to ensure that all relevant taxpayers are registered and can be identified, as necessary, both quickly and securely. ***Chapter 3*** sets out the work of tax administrations in this field, including how they are increasingly involved in whole of government plans on digital identity.

Chapter 4 which looks at the tax assessment function, including all activities related to processing tax returns and payments. This chapter examines the use of e-channels for filing and paying, and outlines administrations' efforts to provide pre-filled returns, as well as the levels of on-time return filing and payment.

Providing services aligned with taxpayer expectations and supporting them in meeting their tax obligations, is essential for high levels of voluntary compliance. ***Chapter 5*** highlights the work of tax administrations in this space, and how they are encouraging "self-service" by taxpayers. This is part of a more fundamental change whereby tax administration becomes a seamless process, with non-compliance and administrative burdens increasingly "designed out".

Managing compliance is at the centre of ***Chapter 6*** which explores how tax administrations are identifying compliance risks, often through the use of data and new technology tools. This chapter further comments on the actions taken against those who fail to meet their obligations, looking at approaches used to prevent and address non-compliance before and after tax returns are filed.

Chapter 7 looks at how tax administrations manage the collection of outstanding taxes, and examines the features of a modern tax debt collection function. This chapter also provides an overview of available collection powers and how they are used.

However, inevitably, disputes between taxpayers and tax administrations do arise, and ***Chapter 8*** considers those processes, including how taxpayer rights are safeguarded, as well as the checks and balances on the exercising of tax powers by administrations.

Like all government bodies, tax administrations are ultimately accountable to the citizens they serve. Operating in a fair and impartial manner and being subject to checks and balances is necessary for a well-functioning tax system. ***Chapter 9*** looks at the framework within which this accountability operates, including the institutional arrangements and government structures in place.

Underpinning all this work are the resources that are available to tax administrations. ***Chapter 10*** provides information on the resources that tax administrations have at their disposal, and describes how tax administrations are managing their people.

Finally, ***Chapter 11*** of this edition of the TAS contains a special feature which explores in great detail how tax administrations are estimating tax gaps, including looking at key tax gap concepts and examples of international experiences in tax gap research.

References

OECD et al. (2024), *Inventory of Tax Technology Initiatives*, https://web-archive.oecd.org/tax/forum-on-tax-administration/tax-technology-tools-and-digital-solutions/index.htm (accessed on 10 September 2024). [1]

2 Responsibilities and collection

This chapter looks at the performance of tax administrations in their primary role of collecting taxes as well as other responsibilities given to them. It provides figures on the aggregate net tax revenues collected and other key information related to the activities of the administrations covered in this publication.

Introduction

The primary purpose of a tax administration is the collection of tax revenue to fund public services, but over time, many tax administrations have also been tasked with other responsibilities. Confidence in the proven ability of tax administrations to deliver complex administrative processes on a large scale undoubtedly plays a significant part in such decisions. This chapter provides an overview of all the responsibilities given to tax administrations and the net revenues collected. It also looks at the importance of withholding regimes to support overall compliance.

Responsibilities of tax administrations

With few exceptions, jurisdictions have unified the collection of direct and (most) indirect taxes within a single body for tax administration, and Table 2.1. summarises for which revenue types the tax administrations participating in this publication have responsibility. (More detail on institutional setups of tax administrations can be found in Chapter 9.)

Table 2.1. Revenue types for which the tax administration has responsibility, 2022

Percentage of administrations that have responsibility for the following revenue types

Personal income tax	Corporate income tax	Value added tax	Excises - domestic	Motor vehicle taxes	Real property taxes	Wealth taxes	Estate, inheritance, gift and other taxes	Other taxes on good and services	Social security contributions	Customs
98.3	100.0	94.8	63.8	46.6	44.8	24.1	48.3	55.2	39.7	44.8

Source: CIAT, IOTA, IMF, OECD, International Survey on Revenue Administration, Tables A.1 Revenue types for which the administration has responsibility: Income tax and taxes on goods and services, A.2 Revenue types for which the administration has responsibility: Other taxes, A.3 Revenue types for which the administration has responsibility: Other taxes (continued), SSC and non-tax revenue, A.4 Employer withholding taxes and combined tax and customs administrations, https://data.rafit.org/regular.aspx?key=74180893 (accessed on 10 September 2024).

Roles in addition to revenue collection

In addition to the traditional tax roles, many governments have given tax administrations other areas of responsibility (including shared responsibility in some areas). While some of these additional roles are relatively closely aligned to the core work of tax administration, some administrations report that they are being tasked with managing wider programmes and activity.

Table 2.2. illustrates some of the roles that tax administrations have in addition to revenue collection. The most common are:

- Administration of property valuation functions for other parts of government that, for some jurisdictions, is also linked to the administration of real property taxes;
- Collection of revenues from lotteries, gambling, gaming and casinos;
- Payment of benefits under various social or welfare programmes, some of which are integrated with elements of the tax system; and
- Management of government's retirement saving plans.

Some of these roles entail use of the tax legislation framework of the jurisdiction, as well as the administrative process of the tax administration. Typically, these may be to provide economic benefits to taxpayers (e.g. welfare-type benefits) or to collect loans or debts owing to government (e.g. student loans or child support). In other situations, the role/ function is less directly related to the tax system, for example oversight of certain gambling activities or population registries.

Table 2.2. Tax administration roles in addition to revenue collection, 2022

Percentage of administrations that have responsibility for the following roles

Welfare benefits	Child support	Property valuation	Student loans	Population register	Retirement savings	Lotteries, gambling, gaming, casinos	Maintaining government's property register	Motor vehicle register
13.8	8.6	27.6	8.6	5.2	12.1	27.6	6.9	1.7

Source: CIAT, IOTA, IMF, OECD, International Survey on Revenue Administration, Table B.2 Roles in addition to revenue collection, https://data.rafit.org/regular.aspx?key=74180913 (accessed on 10 September 2024).

An expansion of responsibilities, while it can bring useful economies of scale and scope, can also potentially increase risks to the core task of raising the tax revenue needed to fund public services and public goods. It therefore requires strong governance, risk management and appropriate resourcing.

Box 2.1. Examples – Wider roles of tax administrations

Brazil – Sinter Programme: National system for territorial information management

The Sinter Programme is a public management system administered by the Brazilian Federal Revenue Service (RFB), integrating geospatial and fiscal data of urban and rural properties. It also includes legal data produced by notaries and land registries, as in Brazil the ownership of property is only acquired through the registration of the deed at the real estate registry office.

It was created to meet the Brazilian state's need for reliable and comprehensive information on urban and rural real estate. This information was fragmented in thousands of systems distributed across the structures of the Federal Government, the states, the Federal District, municipalities and land registries offices.

This marks the beginning of the Brazilian Real State Cadastre (CIB) - a unique nationwide identifier code - assigned to properties that have geospatial information when the data is integrated into the system.

Given that Sinter uses geo-referenced data to correctly locate the properties registered with it, it has produced the following benefits:

- Improved business environment;
- Information about land regularisation efforts and mapping areas of deforestation and illegal fires hotspots in the Amazon rainforest, indigenous peoples and other traditional communities.
- Assistance in combating land grabbing, money laundering, tax evasion and mineral smuggling;
- Greater legal certainty for the parties involved in a negotiation regarding properties with a georeferenced CIB registration code; and
- Timely availability of reliable and comprehensive information on real estate for strategic and effective planning of public policies.

Italy – Real estate digital services

The Italian Revenue Agency has taken steps to improve its real estate services, to improve the transparency of the market and improve digital services to taxpayers.

On the Agency's website, it is possible to authenticate the prices declared in real estate sales made since 2019, along with the main characteristics of the properties sold. By browsing the national map and selecting the relevant filter (time period, size, location etc), the real estate units that have been bought and sold will be displayed, along with the price they were bought and sold for.

There is also the OMI mobile application, which provides details on the average sale and rental prices for different types of properties, and is updated every six months by the Real Estate Market Observatory of the Italian Revenue Agency. The interface allows the user to explore properties of interest through an interactive map, and get preliminary quotations on how much they cost.

Korea – Tax-Benefit Management Bureau

To support its more vulnerable citizens, Korea is actively promoting the establishment of a cross-government welfare infrastructure. To align with this trend, the National Tax Service (NTS) has reinforced its tax benefit management functions by establishing the Tax-Benefit Management Bureau.

The Tax-Benefit Management Bureau is responsible for the operation of both the Earned Income Tax Credit (EITC) and Child Tax Credit (CTC) programmes, designed to support low-income households. The EITC focuses on encouraging low-income earners' participation in the labour market through work-linked income, whereas the CTC aims to support childcare expenses. In addition, this Bureau manages a "Real-time Income Identification Programme," which collects income information of workers in need of welfare benefits in a timely manner and provides it to the relevant agencies.

By 2023, the number of households receiving EITC and CTC increased eightfold, benefiting one in five households nationwide. Recent enhancements include leveraging IT technology to facilitate EITC and CTC applications for the elderly and people with disabilities, continually strengthening welfare tax services.

Through the real-time income identification system, the NTS collects income information on a monthly basis not only for full-time wage-earning employees, but also for workers in non-standard employment arrangements such as platform-based service providers. By providing this information to social insurance agencies, the NTS supports the timely identification of individuals in need of welfare benefits.

Sources: Brazil (2024), Italy (2024) and Korea (2024).

Tax crime investigation responsibilities

Finding ways to fight tax crime is a high priority as money laundering, corruption, terrorist financing, and other financial crimes can threaten the strategic, political and economic interests of jurisdictions. Tax administrations, as gatekeepers to a sound financial system, play a critical role in countering these activities and are in possession of information that could be crucial for a successful criminal tax investigation.

There is a range of organisational approaches for conducting tax crime investigations, and the ISORA survey continues to look at the role of tax administrations in this process. As can be seen from the data, slightly more than half of the tax administrations covered in this publication are involved in conducting tax crime investigations (Table A.87.). The majority of those administrations have responsibility for both conducting and directing tax crime investigations, while the others have responsibility for solely conducting investigations, under the direction or authority of another agency, such as the police or public prosecutor (see Table 2.3.).

In situations where administrations do not have any responsibility for conducting tax crime investigations, this work is done by another agency, such as the police or public prosecutor. This could also be a specialist agency, established outside the tax administration.

Table 2.3. Role of administrations in tax crime investigations, 2022

Percentage of administrations

Tax administration has responsibility for directing and conducting tax crime investigations	Tax administration has responsibility for conducting investigations, under the direction or authority of another agency	Another agency outside of tax administration has responsibility for conducting tax crime investigations
43.1	17.2	44.8

Note: In some jurisdictions, the organisational approach for tax crime investigations may depend on the tax offence or tax-related criminal proceedings. In those cases, an administration may have selected multiple answer options. This is why the percentages add up to more than 100 percent.
Source: CIAT, IOTA, IMF, OECD, International Survey on Revenue Administration, Table A.87 Tax crime investigations: Role of the administration, https://data.rafit.org/regular.aspx?key=74180895 (accessed on 10 September 2024).

More information on the rationale for adopting a national strategy for countering tax crime and on the design of such strategies, is included in the 2024 OECD report *Designing a National Strategy against Tax Crime: Core Elements and Considerations* (OECD, 2024[1]). The report draws on the practices of members of the OECD's Task Force on Tax Crimes and other Crimes (TFTC), which includes officials from many tax administrations.

Box 2.2. Australia – Fraud Surge Response Framework

The Australian Taxation Office (ATO) has established a proactive framework that identifies and responds to significant fraud outbreaks which have the potential to cause systemic failure of controls and significant impacts.

The framework places accountability with a senior officer in the ATO for the management of significant external fraud events. Combined with a clear committee structure that is enacted during a fraud surge, this provides a governance framework and accountability that enables the organisation to work together to mitigate against the fraud event.

The framework is built to prevent fraud events from happening. The framework relies upon intelligence and data that is drawn together in an early warning system, looking for patterns to identify fraud early. This approach means that projections can be made, and possible scenarios can be tested. The ability to foresee possible future fraud events means that the ATO can start to position responses early – either changing approaches and controls immediately to respond to potential events, or monitoring and preparing a response should the worst-case scenario happen.

In containing an instance of fraud, the ATO also considers future prevention activity by enhancing systemic controls. Where necessary, investment cases are developed to support this activity.

The fraud surge response framework design leverages experience from previous large fraud responses and data breach events, as well as best practice drawn from international and Commonwealth incident management frameworks.

Source: Australia (2024).

Revenue collections

This section looks at the net revenue collection of tax administrations, as well as a number of other key figures related to their activities.

Overall, the increase in revenue collections that was noted in the last edition of this publication has continued. Between 2021 and 2022, revenue collections increased in almost all jurisdictions covered. The average increase remains quite significant (+17.3% on average, see Table 2.4.) continuing the substantial recovery of economic activity following the COVID-19 pandemic during which lockdown measures were introduced by many governments and the forced closure of many businesses negatively affected taxable income and sales.

Table 2.4. Change in total net revenue collections, 2018-22

Change	From 2018 to 2019	From 2019 to 2020	From 2020 to 2021	From 2021 to 2022
Increase (percentage of administrations)	96.5	22.8	94.7	96.5
Decrease (percentage of administrations)	3.5	77.2	5.3	3.5
Average change in percent	+6.2	-3.8	+17.2	+17.3

Note: The table is based on the data from jurisdictions covered in this publication. Data for India was excluded as the Indirect Tax Board information was only available from fiscal year 2021.

Source: CIAT, IOTA, IMF, OECD, International Survey on Revenue Administration, Table A.5 Net revenue collected by the tax administration: Total, https://data.rafit.org/regular.aspx?key=74180904 (accessed on 10 September 2024).

Net collections by tax administrations averages 22% of jurisdiction GDP

Through its Global Revenue Statistics Database (OECD, 2023[2]), the OECD generally seeks to publish internationally comparable data on the tax revenues of its members, as well as a number of other jurisdictions for all levels of government. As the information contained in the Global Revenue Statistics Database reports data at a jurisdiction and not an administration level, tax administrations were asked in the ISORA survey to provide a range of information on their revenue collection activity. This information aptly demonstrates the importance of tax administrations to their respective economies.

Net revenue collected by tax administrations participating in this report, as a percentage of gross domestic product (GDP) in 2022, ranges from less than 10% to reach more than 40% in the case of Denmark and Sweden. Average net revenue collected by administrations in this report is 22% of GDP (see Figure 2.1.).

Figure 2.1. Net revenue collected as a percentage of gross domestic product, 2022

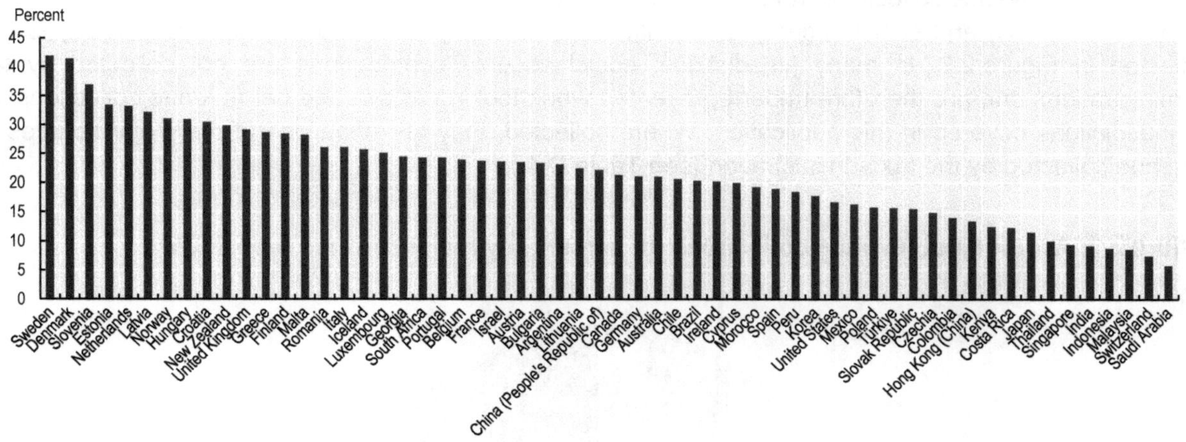

Source: CIAT, IOTA, IMF, OECD, International Survey on Revenue Administration, Table D.1 Revenue related ratios: Revenue to total government revenue and GDP, https://data.rafit.org/regular.aspx?key=74180898 (accessed on 10 September 2024).

StatLink https://stat.link/1r0qgv

Net collections by tax administrations averages 62% of total jurisdiction revenue

Forty-two tax administrations report net revenue collections exceeding more than 50% of total government revenue in 2022, making tax administrations the principal government revenue collection agency in almost three-quarters of jurisdictions covered in this report. Average net revenue collected by administrations in this report is 62% of total jurisdiction revenue (see Figure 2.2.)

Figure 2.2. Net revenue collected as a percentage of total government revenue, 2022

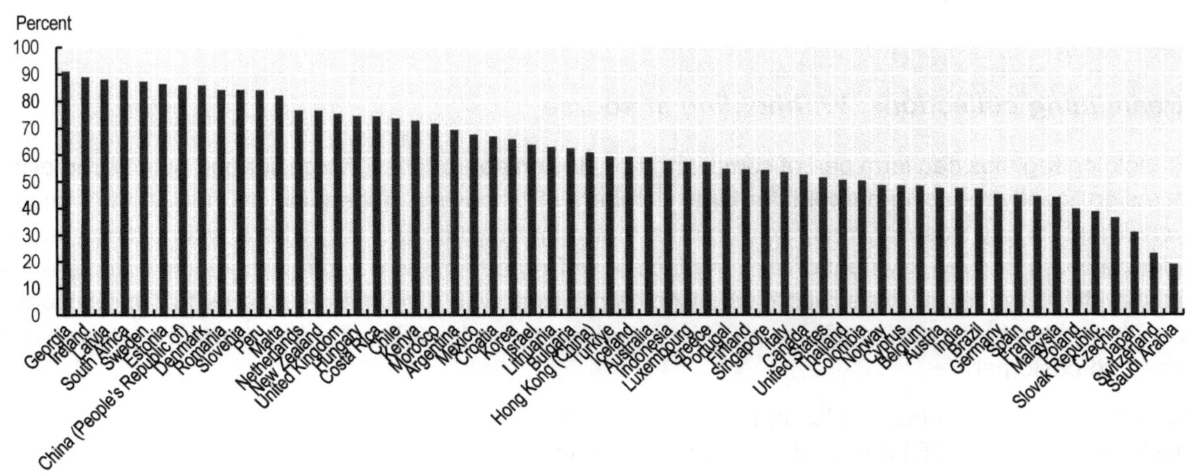

Source: CIAT, IOTA, IMF, OECD, International Survey on Revenue Administration, Table D.1 Revenue related ratios: Revenue to total government revenue and GDP, https://data.rafit.org/regular.aspx?key=74180898 (accessed on 10 September 2024).

StatLink https://stat.link/r3teq8

Value added tax accounts for 30% of net revenue collections and is the major tax type collected by 43% of the tax administrations covered in this report. This is followed by personal income tax, which accounts for 26% of net revenue collections, and is the major tax type collected by 36% of administrations. Corporate Income Tax (19%) and social security contributions (10%) comprise the other major revenue types as reflected in Figure 2.3. In many jurisdictions, social security contributions are not collected by tax administrations and are therefore underrepresented when looking at average net revenue collections for all jurisdictions covered in this publication. Where collected, they are often one of the major sources of revenue collected by the tax administration (see Table D.4.).

Figure 2.3. Average net revenue collections (in percent) by major revenue type, 2022

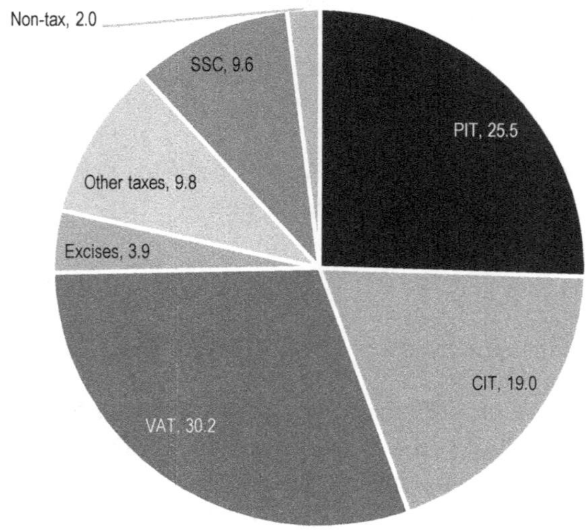

Sources: CIAT, IOTA, IMF, OECD, International Survey on Revenue Administration, Tables D.2 Revenue related ratios: Tax to GDP and non-tax revenue to total revenue, D.3 Tax structure and SSC proportions: PIT, CIT and VAT, and D.4 Tax structure and SSC proportions: Excises, Other taxes and SSC, https://data.rafit.org/regular.aspx?key=74180898 (accessed on 10 September 2024).

StatLink https://stat.link/31tlc7

Streamlining collections: Withholding at source

Withholding regimes can form part of compliance-by-design approaches, which support overall compliance while significantly reducing burdens for large numbers of taxpayers, depending on the extent of taxpayer involvement in any post-payment adjustments that might be needed (i.e. where withholding results in under-payment or over-payment of tax). In place of self-reporting and paying, withholding taxes are taxes paid directly to the tax administration, usually by a principal who pays the net income to the recipient (for example withholding by an employer on salary paid to an employee), or by an intermediary between the payer and customer.

The most common withholding tax in operation globally is income tax on employment income (so called Pay-As-You-Earn (PAYE) approaches). Other examples include withholding taxes on interest, dividends or royalties. Depending on the underlying tax regime and nature of the payments, withholding can vary from a simple system, at a universal set rate, to a more complex system that is responsive to the customer's wider circumstances. Table 2.5. shows the types of income that are generally subject to tax withholding at source for jurisdictions covered in this publication.

Table 2.5. Types of income generally subject to tax withholding at source, 2022

Percentage of jurisdictions

Wage and salary	Dividends	Interest	Rents	Specified business income	Royalties, patents	Sales / purchases of shares	Sales / purchases of real estate	Other types of income
91.4	82.8	77.6	39.7	34.5	67.2	29.3	25.9	43.1

Source: CIAT, IOTA, IMF, OECD, International Survey on Revenue Administration, Table B.49 Withholding at source, https://data.rafit.org/regular.aspx?key=74180917 (accessed on 10 September 2024).

In addition to minimising burdens, withholding regimes can also reduce misreporting and underpayment as the principals or intermediaries responsible for forwarding taxes to the administration have no right over the respective amounts. Of course, there remains scope for failures in such approaches by misapplication of rules or errors by principals or intermediaries where the system relies on them providing information. However, increased automation, greater cross-checking of data and whole of government approaches have the potential to reduce such risks.

To understand the importance of withholding at source for personal income taxes, the ISORA survey asked participating administrations to estimate the percentage of total personal income tax withheld by third parties and subsequently paid to the administration. Administrations that were able to provide this information estimate that around 80% of total personal income tax collections were withheld at source in 2022, a figure that remained stable over the past five years (see Table 2.6.).

Table 2.6. Average percentage of personal income tax withholding, 2018-22

2018	2019	2020	2021	2022
79.2	78.7	80.7	80.6	80.5

Note: The table shows the average percentage of personal income tax withholding for 39 jurisdictions that were able to provide the information for the years 2018 to 2022.
Source: CIAT, IOTA, IMF, OECD, International Survey on Revenue Administration, Table D.40 Electronic payment proportions and third party withholding, https://data.rafit.org/regular.aspx?key=74180902 (accessed on 10 September 2024).

Box 2.3. Examples – Supporting withholding processes

Korea – Streamlining the process of income tax payments using digital technology

The Korean NTS has been expanding taxpayer convenience services, starting with earned income tax and extending to the declaration of business income to streamline the income tax payment process.

In 2006, to facilitate the reporting of income deductions and tax credits for year-end tax settlement on salary and wage earners, the NTS began digitally compiling supporting documents such as insurance premiums, medical expenses, and credit card usage for taxpayers, providing them in electronic file formats. This service relieved taxpayers from the burden of personally collecting supporting documents, as they could submit the compiled data received from the NTS to their withholding agents (employers).

Since 2022, with taxpayer consent the NTS initiated a service where it directly provides year-end settlement data to withholding agents. This streamlines the withholding process for employers, allowing them to complete income tax withholding tasks more efficiently. Taxpayers, particularly those with earned income, can finalise their income tax reporting by simply verifying income deduction and tax credit results. The need for taxpayers to access the NTS portal site (Hometax) or visit tax offices to obtain supporting documents for deductions diminished significantly, reducing the tax compliance costs associated with year-end settlements.

Through these efforts, NTS is moving one step closer to Tax Administration 3.0. The taxation processes will become more seamless and frictionless, embedded within the natural system of taxpayers.

United Kingdom – Improvements to the Pay As You Earn system

There are nearly 18 million new job starters each year, and around one in seven of them are initially put on an incorrect tax code due to wrong or missing information. The United Kingdom's HM Revenue & Customs (HMRC) get around 1 million calls a year from new starters regarding this.

HMRC has made improvements to the system that holds customers' Pay As You Earn records to spot when a tax code does not look right, and then automatically issues a new code if HMRC holds enough information to do so, without the need for further contact. This means the employee receives the correct pay and pays the correct tax much sooner.

HMRC is also testing how best to reassure new starters when this happens, and are trialling contacting some customers via email and text message to let them know that HMRC are aware of the issue and working to correct it. During testing, 681 SMS messages and emails were sent to customers. The contact rates from customers who received the emails/SMS messages dropped considerably – down from an average of 28% of people to just 1.2% from the sample group. Given this was a small sample, further analysis is being undertaken to test this correlation.

Sources: Korea (2024) and the United Kingdom (2024).

References

OECD (2024), *Designing a National Strategy against Tax Crime: Core Elements and Considerations*, OECD Publishing, Paris, https://doi.org/10.1787/0e451c90-en. [1]

OECD (2023), *Global Revenue Statistics Database*, https://www.oecd.org/en/data/datasets/global-revenue-statistics-database.html (accessed on 10 September 2024). [2]

3 Registration and identification

Taxpayer registration and identification is critical for the effective operation of a tax system. This chapter comments on some of the significant characteristics of these processes.

Introduction

A comprehensive system of taxpayer registration and identification is at the foundation of an effective tax system. It is the basis for supporting a wide range of core tax administration work such as self-assessment, value-added tax and withholding tax regimes, as well as third party reporting and matching. This chapter picks out several issues of significance in taxpayer registration and identification, including levels of registration, registration channels and identity management, and how digital transformation affects these services.

Levels of registration

The fundamental importance of an effective tax registration system cannot be overstated. These processes need to both manage those taxpayers that are "part of the system" and to help identify those yet to register. Furthermore, they need to be able to monitor and determine actions and interventions to establish any liability to tax for both individuals and corporate bodies, even in systems where filing is not mandatory.

Figure 3.1. provides information on the rate of registered personal taxpayers as a percentage of the total population. This shows a wide range of registration rates, often reflecting the level of integration the tax administration has with other parts of government, as well as income thresholds for tax purposes.

Figure 3.1. Registration of active personal income taxpayers as percentage of population, 2022

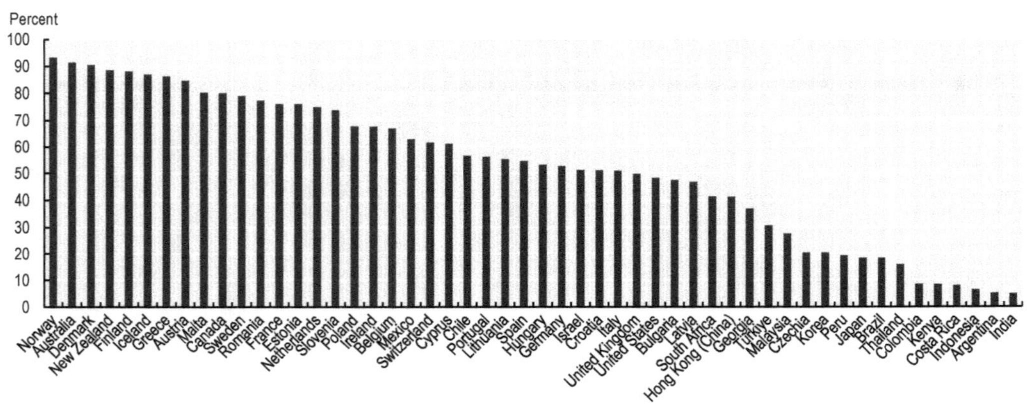

Source: CIAT, IOTA, IMF, OECD, International Survey on Revenue Administration, Table D.19 Registration of personal income taxpayers, https://data.rafit.org/regular.aspx?key=74180900 (accessed on 10 September 2024).

StatLink https://stat.link/kml5to

Registration channels

While the majority of administrations are solely responsible for the system of registration for tax purposes within their jurisdictions, previous editions of this series have shown that in many jurisdictions the registration processes can also be initiated outside of the tax administration through other government agencies (OECD, 2019[1]).

In looking at how taxpayers can register, almost all administrations reported they provide more than one channel for taxpayers to use and 97% report that it is possible to register online (see Table 3.1.). Compared to data from the 2017 edition of this series (OECD, 2017[2]), this is a 27-percentage point increase. Although in-person registration continues to be an important channel or element of the registration process (often due to the need to provide physical evidence of identity), it is expected that as digital identity systems become more sophisticated, the dominance of online channels will grow.

Table 3.1. Availability of registration channels for taxpayers, 2022

Percentage of administrations that provide the respective registration channel

Online	Telephone	Email	Mail / post	In-person	Other channel
96.6	53.4	56.9	63.8	93.1	37.9

Note: The registration channels may not always be available for all tax types or taxpayer segments.
Source: CIAT, IOTA, IMF, OECD, International Survey on Revenue Administration, Tables A.94 Registration channels: Online, Telephone, Email, and A.95 Registration channels: Mail / post, In-person, other, https://data.rafit.org/regular.aspx?key=74180896 (accessed on 10 September 2024).

While the underlying survey does not allow identification of whether the online registration channel is available for all tax types or taxpayer segments, jurisdictions report that it is being integrated in their ongoing digital transformation process. Indeed, in one jurisdiction (Saudi Arabia), taxpayers can only register online (see Tables A.94. and A.95.). This shift to digital channels may also help drive further efficiencies, though as the shift to digital gathers pace further attention is being paid to those who may not have access to digital services.

Integration with other parts of government

Given the pivotal role that registration and taxpayer identification play in underpinning the tax system, having up-to-date tax registers remains a high priority for most tax administrations. As past editions have shown, the large majority of administrations have formal programmes in place to improve the quality of the tax register (OECD, 2019[1]).

Therefore, it is unsurprising that other government bodies may wish to use the tax administration register for their own purposes to provide services or ensure compliance with laws and regulations. This is leading to the creation of cross government databases. As Table 3.2. illustrates, 70% of administrations report the existence of a range of such databases, for example, population or business registers. As noted in Chapter 2, a few administrations also reported being responsible for maintaining cross government databases, such as the government's population and/ or property register (see Table 2.2.).

Box 3.1. Examples – Integration with other parts of government

Brazil – National Identity Card Project

Brazil has advanced the implementation of a National Identity Card (CIN), a new identification document available in physical and digital formats which aims to provide secure self-identification for its citizens and allows the link up of public services, including on taxation. This has centralised Brazil's civil identification system, where previously identification cards were issued at the state level and more susceptible to fraud and other illegal activities. As of January 2024, around 3 million CINs have been issued.

The project has relied heavily on input from the Federal Revenue Office (RFB), with each card using the Individual Taxpayer Registry number as its identifying number. Once a physical CIN is issued, the holder can also obtain a digital version through the government's online portal, which has a single login authentication for all government websites and applications, facilitating citizen access to public services. The CIN comes with a QR Code that can be read easily and quickly, which provides more security for citizens. It makes it possible to identify the authenticity of the card, and to know if it was stolen or lost. The card also allows an easier identification process for people with special needs.

Brazil – REDESIM Business Portal

The REDESIM Business Portal (PNR) has reformulated the traditional interaction model between the Brazilian tax administration and citizens in the processes of opening, legalising and registering legal companies.

All functionalities have been standardised across Brazil regardless of the state, with automatic validations and the option to evaluate services. All stages of registration regularity, viability, registration, tax registrations and licensing process are carried out in a single, linear procedure and each company has been given a unique identity number. The PNR is fundamental to the implementation of tax reforms on consumption, enabling data sharing, the facilitation and simplification of services, the integration of public agencies and more accurate databases. This in turn will provide a better experience for the user and an improvement in the provision of public services.

Source: Brazil (2024).

Table 3.2. Cross government databases: Availability and database types, 2022

Percentage of jurisdictions

Cross government databases exist	If yes, type of cross government databases				
	Population register	Property register	Business register	Motor vehicle register	Other
70.0	71.4	62.9	82.9	68.6	28.6

Note: The percentages are based on data from 52 jurisdictions that are covered in this report and that are included in the ITTI database.
Source: OECD et al (2024), Inventory of Tax Technology Initiatives, https://web-archive.oecd.org/temp/2023-03-09/618463-data-management.htm, Table DM3 (accessed on 10 September 2024).

This integration across government is further increasing as governments see the potential in using information maintained by tax administrations, such as taxpayer address and bank information, to contact citizens and businesses or to make direct benefit or support payments (OECD, 2020[3]). As a result of this closer collaboration between government agencies, many of them are integrating (parts of) their IT systems to make tax registration part of other actions taxpayers undertake. For example, registering for tax at the same time as registering a company or registering the birth of a child. Further, there is a growing trend that the digital identities that taxpayers create as part of the registration process provides access to services from other parts of government or third parties (see Table 3.3.).

Table 3.3. Use of digital identities, 2022

Percentage of administrations that have the respective process in place

Taxpayer type	Taxpayers are required to use an approved digital identity (DI) to access secure digital services	DI used to access the services can be provided by *(multiple answers possible)*			DI offered by the tax administration can also be used to access services from	
		Tax administration	Another government body	Private sector body	Another government body	Private sector body
Individual	100.0	68.6	62.7	39.2	37.1	14.3
Business	94.1	66.7	50.0	35.4	46.9	9.4

Note: The table is based on data from 52 jurisdictions that are covered in this report and that are included in the ITTI database. For the purpose of the ITTI survey, digital identity is defined as an electronic representation of an individual or business which enables them to be sufficiently distinguished when interacting online. The digital identity includes attributes which are bound to a credential that is used to authenticate the individual or business.
Source: OECD et al. (2024), Inventory of Tax Technology Initiatives, https://web-archive.oecd.org/temp/2023-03-09/618377-digital-identity.htm, Tables DI1 and DI2 (accessed on 10 September 2024).

Identity management

All tax administrations, whether required to by law or as a matter of sound business practice, put considerable effort into ensuring the security of taxpayer information. In addition to internal processes to prevent unlawful attempts to obtain information and to ensure taxpayers' rights are protected, all administrations have processes to ensure the person they are dealing with is in fact the taxpayer or their authorised representative. Increasingly these approaches, which in many instances have now been extended to multi-factor authentication, are making use of biometric information, unique to the taxpayer.

For example, in relation to online services, Table 3.4. shows that administrations use some type of authentication method to verify the digital identity. The type of verification method varies. As can be seen in Table 3.4., password-based authentication is used by 87% of administrations, followed by multi-factor authentication and mobile app. A few administrations also reported using facial recognition or fingerprint recognition to authenticate the digital identity of a taxpayer. Half of the administrations reported that their use of different authentication methods is based on the level of security required for certain types of interactions.

Table 3.4. Digital identity authentication and authorisation, 2022

Percentage of administrations that have the respective process in place

Authentication methods used by the tax administration						Use of different authentication methods based on the level of security required for certain types of interactions	Taxpayers can authorise third parties to access digital services
Password-based authentication	ID card	Mobile app	Facial recognition	Finger print	Multi-factor authentication		
86.5	38.5	42.3	13.5	13.5	61.5	50.0	86.5

Note: The figure is based on data from 52 jurisdictions that are covered in this report and that are included in the ITTI database.
Source: OECD et al. (2024), Inventory of Tax Technology Initiatives, https://web-archive.oecd.org/temp/2023-03-09/618377-digital-identity.htm, Tables DI5 and DI6 (accessed on 10 September 2024).

Tax administrations face similar challenges to other organisations in dealing with individuals or organisations that may misuse personal information to impersonate taxpayers in order to commit fraud. The rise of artificial intelligence (AI) enabled image and audio generators will complicate this even further. The on-going and, in many cases, organised nature of this activity is requiring administrations to devote considerable effort to the prevention of identity theft.

Box 3.2. Examples – Identity management

Chile – Platform for Digital Representatives

Chile has introduced a new system called "Platform for Digital Representatives". This platform allows users (both individuals and legal entities) to delegate the completion of tax procedures to authorised third parties, known as digital representatives.

The platform has been integrated with broader government digital services and aims to:

- Standardise the experience of those engaging with digital services from the tax administration and other government institutions;
- Enhance the traceability of government digital procedures;
- Create a unified IT system across government to avoid duplication and reduce costs;
- Provide citizens with a unique digital identity to access all government services.

India – e-Verification system

India has made it possible for taxpayers to meet all their compliance requirements digitally through introducing e-Verification, an online system that allows users to confirm their identity and perform tasks online.

Users can verify their Income Tax Return (ITR) online, as well as other functions such as submissions, responses and requests related to ITRs. This saves taxpayers from having to physically submit their returns and having to physically go to an office to identify themselves. The identity verification process is also much quicker because it is automated.

The user can use any one of the following modes to verify their identity:

- Digital Signature Certificate using Hard Token.
- One-Time Password (OTP) issued by the Unique Identification Authority of India, shared via text message.
- Electronic Verification Code using a verification service enabled by the taxpayer's bank or a Bank ATM (offline method).

Since the introduction of e-Verification, compliance levels have significantly increased, from 13% in 2014-15 to 93% in 2022-23. The average processing time of ITR has reduced from 84 days in 2019-20 to 10 days in 2023-24.

Netherlands – Company Passport

The Dutch Tax Administration has collaborated with the Dutch Blockchain Coalition, the Chamber of Commerce, Notary Association and the banks in a public-private initiative to investigate how introducing the Company Passport can simplify the process of both founding a company and enabling that company to trade with other businesses and consumers.

The Company Passport is a trust framework setting the rules for an online interface that allows entrepreneurs to share and verify data with relevant parties such as banks, insurance firms and the tax administration. It can be set up through an online appointment with a notary. The interface, consisting of guidance app, a wallet and digital identity for a legal entity, allows the entrepreneur to store and receive information in one place, such as a VAT number. This information can easily be shared with third parties, such as banks when requesting a bank account.

This has significant benefits for the customer, such as legal certainty of the identities of business partners, a reduction in duplicate paperwork requests from the various parties and the ability to securely share data with business partners.

Sources: Chile (2024), India (2024) and the Netherlands (2024).

Common approaches to digital identity

As the importance of digital identity grows for the operation of the tax system, so does the need to create digital identities that can be:

- Shared across government,
- Are interoperable between governments, and
- Can be used between government and third parties.

Creating these common approaches will increasingly allow new services to be developed which can reduce burdens on taxpayers as well as allowing third parties to supply information direct to tax administrations, providing richer and more accurate pools of data to tax administrations.

For example, once the domain of multi-national businesses and those involved in international trade, small and medium-sized enterprises and individual taxpayers are now increasingly earning income sourced outside their jurisdiction of residence. As a result of the proliferation of online market-places and sharing/ gig economy platforms, it is now easier than ever for example, to rent out holiday homes or sell goods and services abroad through online platforms.

Tax administrations and businesses are facing a raft of issues in supporting and responding to this which is centred around a platform and a tax administration agreeing the identity of a mutual customer. As a result, work is currently ongoing under the Tax Administration 3.0 umbrella (OECD, 2020[4]) to explore how co-operation between administrations and platforms can be deepened by integrating a tax administration's digital identification systems into the applications used by the platforms. Through this, greater confidence can be placed in the identity of a mutual customer, which can support tax compliance by platform sellers as well as reducing burdens for business.

Box 3.3. United Kingdom – Distributed Identifiers

HMRC is investigating using Distributed Identifiers (DIDs), an innovation in web technology that allows individuals and organisations to generate and store their own unique identifiers using a system they trust, and then use these to verify their identity. This allows simpler, more direct access to services by, for example, allowing sign-in to a service without the need to provide a username, password, or other details. This has major implications in the field of data security and privacy.

DIDs are currently an exploratory piece of work to understand and demonstrate potential opportunities and implications for HMRC, should this technology become more widely accepted and used.

HMRC plans to test a concept that would allow external individuals and organisations to use DIDs to sign in and gain access to government services. This will focus on identity, but they are looking at other tax use cases as well. Multiple frameworks that enable distributed identity already exist.

This is a fast-developing landscape, with rapidly developing open source as well as proprietary software. At the end of this exercise, HMRC will better understand the capability DIDs offer.

Source: United Kingdom (2024).

References

OECD (2020), *Tax Administration 3.0: The Digital Transformation of Tax Administration*, OECD Publishing, Paris, https://doi.org/10.1787/ca274cc5-en. [4]

OECD (2020), "Tax administration responses to COVID-19: Assisting wider government", *OECD Policy Responses to Coronavirus (COVID-19)*, OECD Publishing, Paris, https://doi.org/10.1787/0dc51664-en. [3]

OECD (2019), *Tax Administration 2019: Comparative Information on OECD and other Advanced and Emerging Economies*, OECD Publishing, Paris, https://doi.org/10.1787/74d162b6-en. [1]

OECD (2017), *Tax Administration 2017: Comparative Information on OECD and Other Advanced and Emerging Economies*, OECD Publishing, Paris, https://doi.org/10.1787/tax_admin-2017-en. [2]

OECD et al. (2024), *Inventory of Tax Technology Initiatives*, https://web-archive.oecd.org/tax/forum-on-tax-administration/tax-technology-tools-and-digital-solutions/index.htm (accessed on 10 September 2024). [5]

4 Assessment

This chapter looks at the tax assessment function, which includes all activities related to processing tax returns and payments. It examines the use of e-channels for filing and paying, outlines administrations' efforts to provide pre-filled returns, and discusses the level of on-time return filing and payment.

Introduction

The tax assessment function includes all activities related to processing tax returns, including issuing assessments, refunds, notices and statements. It also includes the processing and banking of payments. These activities continue to be an area of significant change and focus as administrations look to take costs out of high-volume processes.

As reported in previous editions of this series, the widespread enabling of electronic filing and payment by taxpayers has helped administrations to reduce their costs and improve the services they provide. This trend continues with an increasing range of supporting services and options being made available.

Tax administrations are also managing an expanding range of data that administrations are collecting electronically, including from a growing number of third-party organisations. This is facilitating a shift towards more intelligent use of data, and more complete pre-filled returns, increasingly driven by the use of artificial intelligence and machine learning. This is also helping to create more upstream compliance approaches that can minimise or prevent errors in returns. As well as updating information on the channels used for filing and paying, this chapter will outline:

- Administrations' efforts to provide pre-filled returns for individual and corporate taxpayers, including the expansion of this approach by some into completely pre-filled returns for individuals and businesses;
- The levels of on-time return filing and payment; and
- Examples of how technology and the application of data sciences have improved filing, payment and refund processes.

Use of e-channels for filing and paying

To increase uptake in the use of e-filing and e-payment channels, many jurisdictions have also mandated the use of electronic channels for most taxpayers (or most employers in the case of employer withholding taxes). Table 4.1. shows that across the jurisdictions covered in this publication, e-filing and e-payment has been mandated more often for business taxpayers than for individuals. Around three-quarters of jurisdictions make the use of e-filing channels mandatory for corporate income tax (CIT), employer withholding tax (PAYE) and value added tax (VAT), whereas for personal income tax (PIT) this is only the case in half of the jurisdictions. Similarly, e-payment is mandatory for CIT, PAYE and VAT in around two-thirds of jurisdictions, and for PIT again in around half.

Table 4.1. Mandatory use of e-filing and e-payment for most taxpayers by tax type, 2022

Percentage of jurisdictions

E-filing				E-payment			
Personal income tax	Corporate income tax	Employer withholding	Value added tax	Personal income tax	Corporate income tax	Employer withholding	Value added tax
52.6	74.1	75.9	81.8	47.4	60.3	63.0	69.1

Source: CIAT, IOTA, IMF, OECD, International Survey on Revenue Administration, Table B.30 Taxpayer gender recorded; and mandatory electronic filing and payment, https://data.rafit.org/regular.aspx?key=74180917 (accessed on 10 September 2024).

Despite mandating the use of e-channels, with digitalisation continuing to transform everyday life, it is unsurprising that the actual use of e-filing and e-payment channels is significantly higher and continues to grow. As the high rates show, the implementation of those channels is now embedded across a wide range of administrations and as a result these rates are expected to remain stable with only incremental increases going forward.

Table 4.2. outlines average e-filing rates from jurisdictions that provided details of channels used by taxpayers to file for the years 2018 to 2022. Over that period, around 95% of business taxpayers filed their returns electronically. For personal income tax return filers this figure is around 90% as well. Also, it should be noted that for a significant number of administrations a 100% e-filing rate is the reality across the main tax types (see Tables D.26 and D.27).

Table 4.2. Average e-filing rates (in percent) by tax type, 2018-22

Tax type	2018	2019	2020	2021	2022
Personal income tax (46 jurisdictions)	82.1	84.5	87.8	88.2	89.5
Corporate income tax (45 jurisdictions)	91.8	92.5	93.5	94.2	94.7
Employer withholding (35 jurisdictions)	–	–	–	–	94.4
Value added tax (41 jurisdictions)	94.0	95.8	96.7	97.4	98.2

Note: The table shows the average e-filing rates for those jurisdictions that were able to provide the information for the years 2018 to 2022. The number of jurisdictions for which data was available is shown in parentheses. As regards Employer withholding (i.e. PAYE) return, the underlying question was introduced in ISORA 2023 and therefore data is only available for the year 2022.
Source: CIAT, IOTA, IMF, OECD, International Survey on Revenue Administration, Tables D.26 Electronic filing: CIT and PIT, and D.27 Electronic filing: PAYE and VAT, https://data.rafit.org/regular.aspx?key=74180901 (accessed on 10 September 2024).

Looking at the evolution of e-filing rates over the period 2014 to 2022 shown in Table 4.3., it is clear that e-filing rates have increased significantly – between 17 and 23 percentage points – across the three main tax types. (It should be noted that the table only takes into account information from jurisdictions for which data was available for both years 2014 and 2022, which explains the differences in 2022 averages shown in Tables 4.2. and 4.3.)

Table 4.3. Average e-filing rates (in percent) by tax type, 2014 and 2022

Tax type	2014	2022	Difference in percentage points
Personal income tax (31 jurisdictions)	64.5	87.4	+22.9
Corporate income tax (31 jurisdictions)	78.4	95.2	+16.8
Value added tax (29 jurisdictions)	81.8	99.0	+17.2

Note: The table shows the average e-filing rates for those jurisdictions that were able to provide the information for the years 2014 and 2022. The number of jurisdictions for which data was available is shown in parentheses.
Sources: CIAT, IOTA, IMF, OECD, International Survey on Revenue Administration, Tables D.26 Electronic filing: CIT and PIT, and D.27 Electronic filing: PAYE and VAT, https://data.rafit.org/regular.aspx?key=74180901 (accessed on 10 September 2024), and OECD (2017), *Tax Administration 2017: Comparative Information on OECD and Other Advanced and Emerging Economies*, Table A.8., https://doi.org/10.1787/tax_admin-2017-en.

As for electronic payments rates, as can be seen in Table 4.4., around 90% of payments, measured by number and value, were made electronically in 2022. This represents a significant increase since 2018. The percentage of e-payments by value is slightly higher than the percentage of e-payments made by number, suggesting that particularly larger taxpayers make use of this payment channel. (Due to a change in the definition of the underlying survey question, comparisons that examine the evolution of e-payment rates since 2014 would not be reliable.)

Table 4.4. Average e-payment rates (in percent) by number and value of payments, 2018-22

Measurement type	2018	2019	2020	2021	2022
Percentage by number of payments (48 jurisdictions)	80.3	82.5	86.6	88.7	90.0
Percentage by value of payments (48 jurisdictions)	84.8	86.1	88.6	90.4	91.9

Note: The table shows the average e-payment rates for those jurisdictions that were able to provide the information for the years 2018 to 2022. The number of jurisdictions for which data was available is shown in parentheses.
Source: CIAT, IOTA, IMF, OECD, International Survey on Revenue Administration, Table D.40 Electronic payment proportions and third party withholding, https://data.rafit.org/regular.aspx?key=74180902 (accessed on 10 September 2024).

There remain a number of jurisdictions where the volume of returns filed using paper as well as payments through non-electronic means remains high. Among those jurisdictions that provided data, more than 70 million returns (for PIT, CIT, PAYE and VAT) were still filed on paper (see Tables A.48, A.52, A.56 and A.61).

It is to be expected that this figure will further decline over time as more administrations take steps to encourage more taxpayers to use electronic platforms where possible. This will not only lower administration costs but could also reduce the administrative burden on taxpayers over time.

Box 4.1. Examples – E-channels for filing and paying

Canada – Underused Housing Tax webform

The Underused Housing Tax (UHT) is an annual 1% tax on the value of the property of vacant or underused housing in Canada. The tax is expected to largely apply to non-resident, non-Canadian owners.

Previously, the Canada Revenue Agency (CRA) did not have electronic filing options available for non-residents unless they were set up in one of CRA's digital portals. To encourage and facilitate electronic filing of the UHT return, a webform was developed to allow electronic filing using a Digital Access Code (DAC). This filing method is more efficient than filing by paper and represents a pathfinder initiative for the CRA, as the webform data links directly to the processing system without the necessity for manual data capture.

Individuals and corporations can instantly obtain a DAC online by providing specific information. If the taxpayer has any difficulty, they are prompted to call a help desk specifically set up to handle these enquiries. If all pre-determined system checks are met, the return can be automatically assessed with no manual intervention required.

As of November 2023, the CRA has received approximately 30 000 returns using this filing method.

Spain – Single European Payment Area Direct Debits

Spain have introduced measures to make it easier for taxpayers to comply with their payment obligations to the Spanish Tax Agency (AEAT) when living abroad.

Regulatory and technical advances have been made so that taxpayers can pay their taxes by direct debit from accounts located in their jurisdictions of residence, provided that the entity is located within the Single Euro Payments Area (SEPA). This has resolved the issue of needing to have a bank account in Spain.

For further information, please see here:

https://sede.agenciatributaria.gob.es/Sede/en_gb/ayuda/consultas-informaticas/pago-impuestos-deudas-tasas-ayuda-tecnica/aplazamiento-fraccionamiento-deudas.html (accessed on 10 September 2024).

Sources: Canada (2024) and Spain (2024).

Pre-filled returns

One of the significant innovations in tax return process design over the last two decades has been the development of pre-filled tax returns, often for personal income taxpayers. The pre-filled approach involves administrations "pre-populating" the taxpayer's return or on-line account with information from third parties. The pre-filled return can be reviewed by the taxpayer and either filed electronically or in paper form. (Table 4.5. shows that an increasing number of administrations are pre-filling PIT returns.)

As the extent of pre-population is generally determined by the range of electronic data sources available to the administration, it is critical to this approach that the legislative framework provides for extensive and timely third-party reporting covering as much relevant taxpayer information as possible. The complexities of the legal frameworks governing tax can be a barrier to more automated tax calculations, and to help overcome this some tax administrations are exploring the use of machine-readable legislation which can help automate the calculation process through the use of algorithms. This is leading to reduced errors and reduced burdens for taxpayers.

Table 4.5. Pre-filling of PIT returns, 2018-22

Percentage of administrations that pre-fill PIT returns

2018	2019	2020	2021	2022	Difference in percentage points (2018 - 2022)
78.9	80.7	84.2	87.7	87.7	+8.8

Source: CIAT, IOTA, IMF, OECD, International Survey on Revenue Administration, Table A.99 Pre-fill of PIT returns: Income information - Personal information, and wage and salary, https://data.rafit.org/regular.aspx?key=74180896 (accessed on 10 September 2024).

Advocates of pre-filling initially encouraged its use with individual tax regimes that allowed relatively few deductions and credits, and where they could be verified with third party data sources. Advances in rules-based technologies, information-reporting requirements and the application of data science techniques mean that the approach can now be considered more widely. For example, survey responses show that in many jurisdictions PIT returns are pre-filled with different income information and deductible expenses such as donations, school and university fees and insurance premiums (see Table 4.6. and Table 4.7.).

Table 4.6. Categories of third-party income information used to pre-fill PIT returns or assessments, 2022

As a percentage of administrations that pre-fill PIT returns

Taxpayer personal information	Wage and salary	Pension	Interest	Dividends	Capital gains/ losses	Other income
98.0	88.0	82.0	54.0	50.0	40.0	72.0

Source: CIAT, IOTA, IMF, OECD, International Survey on Revenue Administration, Tables A.99 Pre-fill of PIT returns: Income information - Personal information, and wage and salary, A.100 Pre-fill of PIT returns: Income information - Pension, interest, and dividends, and A.101 Pre-fill of PIT returns: Income information - Capital gains / losses, and other income, https://data.rafit.org/regular.aspx?key=74180896 (accessed on 10 September 2024).

Table 4.7. Categories of tax deductible expenses used to pre-fill PIT returns or assessments, 2022

As a percentage of administrations that pre-fill PIT returns

Donations	School and university fees	Childcare expenses	Certain insurance premiums	Health and medical expenses (other than premiums)	Pension/ retirement contributions and savings	Interest on loans and mortgages	Other expenses
36.0	30.0	26.0	48.0	30.0	52.0	40.0	48.0

Source: CIAT, IOTA, IMF, OECD, International Survey on Revenue Administration, Tables A.102 Pre-fill of PIT returns: Expense information - Donations, school and university fees, and childcare expenses, A.103 Pre-fill of PIT returns: Expense information - Insurance premiums, health and medical expenses, and retirement contributions, and A.104 Pre-fill of PIT returns: Expense information - Interest, and other expenses https://data.rafit.org/regular.aspx?key=74180896 (accessed on 10 September 2024).

In a growing number of jurisdictions, this concept now goes as far as totally pre-filling PIT returns, which the taxpayer then has to either agree (which may be by deemed agreement after a certain period of elapsed time) or provide further information which may lead to an upwards or downwards adjustment (see Table A.53). In their most advanced form, complete pre-filled returns are being generated for large proportions of the individual tax base. In addition, the availability of technology solutions and approaches, such as electronic invoicing systems, allows tax administrations to start to go beyond PIT returns and pre-fill CIT, PAYE and VAT returns (see Tables A.49, A.57 and A.62).

The latest pre-filling developments in some jurisdictions are described in Box 4.2.

Box 4.2. Examples – Pre-filling developments

Australia – Activity statement prefill

The Australian Taxation Office (ATO) is harnessing employer-provided data to improve the employer reporting experience and simplify tax obligations.

An activity statement is used by businesses to report certain information to the ATO throughout the year, if the business is registered for Goods and Sales Tax, Pay As You Go instalments or Withholding Tax. When a taxpayer lodges an activity statement online through ATO services, the amount of Pay As You Go Withholding (PAYGW) Tax that they have reported to the ATO is prefilled at the appropriate label in the activity statement. The employer can choose to accept this amount or change it where the amount needs to be adjusted up or down.

The ATO is also piloting the use of employer-provided single touch payroll (STP) data to bring PAYGW amounts to account where a client has not lodged their activity statement by the due date. Where an employer has reported PAYGW amounts through STP and has not lodged their activity statement for the period, the ATO will remind the employer via a letter nudge to lodge the activity statement, or if there are no changes to the PAYGW amount, we will put that amount on their client account for them.

If there is no response the PAYGW amount will be put on account, and if the employer has no other reportable obligations, the activity statement will be set to finalised. The client will still need to lodge the activity statement if they have other reportable obligations, like Goods and Services Tax.

This strategy levels the playing field between compliant and non-compliant employers. Those who delay lodgement of their activity statements to avoid reporting and payment of PAYGW liabilities will no longer obtain an unfair advantage over those who report and pay in a timely manner.

Canada – Fully digital Disability Tax Credit application process

In May 2023, the CRA made it faster and easier for persons with disabilities and their Medical Practitioners (MPs) to complete the Disability Tax Credit (DTC) application form, by introducing a new fully digital application process.

Applicants can now complete the first part of the application form online via My Account. To simplify the application process further and save time, the applicant's portion of the form is prepopulated with information already on file at the CRA. Once completed, the applicant will receive a unique, one-time use reference number to give to their MP who can use it to complete the second part of the form.

Based on previously received feedback from MPs that the current DTC form was not transparent enough about what information was required, the CRA introduced psychometric scales, drop-down menus, radio-buttons to make it more dynamic and to gather more relevant information through targeted questions using proactive disclosure techniques. By applying client and user experience design concepts, the digital application is more responsive to client needs.

Feedback from the medical community has been extremely positive with the most measurable results being a decrease of 60% to the number of clarification letters issued.

China (People's Republic of) – Annual reconciliation of corporate income tax

To reduce the time that tax assessments take and to provide more convenient taxpayer services, the People's Republic of China launched a new model for the refunds resulting from the annual reconciliation of corporate income tax. This includes:

- Simplifying the tax refund process so that after a taxpayer has filed, the system estimates the tax refund and sends the notification to the taxpayer, and as a result the taxpayer only needs to accept this through "one-click" in the system, instead of filling in the tax refund application information item by item. This information is also automatically transmitted to the treasury department, which also greatly increases efficiency.
- Introducing the intelligent review mechanism where the system can automatically check the taxpayer's risk, and if they can meet the requirement for a tax refund the tax refund will be handled automatically as described above; otherwise, it will be transferred to the traditional tax refund process by tax officials.
- Shortening the tax refund cycle so the tax refund review could be completed on the day when the taxpayer files, which is much shorter than the traditional 30-day cycle.

Not only has this model improved the operational experience for taxpayers, it has also removed administrative burdens for tax officials.

Netherlands – Simplified tax return

Since 2022, the Netherlands has issued a simplified electronic tax return (PIT) for taxpayers with a straightforward fiscal situation.

In the past, these taxpayers had to fill out a tax return form with all possible questions about income, that were only partly pre-filled. Now these taxpayers only need to answer a minimal number of yes/no questions and confirm the pre-filled information about their income and, if applicable, their home ownership. If taxpayers disagree with the pre-filled information, they can switch to a normal tax return.

This has significantly reduced the compliance burden for taxpayers, with 86.5% stating that the new service is an improvement.

Source: Australia (2024), Canada (2024), China (People's Republic of) (2024) and the Netherlands (2024).

As the levels of data available to support pre-filling grows, tax administrations are able to develop predictive techniques that can spot errors that taxpayers make as they finalise their return, and also prevent non-compliance. Examples of this have been included in previous editions. See, for example, Box 4.3. in Tax Administration 2022 (OECD, 2022[1]). These can be combined with techniques to prompt action, creating whole new approaches to compliance which are bringing the compliance work 'upstream' into tax administration processes, as Box 4.3. highlights.

Box 4.3. Examples – Spotting errors

Hungary – e-VAT system

On 1 January 2024, the National Tax and Customs Administration (NTCA) of Hungary launched the e-VAT system, which aims to reduce the administrative burden related to the preparation of VAT returns. The new return filing solution combines three innovations:

1. The transaction-based data collected by the NTCA will be sent back to the customer. This allows users to view and sort data from online cash registers, online invoice data reporting and customs declarations into a tax return.
2. Based on an algorithm for the available data, customers will receive a recommendation from the NTCA as to which line of the tax return each transaction should be included in.
3. In the context of the so-called pre-audit function, validation rules are run on the list of supporting documents and the draft tax return prepared as described above, which - before the return is submitted - draws attention to errors that were previously identified from a post-audit. This service should significantly reduce the number of incorrectly filed returns.

The system aims to meet the needs of a wide range of customers with two different interfaces. A user-friendly web interface has been developed for micro and small businesses, while a machine-to-machine solution is available for larger businesses, ensuring the compatibility required for automated communication between the e-VAT system and management software. The usage of the newly introduced service is currently optional for customers.

For further information, please see here: https://youtu.be/zqr8gHiBMnI (accessed on 25 October 2024).

Spain – Self-correction of errors for personal income tax returns

To increase compliance levels and reduce the administrative burden on taxpayers, from 2024 taxpayers have been offered the possibility to correct certain errors made when filing their personal income tax return. This is done through a complementary self-assessment pre-filled by AEAT, which the taxpayer is notified about upon receipt and can choose whether to accept or not. This will be offered both in the voluntary period and once the voluntary period has ended.

Not all self-assessment errors will be corrected through this system, instead it will only be those that arise from discrepancies between the data directly included in the personal income tax return calculated by AEAT, and those declared by the taxpayer.

Sources: Hungary (2024) and Spain (2024).

On-time return filing

Even allowing for changes occurring because of pre-filled or no-return regimes, the filing of a tax return is still the principal means by which a tax liability is established and becomes payable. As a result, the on-time filing rate is seen as an effective measure of the health of the tax system as well as the performance of the tax administration itself.

Traditionally, the ISORA survey measured on-time return filing by putting the number of returns received on-time in relation to the total number of returns expected. ISORA 2023 introduced a new data point which allowed on-time return filing rate also to be measured in relation to the total number of returns received.

Table 4.8. summarises on-time return filing for those administrations able to supply information by tax type. As regards the on-time filing rate in relation to the number of **returns expected**, apart from CIT, the rates are around 85%. The picture is similar when calculating the on-time filing rate in relation to the number of **returns received**, where the rates for PIT, PAYE and VAT on-time return filing are around 90% while the CIT on-time filing rate is 5 percentage points lower. The lower rates for CIT may be explained through more complexity in the corporate income tax system and the preparation of financial statements and year-end reports.

As anticipated, the on-time filing rates expressed as the number of returns received on-time as a percentage of returns received, are noticeably higher than the on-time filing rates expressed in relation to the number of returns expected.

Table 4.8. Average on-time filing rates (in percent) by tax type, 2018-22

	Returns received on-time as a percentage of **returns expected**						Returns received on-time as a percentage of **returns received**	
Tax type	# of jurisdictions	2018	2019	2020	2021	2022	# of jurisdictions	2022
Personal income tax	36 jurisdictions	88.3	85.7	85.6	84.8	84.3	50 jurisdictions	90.3
Corporate income tax	39 jurisdictions	76.6	77.4	76.5	77.4	75.9	50 jurisdictions	85.4
Employer withholding	25 jurisdictions	88.0	87.6	86.3	87.1	86.9	39 jurisdictions	93.2
Value added tax	42 jurisdictions	86.7	85.9	85.5	84.6	85.8	49 jurisdictions	89.4

Note: The table shows the average on-time filing rates for those jurisdictions that were able to provide the information for the years 2018 to 2022 in relation to returns expected, and for the year 2022 in relation to returns received. The number of jurisdictions for which data was available is shown in the table.

Source: CIAT, IOTA, IMF, OECD, International Survey on Revenue Administration, Tables D.22 Rate of returns received on-time: CIT, D.23 Rate of returns received on-time: PIT, D.24 Rate of returns received on-time: PAYE, and D.25 Rate of returns received on-time: VAT, https://data.rafit.org/regular.aspx?key=74180900 (accessed on 10 September 2024).

Table 4.9. shows the evolution of on-time filing rates which, due to the available time series, is expressed as a percentage of returns expected. On average, this has remained broadly static between 2014 and 2022, although the underlying data for on-time filing shows significant variation in the evolution of on-time filing rates between jurisdictions. It should be noted that the table only takes into account information from jurisdictions that were able to provide data for both years 2014 and 2022, which explains the differences in 2022 averages shown in Table 4.8. and Table 4.9.

Table 4.9. Average on-time filing rates (in percent) by tax type, 2014 and 2022

Returns received on-time as a percentage of returns expected

Tax type	2014	2022	Difference in percentage points	No. of jurisdictions with a **decreasing** on-time filing rate	No. of jurisdictions with an **increasing** on-time filing rate
Personal income tax (38 jurisdictions)	86.1	85.7	-0.4	18	20
Corporate income tax (36 jurisdictions)	80.0	78.5	-1.5	17	19
Employer withholding (18 jurisdictions)	86.9	90.0	+3.1	10	8
Value added tax (37 jurisdictions)	86.0 (2016)	85.8	-0.2	23	14

Note: The table shows the average on-time filing rates for those jurisdictions that were able to provide the information for the years 2014 and 2022. The number of jurisdictions for which data was available is shown in parenthesis. For VAT, the table compares information for the years 2016 and 2022, as the underlying question was changed with ISORA 2018.
Sources: CIAT, IOTA, IMF, OECD, International Survey on Revenue Administration, Tables D.22 Rate of returns received on-time: CIT, D.23 Rate of returns received on-time: PIT, D.24 Rate of returns received on-time: PAYE, and D.25 Rate of returns received on-time: VAT, https://data.rafit.org/regular.aspx?key=74180900 (accessed on 10 September 2024), OECD (2017), *Tax Administration 2017: Comparative Information on OECD and Other Advanced and Emerging Economies*, Table A.6., https://doi.org/10.1787/tax_admin-2017-en, and OECD (2019), *Tax Administration 2019: Comparative Information on OECD and Other Advanced and Emerging Economies*, Table D.12., https://doi.org/10.1787/74d162b6-en.

The variation of on-time filing rates (expressed as a percentage of returns received) by jurisdiction are also visible in:

- Figure 4.1. which shows the range of on-time filing rates across major tax types. For a number of jurisdictions this range is significant.
- Figure 4.2. which shows the PIT and CIT on-time filing rates.

Figure 4.1. Range in on-time filing performance across major tax types, 2022

Returns received on-time as a percentage of returns received

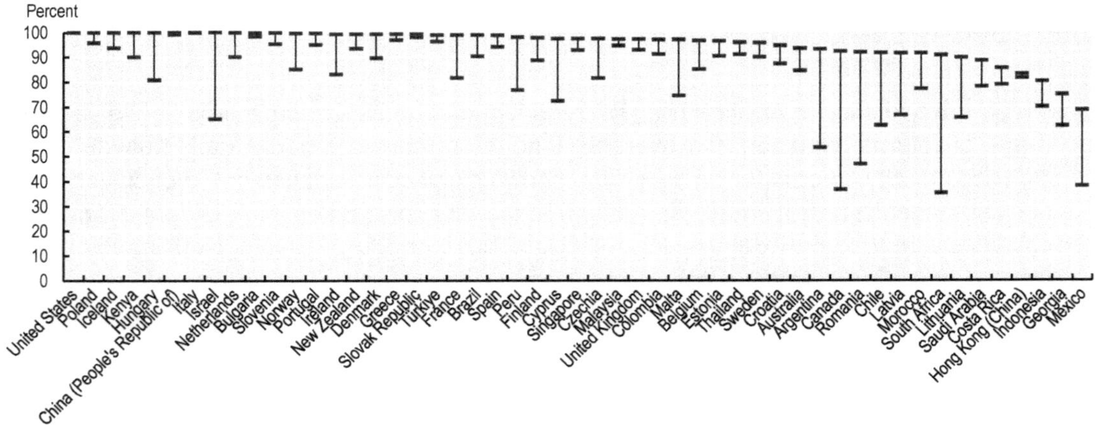

Note: The figure shows for each jurisdiction the range in on-time filing performances in 2022 across the four tax types: PIT, CIT, Employer withholding and VAT (where applicable). It only includes jurisdictions for which information was available for at least two tax types.
Source: CIAT, IOTA, IMF, OECD, International Survey on Revenue Administration, Tables D.22 Rate of returns received on-time: CIT, D.23 Rate of returns received on-time: PIT, D.24 Rate of returns received on-time: PAYE, and D.25 Rate of returns received on-time: VAT, https://data.rafit.org/regular.aspx?key=74180900 (accessed on 10 September 2024).

StatLink https://stat.link/iy8kmr

Figure 4.2. PIT and CIT on-time filing rates, 2022

Returns received on-time as a percentage of returns received

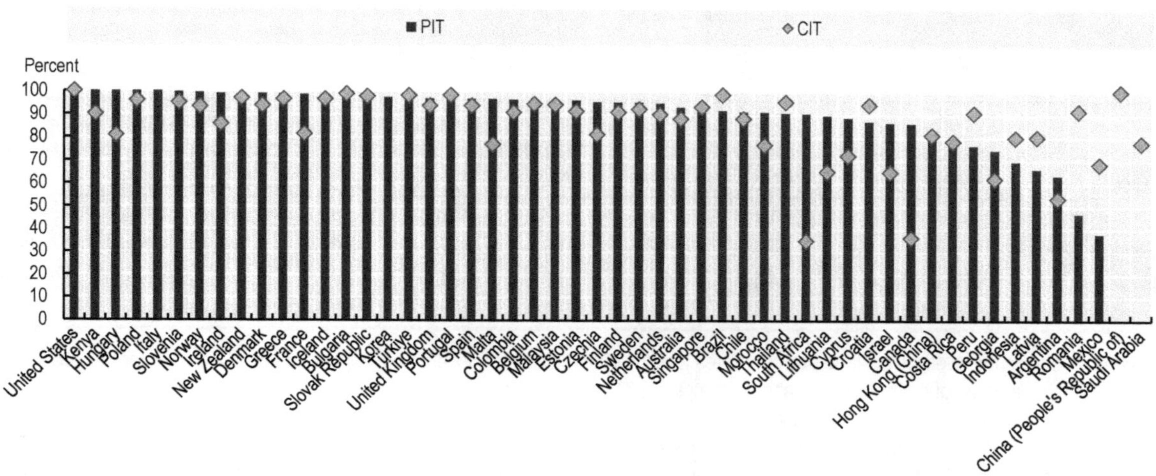

Source: CIAT, IOTA, IMF, OECD, International Survey on Revenue Administration, Tables D.22 Rate of returns received on-time: CIT, and D.23 Rate of returns received on-time: PIT, https://data.rafit.org/regular.aspx?key=74180900 (accessed on 10 September 2024).

StatLink https://stat.link/6rzne4

Given the impact on compliance rates, many tax administrations are turning to behavioural insight techniques to try and encourage more timely and accurate filing. This is seeing promising results, with tax administrations reporting that 'nudges' at key points in the filing process can increase the timeliness of filing. Not only is this improving compliance rates, but it is also freeing up resources that can be used elsewhere. Chapter 6 contains further information on the use of behavioural insights.

On-time payment

Payment of tax constitutes one of the most common interactions between taxpayers and tax administrations, especially for businesses that are typically required to regularly remit a variety of payments covering both their own tax liabilities and those of their employees. Administrations continue to make progress in increasing the range of e-payment options available to taxpayers and to increase their use. This progress not only lowers the cost to the administration, it can also increase on-time payments and reduce the number of payment arrears cases by providing improved access and a better payment experience. One significant development is the growth of payment facilities being built into the natural systems of taxpayers. This is making payment more seamless for taxpayers, as they can use their existing banking or accounting software to make payments.

Traditionally, and similar to on-time return filing, the ISORA survey measured on-time payment by putting the value of payments received on-time in relation to the total value of payments due. ISORA 2023 introduced a new data point allowing the on-time payment rate to also be measured in relation to the total value of payments received.

On-time payment rates for those administrations able to supply information by tax type are summarised in Tables 4.10. and 4.11. Table 4.10. shows that the slight reduction in on-time payment rates (expressed as a percentage of **payments due**) that can be observed for years 2020 and 2021 is also visible in 2022 for

PIT, PAYE and VAT. Only the average on-time payment rate for CIT is back to its pre-pandemic value. Apart from PIT, the rates are in the mid to high-80s. Similarly, when looking at the on-time payment rates in relation to **payments received**, the rates for CIT, PAYE and VAT are around 90%, while the rate for PIT is around 85%.

Table 4.10. Average on-time payment rates (in percent) by tax type, 2018-22

	Payments made on-time as a percentage of **payments due**						Payments made on-time as a percentage of **payments received**	
Tax type	# of jurisdictions	2018	2019	2020	2021	2022	# of jurisdictions	2022
Personal income tax	29 jurisdictions	81.7	81.1	78.7	75.8	76.8	35 jurisdictions	84.4
Corporate income tax	31 jurisdictions	84.4	84.2	81.5	82.3	83.8	36 jurisdictions	89.2
Employer withholding	28 jurisdictions	94.4	94.2	91.0	90.8	89.7	32 jurisdictions	91.6
Value added tax	31 jurisdictions	87.8	87.9	86.3	86.1	85.5	33 jurisdictions	89.5

Note: The table shows the average on-time payment rates for those jurisdictions that were able to provide the information for the years 2018 to 2022 in relation to the value of payments due, and for the year 2022 in relation to the value of payments received. The number of jurisdictions for which data was available is shown in the table.
Source: CIAT, IOTA, IMF, OECD, International Survey on Revenue Administration, Tables D.36 Rate of payments received on-time: CIT, D.37 Rate of payments received on-time: PIT, D.38 Rate of payments received on-time: PAYE, and D.39 Rate of payments received on-time: VAT, https://data.rafit.org/regular.aspx?key=74180902 (accessed on 10 September 2024).

Looking at Table 4.11. which shows the changes in average on-time payment rates between 2014 and 2022, it seems that the rates have declined across all tax types. However, looking at the data by jurisdiction it becomes obvious that number of jurisdictions with decreasing rates and those with increasing rates are almost split evenly. Also, the number of administrations that were able to provide on-time payment data is very low.

Table 4.11. Average on-time payment rates (in percent) by tax type, 2014 and 2022

Payments received on-time as a percentage of payments due

Tax type	2014	2022	Difference in percentage points	No. of jurisdictions with a **decreasing** on-time payment rate	No. of jurisdictions with an **increasing** on-time payment rate
Personal income tax (16 jurisdictions)	80.7	77.3	-3.4	10	6
Corporate income tax (16 jurisdictions)	90.1	86.7	-3.4	8	8
Employer withholding (14 jurisdictions)	93.0	90.2	-2.8	6	8
Value added tax (18 jurisdictions)	88.8	88.3	-0.5	8	10

Note: The table shows the average on-time filing rates for those jurisdictions that were able to provide the information for the years 2014 and 2022. The number of jurisdictions for which data was available is shown in parenthesis. Data for Costa Rica has been excluded from the calculations as it would distort the average ratios.
Sources: CIAT, IOTA, IMF, OECD, International Survey on Revenue Administration, Tables D.36 Rate of payments received on-time: CIT, D.37 Rate of payments received on-time: PIT, D.38 Rate of payments received on-time: PAYE, and D.39 Rate of payments received on-time: VAT, https://data.rafit.org/regular.aspx?key=74180902 (accessed on 10 September 2024), and OECD (2017), *Tax Administration 2017: Comparative Information on OECD and Other Advanced and Emerging Economies*, Table A.9, https://doi.org/10.1787/tax_admin-2017-en.

The range of on-time payment depicted in Figure 4.3. shows a significant gap in on-time payment across the main tax types for a number of jurisdictions, in some cases above 30 percentage points.

Figure 4.3. Range in on-time payment performance across major tax types, 2022

Payments received on-time as a percentage of payments received

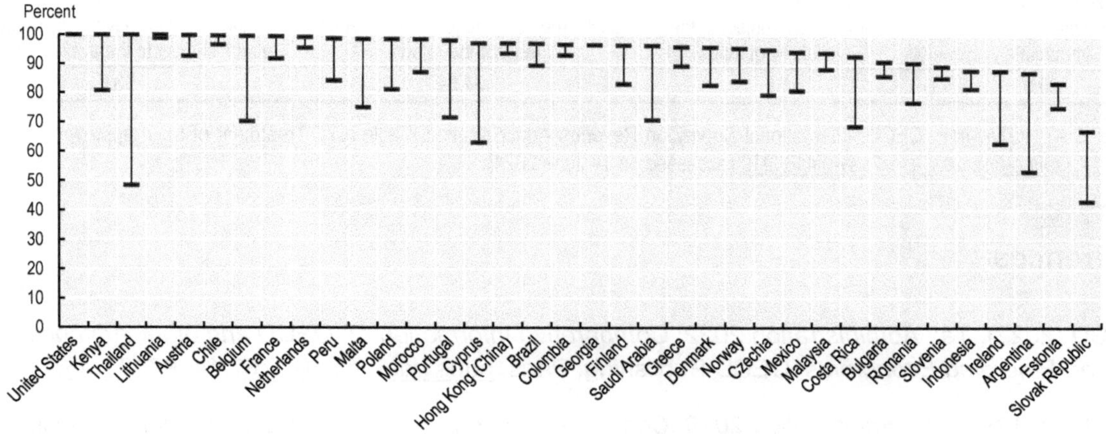

Note: The figure shows for each jurisdiction the range in on-time payment performances in 2022 across the four tax types: PIT, CIT, Employer withholding and VAT (where applicable). It only includes jurisdictions for which information was available for at least two tax types.
Source: CIAT, IOTA, IMF, OECD, International Survey on Revenue Administration, Tables D.36 Rate of payments received on-time: CIT, D.37 Rate of payments received on-time: PIT, D.38 Rate of payments received on-time: PAYE, and D.39 Rate of payments received on-time: VAT, https://data.rafit.org/regular.aspx?key=74180902 (accessed on 10 September 2024).

StatLink https://stat.link/8af21b

Future editions of this report will continue to track these trends, and recovering and increasing on-time payment rates will no doubt remain an area of focus for administrations given the amounts of revenue involved, with many tax administrations reporting investing additional resources in this area, to make payments easier and more in real time.

Refunds and credits

Given the underlying design of the major taxes administered (i.e. PIT, CIT and VAT), some element of over-payment by a proportion of taxpayers is unavoidable. Excess tax payments represent a cost to taxpayers in terms of "the opportunity cost", which is particularly critical to businesses that are operating with tight margins where cash flow is paramount. Any delays in refunding legitimately overpaid taxes may therefore result in significant "costs" to taxpayers.

Table 4.12. shows the different treatment of VAT refunds, and highlights that the majority of administrations pay out refunds immediately. This is helpful to business, but tax administrations need to continue to be cognisant of fraud risks. Tax regimes with a high incidence of tax refunds are particularly attractive to fraudsters (especially via organised criminal attacks) necessitating effective risk-based approaches for identifying potentially fraudulent refund claims.

Table 4.12. Treatment of VAT refunds, 2022

Percentage of jurisdictions where ...			
VAT refunds are automatically paid out immediately	VAT refunds are paid out immediately subject to the availability of funds	VAT refund are established as a 'credit' in the taxpayer's account, until such time as the taxpayer may legally request the refund	VAT refund are established as a 'credit' in the taxpayer's account, until such time as the taxpayer may legally request the refund, subject to the availability of funds
60.0	1.8	34.5	3.6

Source: CIAT, IOTA, IMF, OECD, International Survey on Revenue Administration, Table A.72 Treatment of most approved VAT refunds, https://data.rafit.org/regular.aspx?key=74180910 (accessed on 14 June 2024).

References

OECD (2022), *Tax Administration 2022: Comparative Information on OECD and other Advanced and Emerging Economies*, OECD Publishing, Paris, https://doi.org/10.1787/1e797131-en. [1]

OECD (2019), *Tax Administration 2019: Comparative Information on OECD and other Advanced and Emerging Economies*, OECD Publishing, Paris, https://doi.org/10.1787/74d162b6-en. [3]

OECD (2017), *Tax Administration 2017: Comparative Information on OECD and Other Advanced and Emerging Economies*, OECD Publishing, Paris, https://doi.org/10.1787/tax_admin-2017-en. [2]

5 Services

This chapter examines how tax administrations' compliance goals are met by providing effective and efficient services to taxpayers, increasingly through technology. This is helping increase voluntary compliance amongst taxpayers by making it easier to understand tax obligations, report taxable income and make payments.

Introduction

A core part of supporting taxpayer compliance is the provision of a wide range of effective and easy to use services for taxpayers - such as educational initiatives, specific guidance, appropriate prompts or calculation tools. Providing the right services, to the satisfaction of taxpayers and other stakeholders, will increase the level of participation, taxpayer trust, and confidence in the tax system as a whole. Consequently, four out of five tax administrations covered in this publication are taking a strategic approach towards taxpayer services and assistance as seen in Table 5.1.

Table 5.1. Service and assistance strategy, and service delivery standards, 2022

Percentage of administrations

Formal taxpayer service and assistance strategy exists	If yes, strategy is published	Formal set of service delivery standards is produced	If yes, set of standards is published
78.9	71.1	84.5	61.2

Source: CIAT, IOTA, IMF, OECD, International Survey on Revenue Administration, Table B.4 Selected governance practices: Plans, reports and standards; and organizational chart, https://data.rafit.org/regular.aspx?key=74180913 (accessed on 10 September 2024); and Table B.46 Gender-based analysis of taxpayer satisfaction, and service and assistance strategy, https://data.rafit.org/regular.aspx?key=74180919 (accessed on 10 September 2024).

Also, as illustrated in Table 5.1, around 85% of tax administrations have adopted a formal set of service delivery standards, with the majority of those making the standards public. Creating a commitment to service provision and keeping themselves accountable against those standards will further enhance trust and confidence among stakeholders, and positively contribute to taxpayer compliance. Some selected links to service standards and commitments are included in Table 5.2.

Table 5.2. Links to selected service delivery commitments and standards

Jurisdiction	Links (accessed on 10 September 2024)
Australia	https://www.ato.gov.au/about-ato/commitments-and-reporting/service-commitments
Canada	https://www.canada.ca/en/revenue-agency/services/about-canada-revenue-agency-cra/service-standards-cra.html
Hong Kong (China)	https://www.ird.gov.hk/eng/abo/pam32.htm
Ireland	https://www.revenue.ie/en/corporate/information-about-revenue/customer-service/service-standards/index.aspx
Italy	https://www.agenziaentrate.gov.it/portale/web/guest/agenzia/amministrazione-trasparente/servizi-erogati/carta-servizi/la-qualita-dei-servizi/il-monitoraggio

Taxpayer compliance can, of course, be heavily affected by elements outside of the control of the tax administration, for example the state of the economy, changes in the reporting environment (for example a shift from salaried work to self-employment) and the perceived fairness of tax policy among other things. There are, though, a number of areas that tax administrations can consider when supporting taxpayer compliance through their service offerings:

- Understanding and meeting taxpayer preferences;
- Supporting self-service;
- Providing educational and support initiatives; and
- Providing collaborative services.

This chapter examines those areas in more detail. It also comments on the importance of providing an inclusive set of services to ensure equitable access for all citizens, including those with disabilities or those without online access.

Understanding and meeting taxpayer preferences

Taxpayer contact volumes are very large scale. Administrations reported more than 3.5 billion incoming contacts via online taxpayer accounts, and there are still more than 300 million incoming telephone contacts (see Table 5.4). However, unlike many other government services, at the individual level taxpayers will often have very limited periodic contact with tax administrations and for some this may be in relatively stressful situations involving significant sums of money or with risks of penalties in the background. For many taxpayers, expectations have also changed as regards the availability of services and response times, particularly following the COVID-19 pandemic and in light of the ongoing digital transformation of the economy.

Taxpayer satisfaction surveys can provide valuable information to tax administrations regarding services' expectations as well as insights into service perception. Table 5.3. shows that around 85% of administrations indicated measuring individual taxpayer satisfaction, and 75% business taxpayer satisfaction. The percentage is lower when it comes to measuring the satisfaction of tax intermediaries, with 56% of administrations conducting satisfaction surveys from this stakeholder group. For those conducting taxpayer satisfaction surveys, slightly more than half publish the results across all three groups. Box 5.1. contains examples of administrations understanding and meeting taxpayer preferences.

Table 5.3. Conduction of taxpayer satisfaction surveys, 2022

Percentage of administrations

Individual taxpayers			Business taxpayers			Tax intermediaries		
	If yes ...			If yes ...			If yes ...	
Survey conducted	External vendor used	Results made public	Survey conducted	External vendor used	Results made public	Survey conducted	External vendor used	Results made public
84.2	64.6	58.3	75.4	58.1	55.8	56.1	62.5	56.3

Source: CIAT, IOTA, IMF, OECD, International Survey on Revenue Administration, Table B.45 Satisfaction surveys, https://data.rafit.org/regular.aspx?key=74180919 (accessed on 10 September 2024).

Box 5.1. Examples – Understanding and meeting taxpayer preferences

Czechia – Functional Currency

A functional currency is typically the currency in which the company conducts the majority of its transactions. Currently in the Czech Republic, this may be the Euro, the US Dollar or the British Pound, in addition to the Czech Crown. The 2024 Accounting Act has been introduced to reduce the administrative burden and make accounting in the Czech Republic more compatible with global accounting frameworks, reducing conflicts with EU law. It allows companies to use a functional currency as the currency of accounting, in addition to the Czech Crown.

Although a taxpayer may keep its accounting records in a currency other than the Czech Crown, the tax base and the tax itself, will continue to be reported in Czech Crowns in the corporate income tax return with the legislation containing special provisions for the conversion of the functional currency when calculating tax. In the future it is expected that the list of functional currencies will be expanded and additionally the tax liability itself will be calculated and further administrated in the functional currency.

United Kingdom – Child Benefit digital transformation

The United Kingdom's HM Revenue and Customs (HMRC) have enabled thousands of parents to claim their Child Benefit payments online – reducing wait times and customer costs. Between February and September 2023 these new services were accessed more than 2.7 million times. HMRC has reduced the need for customers to print or post forms, reducing wait times (from claim to payment) from nineteen days to just three days for most customers.

To improve customer contact and provide reassurance about the progress of online claims, HMRC is developing the use of digital communications to provide customers with the information they need, when they need it, using their channel of choice. One of the main reasons that customers contact HMRC is to 'progress chase' and HMRC has received customer feedback that reassurance is important when interacting online.

New technology introduced in 2024 will enable HMRC to provide targeted support such as text messages and push notifications to customers to take action and provide assurance that the task has been successfully completed, all without having to call HMRC. In January 2024, HMRC started sending a selection of Child Benefit claimant customers an SMS message, reassuring them that their claims were being processed and pointing them to further information online, reducing the need for them to contact HMRC.

Sources: Czechia (2024) and the United Kingdom (2024).

An important aspect of meeting taxpayer preferences is getting the mix of channels right. Table 5.4. highlights the shift to digital that occurred since the COVID-19 pandemic, with use of online channels continuing to grow significantly. The decline of in-person visits to the tax office did not persist during 2022. However, it remains well below pre-pandemic volumes. Digital assistance, for example through chatbots, has become an important channel in many jurisdictions. The data confirms a structural shift away from channels that occur during tax office working hours to channels that can be used 24/7.

Table 5.4. Service demand by channel, 2018-22

Channel type		No. of jurisdictions	2018	2019	2020	2021	2022
Online via taxpayer account	Total number	30	1 076 833 409	1 245 565 136	1 837 708 162	2 418 962 911	3 535 474 264
	Change in %			+15.7	+47.5	+31.6	+46.2
Telephone call	Total number	51	327 203 283	312 515 920	307 606 424	346 034 546	317 564 223
	Change in %			-4.5	-1.6	+12.5	-8.2
In-person	Total number	35	109 620 990	109 052 857	48 699 279	41 594 555	51 484 632
	Change in %			-0.5	-55.3	-14.6	+23.8
Mail / post	Total number	15	35 039 012	35 166 408	31 998 546	35 602 576	39 389 387
	Change in %			+0.4	-9.0	+11.3	+10.6
E-mail	Total number	27	11 237 613	12 673 006	17 366 766	20 062 665	30 997 857
	Change in %			+12.8	+37.0	+15.5	+54.5
Digital assistance	Total number	30	11 022 155	21 310 120	30 673 147	52 669 925	60 661 905
	Change in %			+93.3	+43.9	+71.7	+15.2

Note: The table only includes jurisdictions for which data was available for 2018 to 2022. The number of jurisdictions for which data was available is shown in the table.

Sources: CIAT, IOTA, IMF, OECD, International Survey on Revenue Administration, Tables A.96 Incoming service contacts: Track keeping and number of contacts by channel - Online and digital assistance, A.97 Incoming service contacts: Number of contacts by channel - Telephone call and e-mail, and A.98 Incoming service contacts: Number of contacts by channel - Mail / post and in-person, https://data.rafit.org/regular.aspx?key=74180896 (accessed on 10 September 2024).

Understanding what channels taxpayers are using and how will allow tax administrations to adjust their service offerings, if needed. As Table 5.5. illustrates, the vast majority of administrations use statistics about service channel usage to create new or improved services, and to anticipate service demand to adjust staff allocation.

Table 5.5. Use of statistics about service channel usage, 2022

Percentage of administrations

Use of statistics about service channel usage to …			
Encourage service adoption by taxpayers (e.g. promote self-service)	Create new or improved services	Anticipate service demand to adjust staff allocation	Reduce information and communication technology service disruptions
86.2	89.7	79.3	75.9

Source: CIAT, IOTA, IMF, OECD, International Survey on Revenue Administration, Table B.39 Service channels: Statistics about service channel usage, https://data.rafit.org/regular.aspx?key=74180919 (accessed on 10 September 2024).

Box 5.2. United Kingdom – Removal of postal outputs

HMRC is reducing the amount of post sent to customers to speed up and simplify customer communication while reducing costs. Business improvements are also being implemented which support a digital journey for the customer.

In 2023/24, HMRC stopped sending letters reminding customers new to the self-assessment system of their first filing deadline, letters relating to self-assessment and Corporation Tax repayment notifications or a Pay As You Earn employers payment booklet. These changes have removed around 5.2 million pieces of HMRC-generated post.

HMRC is developing plans to build on these successes in 2024/25, aiming to:

- Eradicate unnecessary paper outputs;
- Provide digital versions of paper outputs for customers who use our online services;
- Improve content for customers including better signposting to digital channels and guidance, for example, through the use of QR codes.

Source: United Kingdom (2024).

Supporting self-service

The self-service offering from tax administrations continues to grow, with an expanding range of self-services being provided. Common examples of this include the ability to register, file and pay on-line, along with a range of interactive tools. This is leading to efficiency gains in tax administrations, as well as being able to provide a more 24/7-style service to taxpayers. More than 85% of administrations indicated using service channel data to encourage service adoption by taxpayers, for example by promoting self-service (see Table 5.5.).

Table 5.6. illustrates some of the online services that administrations are offering. While the ISORA survey looked at the availability of those online services, there is additional information in the Inventory of Tax Technology Initiatives (ITTI) that shows whether automated responses are sent (when pre-determined criteria are met) to a person requesting, for example, when asking for extensions of deadlines or payment arrangements, see Table 5.7. Providing those automated responses, without human intervention, makes those genuine self-services.

The growth in the use of technology and more personalised services has also seen tax administrations focus more on the experience of taxpayers in using these services. This has also led to taxpayer centred service improvements which help improve outcomes for administrations and taxpayers alike. As mentioned in Chapter 10, a significant number of administrations, around 70%, employ user interface design specialists with the goal of ensuring that services are easy to use (see Table 10.4.).

Table 5.6. Provision of online services, 2022

Percentage of administrations

Virtual assistants (e.g. chatbots)	Tax calculators	Taxpayer portal providing 'whole of taxpayer' view	Requesting extensions of deadlines	Asking for payment arrangements	Secure communication with taxpayer	Uploading files onto the tax administration's systems	Filing tax related objections	Viewing taxpayer information captured from 3rd parties
63.8	82.8	84.5	70.7	79.3	89.7	93.1	87.9	75.9

Source: CIAT, IOTA, IMF, OECD, International Survey on Revenue Administration, Tables B.41 Service channels: Online services - Part 1, and B.42 Service channels: Online services - Part 2, https://data.rafit.org/regular.aspx?key=74180919 (accessed on 10 September 2024), and Table A.110 Innovative technologies: Implementation and usage - Whole-of-government identification, digital authentication technology, and virtual assistants, https://data.rafit.org/regular.aspx?key=74180897 (accessed on 10 September 2024).

Table 5.7. Online services with automated responses, 2022

Percentage of administrations that provide automated responses (when pre-determined criteria are met) as a percent of those that offer the respective online service

Tax type	**Registering for tax:** Registrant receives an automated response with tax registration number	**Filing tax returns:** Returns are automatically processed and the assessments sent to taxpayers without human intervention	**Requesting extensions of deadlines:** Requesting person receives automated response whether extension of deadline has been accepted or rejected	**Asking for payment arrangements**: Requesting person receives automated response whether payment arrangement has been accepted or rejected
Personal income tax	51.0	68.6	5.9	33.3
Corporate income tax	55.8	51.9	5.8	30.8
Value added tax	42.9	49.0	6.1	26.5

Note: The table shows the number of administrations that provide automated responses for online services when pre-determined criteria are met, as a percent of those administrations that offer such online services. The percentages are based on ITTI data from 52 jurisdictions that are covered in this report and that have completed the global survey on digitalisation.
Source: OECD et al. (2024), Inventory of Tax Technology Initiatives, https://web-archive.oecd.org/temp/2023-03-09/618462-taxpayer-touchpoints.htm, Tables TT1, TT2 and TT3 (accessed on 10 September 2024).

Box 5.3. Examples – Enhancing self-service

Bulgaria – Submission of taxpayer data

The National Revenue Agency (NRA) has introduced a new service whereby data can be submitted automatically by the taxpayer through their own systems as opposed to having to enter the NRA portal and upload files. This is done either through a public application programming interface or through communication at the system-system level. This allows for the process to be carried out automatically in the clients' data processing systems and makes it easier for the taxpayer to comply with their obligations.

Canada – Secure exchange of files

The Canada Revenue Agency (CRA) has introduced a Secure Drop Zone (SDZ) initiative to facilitate the secure exchange of files up to 10Gb of data between the CRA and their clients. This initiative helps address the critical need for secure data sharing of large data files.

SDZ provides a cost saving and practical solution that can be implemented in multiple administrative contexts, allowing the exchange of sensitive information in a quick and efficient manner. By introducing SDZ, the CRA has improved the speed and safety of digital file exchanges between its programmes and its clients. This approach ensures that sensitive information is shared securely, reducing the risk of data breaches.

The implementation of this initiative has yielded significant results for the CRA. SDZ has streamlined the receipt of information into one hub, reduced the time required for data sharing, reduced the risk of sharing sensitive tax-related information by less secure methods and ensured that each file transfer has an audit trail.

China (People's Republic of) – Modernising Personal Income Tax collection

The State Tax Administration (STA) has modernised the process of collecting Personal Income Taxes. This approach aims to accelerate the digital transformation and improvement of the personal income tax system, improving the experience for both tax administrations and taxpayers. The key features are:

- Mobile application: The introduction of a mobile tax app has made filing tax returns easier by breaking down complex paper returns into individual, comprehensible components. Innovations such as pre-filled forms and automatic payment calculations have made it easier for people to comply with their obligations, making filing tax returns more efficient and reducing the need for paper forms.
- Information sharing mechanisms across government departments: Sharing information across government departments verifies the data provided by the taxpayer. This makes it easier for taxpayers to claim benefits, get any refunds and qualify for any special additional deductions.
- Behavioural insights: Behavioural insight methods have been used to send personalised prompts and reminders to taxpayers to encourage them to fulfil their obligations. An annual tax review feature helps taxpayers remember important tax events and filings, promoting awareness and changing paying taxes from being a burden to something to be celebrated.
- Online webchat platform: A new platform is under construction to provide personalised assistance when taxpayers have questions around tax policies or system operations. Programmed using artificial intelligence, when taxpayers have a question, a virtual assistant provides answers. This is aimed at improving the taxpayer experience.

Costa Rica – Integrated Tax Administration System

Costa Rica has invested a considerable amount in the implementation of a new tax administration platform – the Integrated Tax Administration System (TRIBU-CR) - to upgrade the tax agency's online services. This will offer services such as registration, declaration, payment, applications processing, consultations and complaints handling. It will also allow for the automatic exchange of information with OECD countries. TRIBU-CR is going to start to work in 2025.

Portugal – Online tax residency certification

Portugal has simplified the procedure for filing the Residence Tax Certificate. This is a compulsory document issued by the Portuguese Tax and Customs Authority attesting tax residence in Portugal, for the purposes of applying double taxation conventions. As of 1 January 2022, taxpayers no longer need to send the forms to the tax office to be signed and stamped.

Instead, taxpayers can request a Certificate of Residency (CoR) from the Portuguese Tax and Customs Authority website, and, as long as they meet the requirements, the CoR becomes immediately available to download or print. This new procedure for obtaining a CoR has significantly reduced the taxpayers' administrative burden, as they no longer have to physically handle any documents given the procedure is handled electronically.

In order to make it a secure form, validation mechanisms have been introduced that can be checked at any time by foreign tax administrations and taxpayers.

This has also reduced the burden on Portuguese taxpayers that need a certification of residency in foreign jurisdictions, as all of Portugal's double taxation agreement partners have been informed about this new procedure. Taxpayers just have to fill in the forms of the foreign jurisdiction they are resident in, attach the Portuguese CoR, and send the documentation to the relevant authorities.

Spain – Multi-channel information and assistance service specifically addressed to non-residents

Spain have introduced a new service to provide information and assistance on taxation matters for non-residents without permanent establishment (Non-Resident Income Tax, non-established VAT, Inheritance and Gift Tax and payment by transfers from abroad), through various non-face-to-face channels (telephone appointment, virtual assistant available in Spanish and English, chat and online forms). The service is provided by specialised officials from 9 am to 7 pm.

Sources: Bulgaria (2024), Canada (2024), China (People's Republic of) (2024), Costa Rica (2024), Portugal (2024) and Spain (2024).

Virtual assistants

The previous editions of this series highlighted how a growing number of administrations are using virtual or digital assistants to help respond to taxpayer enquiries and support self-service. This is confirmed through the data in Table 5.4. on service demand by channel, but also in Table 5.8. which shows that the growth has been significant (plus 29 percentage points between 2018 and 2022) and that these services are now commonly used by many administrations.

Table 5.8. Use of virtual assistants, artificial intelligence and application programming interfaces, 2018-22

Percentage of administrations that use this technology

Status of implementation and use	Virtual assistants (e.g. chatbots)			Artificial intelligence (AI), including machine learning			Application programming interfaces (APIs)		
	2018	2022	Difference in percentage points (p.p.)	2018	2022	Difference in p.p.	2018	2022	Difference in p.p.
Technology is implemented and used	34.5	63.8	+29.3	29.8	63.8	+34.0	79.0	96.6	+17.6
Technology is in the implementation phase for future use	13.8	17.2	+3.4	15.8	24.1	+8.3	7.0	3.4	-3.6
Technology is not used, incl. situations where the implementation has not started	51.7	19.0	-32.7	54.4	12.1	-42.3	14.0	0.0	-14.0

Sources: CIAT, IOTA, IMF, OECD, International Survey on Revenue Administration, Tables A.108 Innovative technologies: Implementation and usage - Blockchain, artificial intelligence, and cloud computing, A.109 Innovative technologies: Implementation and usage - Data science, robotic process automation, and APIs, and A.110 Innovative technologies: Implementation and usage - Whole-of-government identification, digital authentication technology, and virtual assistants, https://data.rafit.org/regular.aspx?key=74180897 (accessed on 10 September 2024).

The success of these services continues to be developed further, with jurisdictions investigating how they can use advances in artificial intelligence (AI) to deliver more sophisticated levels of support. Figure 5.1. shows that 40% of administrations who have a virtual assistant are using AI in some form to improve the service. This can allow the system to cope with more complex questions being asked by taxpayers and/or more personalised answers being given. This is part of the wider trend of the use of AI in tax administration which can be seen throughout this report.

Figure 5.1. Type of virtual assistants, 2022

Percentage of administrations

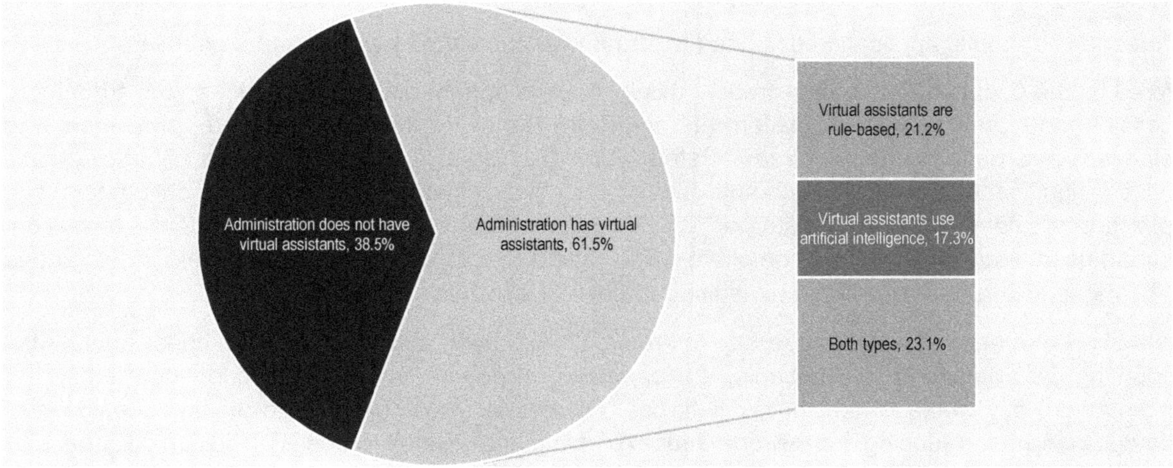

Note: The percentages are based on ITTI data from 52 jurisdictions that are covered in this report and that have completed the global survey on digitalisation.
Source: OECD et al. (2024), Inventory of Tax Technology Initiatives, https://web-archive.oecd.org/temp/2023-03-09/618462-taxpayer-touchpoints.htm, Table TT5 (accessed on 10 September 2024).

StatLink https://stat.link/2a0wxr

Box 5.4. Türkiye – Digital Tax Assistant

Türkiye has introduced an online chat service to provide fast and easily accessible up-to-date information on tax legislation, which in turn aims to increase the efficiency of the administration and improve the customer experiences.

The Digital Tax Assistant (GIBI), is supported by Artificial Intelligence (AI) and has the capacity to provide 24/7 service to users. It provides answers to general, non-personal and non-case-specific legislative questions as well as general guidance on electronic services. It also enables taxpayers to carry out certain functions online, such as making payments.

GIBI can be accessed through the tax administration website, through the GIB mobile app or messenger apps. GIBI is constantly updating and improving its answers through machine learning.

Source: Türkiye (2024).

Mobile applications

The recent trend for the increasing use of mobile applications by tax administrations seen in other editions of this series has continued. Mobile applications allow taxpayers to access services on the go, and thus provide additional flexibility and support self-service.

While the main use often remains the provision of information and guidance, mobile applications are becoming increasingly transactional, and are becoming a primary way for taxpayers to access relevant records and personal tax accounts, communicate with the tax administration, supply information and tax returns and make payments. Box 5.5. provides latest developments in this area.

Box 5.5. Examples – Mobile applications

Croatia – mPorenza: Simplifying tax compliance through mobile convenience

mPorezna is a mobile application designed to streamline and simplify tax-related processes.

Offered by the Croatian Tax Administration, this innovative app marks a significant leap toward a more accessible and user-friendly tax system and improves the way citizens, freelancers, craftsmen, and businesses in Croatia manage their tax-related tasks. The versatile app delivers an array of electronic services, significantly reducing the complexities and costs associated with meeting tax obligations. The application provides real-time updates on tax obligations, deadlines, and other pertinent information, ensuring users stay informed and compliant. mPorezna also supports the digital submission of various tax forms, reducing paperwork and expediting the overall process.

Users of mPorezna gain instant access to tax-related information and services, from checking their tax accounting card balance to downloading 2D barcodes for payments, reviewing submitted forms, the app ensures easy management of tax liabilities. mPorezna also supports the digital submission of various tax forms, reducing paperwork and expediting the overall process. Additionally, the app facilitates fiscal responsibility by enabling users to verify issued invoices via QR code scanning and report inaccuracies directly to the Tax Administration.

This proactive approach aligns with the broader digital transformation goals, making tax compliance more manageable and accessible in an era dominated by mobile technologies. Available on app stores, mPorezna represents a pivotal step towards a more accessible, efficient, and user-friendly tax management system.

Hungary – Mobile application

The National Tax and Customs Administration (NTCA) of Hungary is committed to reducing administrative burdens by taking digitalisation to a higher level.

In 2022, the NTCA Mobile application was used by nearly half a million taxpayers. As a result of recent improvements, taxpayers now have the NTCA's general taxpayer information interface at their fingertips - where they can consult useful information such as their current account data, the quantities of goods they can bring in and take out of the country without paying taxes, the current settlement prices of fuel, and their employment relationship data.

Moreover, further developments of this platform have seen the roll-out of complete services for tax compliance. For example, a simplified user interface was developed and the payment system improved to make it easier for taxpayers to pay vehicle tax, with a legally mandated instalment payment request feature introduced in 2024. A notification functionality was also introduced in the mobile app, which sends push notifications to the taxpayer's smartphone with a notification of changes in the taxpayer's employment details (e.g. hours worked).

For more information, please see here: https://www.youtube.com/watch?v=WBOzHOAzq6Y (accessed on 10 September 2024).

United Kingdom – Storing National Insurance numbers in the mobile application and digital wallets

HMRC has supported more of its customers to self-serve through digital channels. In the last twelve months, 3.28 million customers have used the HMRC App 77.9 million times, a growth of 73% when compared with customers in the previous twelve months. The HMRC App has a rating between 4.7 - 4.8/5 on online app stores.

HMRC has also made it easier for taxpayers to find and store their National Insurance Number (NINO). In a first for HMRC, an innovative feature has been launched enabling individuals to store a NINO in a digital wallet in their devices. More than 335 000 customers have stored their NINO in a digital wallet and around 700 000 customers have also viewed or downloaded a NINO letter. These improvements will help reduce calls from people who have lost their NINOs and help HMRC move away from issuing paper letters.

Sources: Croatia (2024), Hungary (2024) and the United Kingdom (2024).

Educational and support initiatives

Education of taxpayers has two aspects, one around taxpayers' understanding of their own obligations and their abilities to meet them and the other awareness-raising around the role of tax in society. Both are important factors in supporting voluntary compliance. Influencing beliefs, attitudes and norms is generally considered an effective and efficient way to influence compliance behaviour over the long term. In this regard, the majority of tax administrations report carrying out educational initiatives and around half provide free tax services for new businesses and lower income individuals (see Table 5.9.).

In practice, this will include the provision of online material and e-learning, information campaigns (including through social media), and conferences and community outreach among other forms. The importance of social media to inform citizens has been recognised by almost all administrations, with 95%

indicating that they use social media to distribute information, and around 75% reporting using it interactively (see Table B.40).

Table 5.9. Educational and business support initiatives, 2022

Percentage of administrations

Educational services to children, youth, and students	Educational services to new businesses	Free tax services for lower income individuals	Free tax services for new businesses	Taxpayer education or awareness campaigns targeting a particular gender
86.0	66.7	47.4	49.1	8.8

Source: CIAT, IOTA, IMF, OECD, International Survey on Revenue Administration, Table B.47 Taxpayer education, https://data.rafit.org/regular.aspx?key=74180919 (accessed on 10 September 2024).

Previous editions in this series as well as other OECD reports have provided numerous examples of educational and business support initiatives, for example:

- Chapters 6 and 7 of the report *Tax Administration 2019* (OECD, 2019[1]) included detailed descriptions on how Canada and Japan educate future taxpayers.
- The 2021 edition of *Building Tax Culture, Compliance and Citizenship: A Global Source Book on Taxpayer Education* (OECD, 2021[2]) analyses a unique dataset of 140 taxpayer education initiatives and aims to help tax administrations in designing and implementing taxpayer education initiatives. It also shows that increasing tax literacy can play an active role in shaping a country's tax culture and generate an improvement in tax morale, the intrinsic motivation to pay taxes.
- The 2023 report *Communication and Engagement with SMEs: Supporting SMEs to Get Tax Right* (OECD, 2023[3]) examines communication strategies that tax administrations can use to assist small and medium-sized enterprises (SMEs) in fulfilling their tax obligations, and analyses the various tools and channels available to tax administrations, including educational programmes.

Box 5.6. Examples – Educational and support initiatives

Canada – Assisted Compliance Program

The CRA uses an escalating approach to address and deter non-compliance as early as possible with the appropriate level of intervention; this includes communications, education, and outreach to help taxpayers meet their tax obligations.

The CRA approaches its work with the underlying premise that most people - given the opportunity and the right services - will meet their tax obligations. Recognising that the tax system is complex and that voluntary compliance is more cost-effective than enforcement, the CRA is increasingly focused on helping clients comply by using an education-first approach.

When addressing non-compliance, the CRA ensures customer service by adapting interventions to the circumstances, while remaining professional, transparent, fair and honest in how the client is treated. As such, compliance strategies continue to increase the use of an outreach and education-based approach, designed to inform taxpayers of their reporting obligations and their potential entitlements.

One example is the Assisted Compliance Program, which aims to improve voluntary compliance and address non-compliance through an education-first approach. This program bridges the gap between outreach and audit activities, helping individuals and businesses understand and meet their obligations under the tax system, while avoiding costly audit interventions.

The Assisted Compliance Program helps taxpayers to amend incorrectly filed returns by employing a more appropriate intervention than traditional audits. It represents an evolution of taxpayer education activities by engaging them with tailored information and individual support. This way, the CRA can reserve more comprehensive and traditional enforcement efforts, such as audits, for more serious or complicated cases.

Chile – Encouraging social responsibility within business groups

Establishing a sense of responsibility around paying taxes is crucial in Chile. The Internal Revenue Service (SII) has particularly focused on instilling this within business groups.

To encourage awareness and responsible behaviour around paying taxes, the SII has developed tools aiming to minimise potential non-compliance by business groups and underscore the significance of each entity's tax contributions to the country. For instance, the SII has outlined a set of best practices that businesses should take into account to ensure compliance. Additionally, a Tax Contribution Report is published for each business group, detailing how their taxes are used to contribute to state finances.

By creating tools and reports that demonstrate the value of compliance, the SII is fostering a collective effort to contribute towards the progress of the country and creating a sense of social responsibility amongst business groups.

China (People's Republic of) – TaxExpress

In 2023, the STA launched TaxExpress, a service to aid taxpayers in understanding how international taxation works. This aims to facilitate cross-border flows of investment, technology and resource.

The key features are as follows:

- Communication: TaxExpress enables taxpayers to get in touch with the tax administration if they have any issues or queries. Policy updates via email or text are also available to taxpayers if subscribed to.
- Knowledge products: Free knowledge products have been made available and are updated regularly on the STA website, as well as its social media account.
- Transfer pricing: More resources have been allocated to the STA's programmes on Transfer Pricing, generating positive feedback from taxpayers.
- Country profiles: Country profiles on tax have been created for 105 jurisdictions, to help taxpayers do their due diligence when doing business abroad.
- International tax law: Key international tax law cases have been published, which may be helpful when trying to resolve disputes.
- Frequently Asked Questions (FAQs): An FAQs page has been published, compiling answers to the most common questions from the STA's phone service.

France – Using social media to communicate with younger taxpayers

The Directorate General of Public Finances (DGFiP) has started using social media accounts to engage young people, as part of its wider communication strategy.

In 2023, DGFiP published a video explaining how to file a tax return faster than a choreographed dance. DGFiP also produced short musical videos, where a young artist sang along to pop music hits to encourage users to fulfil their tax obligations. The content was intended to be both informative and humorous. Using tailored videos on social media is much more visible to younger taxpayers than the content previously published on DGFiP's website.

These videos have generated tens of thousands of views, as well as media attention. They are a useful addition to DGFiP's communication resources.

India – Taxpayers' Hubs

Taxpayers' Hubs are dedicated spaces designed to serve as centres for spreading tax awareness and financial literacy in the tier 2 and tier 3 cities of India, to showcase the visibility of the Income Tax Department in terms of administering taxpayer services and the ease of voluntary compliance. The Department established Taxpayers' Hubs in various cities across the length and breadth of the country, namely - Gorakhpur, Bhagalpur, Cuttack, Jhansi and Vishakhapatnam. More are due to be set up in Shillong and Udaipur.

The Taxpayers' Hubs are built in areas frequently visited by the public, such as parks, convention centres, community halls, local fairs etc. They feature a diverse range of kiosks, each serving a specific purpose:

- Informational Kiosk to disseminate crucial tax-related information and updates;
- Grievance Kiosk to provide taxpayer assistance and resolve any tax-related concerns or issues;
- Educational Kiosk to promote tax literacy and provide valuable guidance on tax planning and compliance.

Furthermore, the Taxpayers' Hub features a vibrant Children's Corner that houses board games, puzzles, virtual reality games and comics on taxation, laying the foundation for financial literacy at an early age.

In the Taxpayers' Hubs, informative brochures and crucial tax information are available through LED screens, displayed to achieve the objective of educating and enlightening taxpayers visiting the hubs.

Through a combination of interactive and informative brochures, and the powerful tagline "Every Taxpayer is a Nation Builder", the Taxpayers' Hub strives to empower taxpayers with the knowledge to make informed decisions.

Ireland – 'Introduction to Tax' module

Tax compliance relies on taxpayers having a clear appreciation and understanding of the tax system and their compliance obligations. The 'Introduction to Tax' module is a teaching resource that has been developed to provide students with an overview of key taxes that they may encounter throughout their personal and professional lives.

Revenue's analysis of customer contacts identified the 16 to 20-year-old age cohort as a high contact group that was not featured in Revenue's targeted outbound communications. The module aims to improve tax literacy, encourage the use of Revenue's online services, educate young people on the social utility and importance of taxation, and empower them to manage their taxes. The key elements include:

- Identify, engage, and collaborate with relevant stakeholders;
- Conduct pilots with a range of different schools including urban/rural, single gender/mixed gender, public/private;
- Conduct surveys, questionnaires, and focus groups to gather valuable feedback.

The results have been very positive. Students who have undertaken the module demonstrate:

- 49% increase in understanding how to register for tax when starting work;

- 41% increase in understanding how to use Revenue's online services;
- 37% increase in understanding how to read a payslip;
- 29% increase in understanding how to calculate tax.

This may be a young person's first interaction with a government agency. This first positive interaction provides them with confidence and reassurance in future dealings, which in turn builds trust in government leading to lasting benefits for all Public Service Bodies.

Italy – Tax education

In Italy, educating young people about tax is important. The Italian Revenue Agency has partnered with the Ministry for Education since 2004 to promote the 'Tax and School' project. The project includes school visits, visits to the Revenue Agency, competitions and participation in institutional events and at the international level, for example at Global Money Week. Children are introduced to the world of tax through in different interactive formats, such as stories, comics, games and video clips.

Since 2017, the Italian Revenue Agency has also participated in the European Commission's TAXEDU project, which aims to educate young Europeans about taxes and how they affect their lives. There is a portal, aimed at young people aged 9 to 25, to provide information on different aspects related to tax, with the content and language tailored to age. The portal is periodically updated with games, e-learning material and microlearning clips designed to involve young people in the approach to taxation in a fun and engaging way. There are also specific training materials dedicated to teachers.

Italy – Tax digital communication strategy and campaigns

In recent years, the web and social media strategy of the Italian Revenue Agency has gradually changed its focus, becoming increasingly sensitive to taxpayer's needs. This means that the communication strategy is not limited to being informative, but it also fulfils its institutional mission of enhancing services provided to taxpayers.

The Italian Revenue Agency uses a target-oriented approach by adopting integrated communication actions, to adapt to the use of social media by its taxpayers. With its proactive approach, the Agency has spread awareness of the opportunity to use its services in a more agile way.

On this basis, the Italian tax administration has chosen to consolidate its institutional presence online and through social media platforms, achieving encouraging results. For example, online video tutorials helping taxpayers to use new services received over 6 million views.

In line with the Agency's digital communication strategy, the Agency performs integrated communication actions concerning different issues, such as pre-filled tax returns, mandatory e-invoicing and online services.

In recent months, the Agency has used a combination of its website and social media campaigns to promote where taxpayers can find accessible information to help them fulfil their tax obligations.

In reaching millions more taxpayers, the Italian Revenue Agency has increased its credibility and visibility, as well as showing openness and creating more dialogue with taxpayers.

Türkiye – Communication with new taxpayers to increase voluntary compliance

Türkiye has adapted numerous communication approaches to increase the voluntary compliance of recently established personal and corporate income taxpayers. Taxpayers are established on a monthly basis, and the documents are given to taxpayers through a visit from officials.

Taxpayers are provided with the following guidance:

- Letters reminding personal income taxpayers of their basic rights and obligations, and indicating the channels through which they can contact the tax administration.
- Brochures in which taxpayers' rights and obligations are briefly and clearly explained.
- Communication cards containing information on the various ways in which taxpayers can communicate with the tax administration.

Text messages were also sent to congratulate the newly established taxpayers for starting their activities, with a link to the "Information Video for Recently Established Taxpayers" prepared by the tax administration.

Sources: Canada (2024), Chile (2024), China (People's Republic of) (2024), France (2024), India (2024), Ireland (2024), Italy (2024) and Türkiye (2024).

Collaborative services

As the digital services developed by tax administrations grow, more and more administrations recognise that these services bring opportunities:

- To join-up with other government agencies to provide a whole of government service experience; and
- To work with third-party developers to connect with the systems of taxpayers.

Joined-up government services

Tax administrations are reporting joining-up with other government agencies to enhance the overall service experience across government, including through "collect once, use many times" approaches. Tax administrations have a special place within government in this respect since they will often hold up-to-date verified information on identity, will be involved in both receiving and making payments and will receive and send information to third parties (such as financial institutions and employers.)

Table 5.10. shows two examples of joined-up government services. In many jurisdictions registering for tax or making tax payments are now part of wider government processes, thus reducing and simplifying administrative burdens. Also, a number of country examples of such joined-up services have been included in previous editions in this series, for example, in Box 1.7 of the 2019 edition (OECD, 2019[1]). In addition, the example in Box 5.7. illustrates how the Inland Revenue Authority of Singapore has set-up a team that builds linkages between the tax administration and the wider government ecosystem.

Table 5.10. Joined-up government services, 2022

Percentage of jurisdictions that have the respective service

Tax type	Registration for tax is part of a wider government registration process	Making payments is part of a wider government online payment portal
Personal income tax	49.0	39.2
Corporate income tax	63.5	36.5
Value added tax	40.8	34.7

Note: The percentages are based on ITTI data from 52 jurisdictions that are covered in this report and that have completed the global survey on digitalisation.
Source: OECD et al. (2024), Inventory of Tax Technology Initiatives, https://web-archive.oecd.org/temp/2023-03-09/618462-taxpayer-touchpoints.htm, Tables TT1, TT2 and TT3 (accessed on 10 September 2024).

Box 5.7. Singapore – Formation of the Digital Ecosystem Partnership Team

With greater emphasis on transformation within the tax ecosystem and in the spirit of organisational agility, the Inland Revenue Authority of Singapore (IRAS) has piloted the Digital Ecosystem Task Force (TF).

The TF is made up of two cross-divisional project teams to address the supply and demand aspects of digitalisation within the tax ecosystem over two years. Following the successful pilot of the TF, IRAS set up a dedicated team known as the Digital Ecosystem and Partnership Team (DEPT), a highly diverse group of officers with business knowledge, information technology and data management expertise, marketing and stakeholder engagement skills, as well as tax knowledge and grant management expertise.

DEPT spearheaded the engagement of the tax ecosystem and accelerated the development of digital solutions that facilitate seamless fulfilment of tax obligations. For example, DEPT enabled the interoperability of systems by building linkages with the wider government ecosystem, leveraging on existing whole of government initiatives and partnering with other government agencies to facilitate seamless data transmission via accounting or payroll software. The network effect was also achieved by establishing a self-enforcing network, through maintaining a list of software developers who have successfully integrated their software with IRAS.

DEPT has enabled IRAS to foster a more robust and interconnected digital ecosystem, driving the widespread adoption of digital solutions by taxpayers and tax intermediaries, and enhancing the overall efficiency and effectiveness of the tax compliance processes for businesses and individuals.

Source: Singapore (2024).

Working with third-party developers

Embedding services and processes in the natural systems used by taxpayers in their daily lives and businesses will help to improve tax compliance, and also reduce administrative burdens and free up time that owners can use to grow their businesses. Most of those natural systems are prepared by third-party developers and many administrations are driving collaborations with those developers to open up new services. In addition to embedding services, a number of administrations are also creating natural systems that will assist taxpayers to fulfil their tax obligations, either directly or in collaboration with third parties (see Table 5.11.).

Table 5.11. Working with third-party developers, 2022

Percentage of administrations

Creating software packages for use by taxpayers		Integrating tax interactions into third party systems		
Administration creates software packages that assist taxpayers to fulfil their tax obligations	Administration engages in co-creation of software packages with third parties	Administration develops APIs	If yes, Administration makes library of APIs publicly available for third party use	If yes, Administration engages in co-creation of APIs with third parties
57.7	48.1	84.6	75.0	56.8

Note: The percentages are based on ITTI data from 52 jurisdictions that are covered in this report and that have completed the global survey on digitalisation.
Source: OECD et al. (2024), Inventory of Tax Technology Initiatives, https://web-archive.oecd.org/temp/2023-03-09/618462-taxpayer-touchpoints.htm, Table TT7 (accessed on 10 September 2024).

The connection of the tax administration's system to the natural systems of taxpayers is typically done through Application Programming Interfaces (APIs). APIs are allowing connectivity between systems, people and things without providing direct access, and are the critical enablers of many innovative services. It is against this background that around 85% of tax administrations are now creating APIs and three-quarters of them are making the APIs available to third party developers. Further, as part of the process of developing APIs, close to 60% of tax administrations are engaging in co-creation with third parties.

The OECD report *Unlocking the digital economy – a guide to unlocking application programming interfaces in government* (OECD, 2019[4]) provides an overview of the practices, techniques and standards used to deliver contemporary and effective digital services for taxpayers through APIs. As the services delivered become more sophisticated, and play a greater role in delivering a quality service to taxpayers, tax administrations are having to invest more in the management and oversight of their APIs. Box 5.8. contains examples of some of the latest developments in administration regarding APIs and working with third-party developers.

Box 5.8. Example – Using APIs and working with third-party developers to provide better services

Australia – Collaborations with third parties to provide new services

The Australian Taxation Office (ATO) remains committed to strengthening the relationship with its Digital Service Provider (DSP) partners through its engagement framework. DSPs play a critical role in the administration of the tax and superannuation systems, and early collaboration is critical to the success of any new initiatives. The software industry continues to evolve with new technology innovations and a desire to integrate with financial platforms.

The ATO's Strategic Working Group is used to consult with a broad segment of industry representatives on a range of strategic topics impacting the future of the industry. Examples of topics for 2024 include: real time payments aligned to reporting obligations, utilisation of AI in software, improving take up of e-invoicing and continuing to evolve the DSP Operational Security Framework to improve the integrity of ATO services and broader ecosystem.

Australia – Guidance in software concept

The ATO has a vision of developing a digital-first ecosystem that utilises the natural systems of small businesses to support greater awareness and understanding of tax. In line with this, it has introduced a guidance in software concept, which aims to:

- Embed high-quality, system generated tax guidance and tools into the natural systems that small businesses use to run their business;
- Deliver advice in real-time;
- Support better decision making and understanding of the potential tax consequences of transactions.

The ATO is working with its digital partners and tax professionals to co-design a solution to make its existing public advice and guidance more consumable and accessible. This is being achieved through embedding guidance prompts and tools into the software services used by tax professionals and small businesses. The concept is consistent with the OECD building blocks for a future tax system (tax rule management and application) and moving towards the OCED's Tax Administration 3.0 vision.

The guidance in software concept has two parts, testing:

- the overarching concept and framework of co-designing with the ATO's digital partners and tax professionals to encourage innovation in the wholesale market to help taxpayers get it right;
- the concept of focusing on an area of risk or section of law that is complex and difficult for taxpayers or their advisers to understand.

Brazil – Integration with taxpayers' natural systems: Integra Accountant

The "Integra Contador" project aims to digitally integrate private accounting systems with the Brazilian tax administration. By simplifying and speeding up accounting processes - including company registration, invoice processing, payroll calculation, tax form generation, and financial report delivery - the project seeks to reduce processing and response times by contributing to a more efficient and secure environment for companies, service providers and the tax administration.

The project has already shown promising results in 2023, efficiently processing large databases of information, including tax declarations. The continuous development of this project aims to improve tax compliance, while improving public and private sector partnerships.

Singapore – "One-Stop Payroll" solution

The One-Stop Payroll (OSP) initiative represents significant progression in the collaborative efforts of the government with various ecosystem players.

IRAS, the Ministry of Manpower (MOM), the Central Provident Fund Board (CPFB), software developers, and employers, have worked together to create an integrated digital service. This service enables employers to fulfil their payroll-related statutory obligations across multiple agencies through a single payroll software. Presently, employers are required to make multiple separate submissions in varying formats and at different frequencies to different government agencies, resulting in a substantial regulatory burden.

The OSP initiative affords employers a one-stop solution to fulfil these submissions easily through their payroll/HR system, which is integrated seamlessly with IRAS, CPFB and MOM by way of Application Programmable Interfaces. This initiative yields tangible benefits, particularly cost and time savings for businesses. It also enables software developers and ecosystem partners to enhance and expand the functionalities of their solution offerings. From a whole of government perspective, this employer and citizen-centric approach to service delivery is instrumental in facilitating accurate and timely submissions by employers. It effectively reduces the compliance burden for them and minimises the need for downstream compliance and audit processes, ultimately fostering a more efficient regulatory environment.

Sweden – Submitting an income tax return for a limited company through an Application Programme Interface

From initially only offering tax return submissions on paper, the Swedish Tax Agency (STA) has gradually developed their digital services, and there is now the possibility to submit a complete income tax return for a limited company through an API solution. The progress over time can be described in three steps:

- Step 1 – Tax return submission completed via e-service or file transfer, where only certain parts can be submitted digitally.
- Step 2 – From 2021, the tax return submission can be completed via file transfer, including attachments, digital signatures and other details.
- Step 3 – From 2023, the tax return submission can be completed directly via API in the company's own tax return programme, combined with a digital signature.

The STA still offer all the services mentioned above, including paper tax returns. All services are still in use by companies, but the use of more modern services is gradually increasing. The STA have found that the amount of paper returns has decreased every year, alongside the use of services with only partly digital submission.

Sweden – Rules as Code concept

The STA has explored how the Rules as Code (RaC) concept can be applied to facilitate tax compliance for small to medium sized businesses.

The STA now provides a technical solution that creates opportunities for business system developers to enable legal guidance in their systems. The STA creates rule-based machine-readable files, as well as written specifications in different areas of tax specific legislation supplied as open data. When used together with a rule engine, the rule files combined with existing data in the business system could create a more automated compliance process.

A key element of this work is that STA only makes the rule files available for use, and is not obliged to develop any application or services of its own. The internal work process enables legal experts within the STA to independently create rule files and make them publicly available without the need to involve technical assistance. This is made possible by the development of a rule editor that the experts can use to convert decision trees into machine readable code. To date, the STA has made rule files and specifications in three different legal areas as well as an Application Programme Interface available for use.

The concept, even though already available and in production, is still in a development phase and continuously improving with feedback from business system developers.

Sources: Australia (2024), Brazil (2024), Singapore (2024) and Sweden (2024).

Inclusive administration

Tax administrations should consider providing comprehensive services that ensure equitable access for all citizens, including those with disabilities, those without internet access, or those who do not speak any of the official languages of the jurisdiction. Providing accessible formats, multilingual support, and offline service options facilitates bridging gaps in communication and access, promoting a more inclusive society. These measures can assist enhancing the trust in the system and voluntary compliance.

As can be seen in Table 5.12., the majority of administrations are aware of this while designing their services. Almost all administrations make special provisions for taxpayers with disabilities. Also, while there is an increasing shift to the use of electronic services for both convenience and cost-efficiency purposes, a proportion of taxpayers will not have access to, or be comfortable with such services. As a result, more than 80% of administrations offer specific services to support digitally disadvantaged taxpayers. Moreover, more than 60% of administrations ensures that online services are available to users who have visual, auditory motor or cognitive disabilities.[1]

Table 5.12. also shows that the majority of administrations provides services in non-official languages, thus ensuring that all taxpayers can access the essential information required to comply with their tax obligations. Box 5.9. shows an example how authorities are helping foreign employees arriving in Finland.

Table 5.12. Inclusive services, 2022

Percentage of administrations offering such services

Special provision made for taxpayers with disabilities	Special services provided for digitally disadvantaged taxpayers	Telephone services provided in non-official languages	Information on website / mobile applications provided in non-official languages
91.4	81.0	53.4	72.4

Source: CIAT, IOTA, IMF, OECD, International Survey on Revenue Administration, Table B.40 Service channels: Features of the service approach, https://data.rafit.org/regular.aspx?key=74180919 (accessed on 10 September 2024).

Box 5.9. Finland – Work Help Finland application

Work Help Finland is a mobile application co-developed by the Police University College and Finnish public authorities. It provides foreign employees arriving in Finland with information on their rights and obligations around working in Finland. The application helps combat work-related exploitation, human trafficking and undeclared work by providing workers with important, easy-to-understand information all in one place. It is available in twenty-six languages and free to download.

The Finnish Tax Administration participated in the project by contributing taxation-related content for the app. Work Help Finland has basic information on Finland's taxing rights, how the duration of stay affects taxation, explains what the Finnish tax card is and how to get one, and how to apply for a Finnish personal ID. Special regulations concerning certain groups of workers are also discussed. The app also contains links to the Tax Administration's website and to its English-language pages.

Source: Finland (2024).

In addition, tax administrations are also considering how to assist taxpayers in difficult personal circumstances, for example by developing new services or by providing tailored support. Box 5.10. contains two examples, and Chapter 13 of the 2019 edition of this series described the ATO's Dispute Assist which is a service that supports vulnerable individuals and small businesses with the objection process (OECD, 2019[1]).

Box 5.10. Examples – Inclusion

Australia – Vulnerable clients

The ATO is seeing an increasing number of clients in vulnerable positions who cannot make their payments. Although the ATO has focused on debt recovery after the COVID-19 Pandemic, the ATO maintains a balanced approach that helps to both identify and differentiate assistance for vulnerable taxpayers having trouble.

To better assist those in need, the ATO has called for taxpayers who are experiencing difficulties making their payments to contact the ATO early to seek assistance. This enables a new approach of reduced but purposeful contact that provides taxpayers with tailored support and allows them to get back on track.

Vulnerability can impact clients in different ways, and it is difficult to define given the often complex and personal circumstances a client might face. The ATO therefore seeks to understand its taxpayers through the factors or barriers that prevent them from paying, lodging or engaging – such as serious illness, mental health challenges, natural disasters, family or domestic violence and low levels of support or literacy.

The ATO is working to design a simpler framework to support these taxpayers. For example, it has proposed the introduction of new products that pause recovery action while vulnerable taxpayers seek support or professional advice. There is also extra support and assistance teams available for vulnerable taxpayers with more complex and challenging situations.

Canada – Better support for executors to file taxes for deceased taxpayers

Settling the taxes of someone who died can be complex and emotional. In Autumn 2020, the CRA spoke to executors to understand the needs and challenges they faced when filing the taxes of someone who died.

The CRA has ongoing commitments to make it easier to understand and navigate the process. For example:

- Improvements were made to the web content on Canada.ca to make it easier to find, navigate, and use the information to settle the taxes of someone who died. Comparing against the original content, the new content showed:
  - 55% point increase in people finding relevant content
  - 41% point increase in people completing their tasks successfully
  - 31% point increase in self-reported ease of use
- Contact centre agents are better equipped with specialised resources to help executors. Contact centre wait times are available online so executors can make an informed choice on the best time to call.
- Individuals are able to text online with a CRA service representative to obtain answers to general questions on how to settle the taxes of someone who died.

Insights from this client experience project and user feedback is continuing to inform concrete service improvements.

Sources: Australia (2024) and Canada (2024).

Notes

[1] See: OECD et al. (2024), Inventory of Tax Technology Initiatives, https://web-archive.oecd.org/temp/2023-03-09/618462-taxpayer-touchpoints.htm, Table TT4 (accessed on 10 September 2024).

References

OECD (2023), *Communication and Engagement with SMEs: Supporting SMEs to Get Tax Right*, OECD Forum on Tax Administration, OECD Publishing, Paris, https://doi.org/10.1787/f183d70a-en. [3]

OECD (2021), *Building Tax Culture, Compliance and Citizenship: A Global Source Book on Taxpayer Education, Second Edition*, OECD Publishing, Paris, https://doi.org/10.1787/18585eb1-en. [2]

OECD (2019), *Tax Administration 2019: Comparative Information on OECD and other Advanced and Emerging Economies*, OECD Publishing, Paris, https://doi.org/10.1787/74d162b6-en. [1]

OECD (2019), *Unlocking the Digital Economy - A Guide to Implementing Application Programming Interfaces in Government*, OECD Publishing, Paris, https://doi.org/10.1787/56697aa7-en. [4]

OECD et al. (2024), *Inventory of Tax Technology Initiatives*, https://web-archive.oecd.org/tax/forum-on-tax-administration/tax-technology-tools-and-digital-solutions/index.htm (accessed on 10 September 2024). [5]

6 Compliance management

Assessing the accuracy and completeness of taxpayer reported information is a core function of tax administrations. This chapter takes a closer look at tax administrations' work in this area, including what they do to understand and manage compliance risk, and how they prevent and address non-compliance. Finally, this chapter looks at approaches to evaluate taxpayer compliance burdens.

Introduction

The audit, verification and investigation function assesses the accuracy and completeness of taxpayer reported information. This function employs on average 30% of tax administration staff to verify that tax obligations have been met. While this often happens through audits, there is an increasing use of automated electronic checks, validations and matching of taxpayer information. The undertaking and visibility of these and other compliance actions is critical in supporting voluntary compliance, including through their impacts on perceptions of fairness in the tax system, as well as creating a 'deterrent effect'. This chapter therefore looks at:

- How tax administrations manage compliance risks, including the different approaches to prevent and address non-compliance;
- The delivery of compliance actions undertaken by tax administrations, looking at audits as well as tax crime investigations; and
- The importance of evaluating and reducing taxpayer compliance burden.

Compliance risk management

The process of compliance risk management, as described in the 2004 OECD guidance note *Compliance Risk Management: Managing and Improving Tax Compliance* (OECD, 2004[1]), has remained largely unchanged over the years. Its key steps, as illustrated in Figure 6.1., still serve as a blueprint for managing compliance risks. Since then, several OECD reports explored aspects of this framework providing guidance and good practice examples, and the 2017 report *The Changing Tax Compliance Environment and the Role of Audit* (OECD, 2017[2]) looked at a range of incremental changes occurring across tax administrations which, taken together, were changing the nature of the tax compliance environment, allowing for more targeted and managed compliance.

Figure 6.1. Compliance risk management process

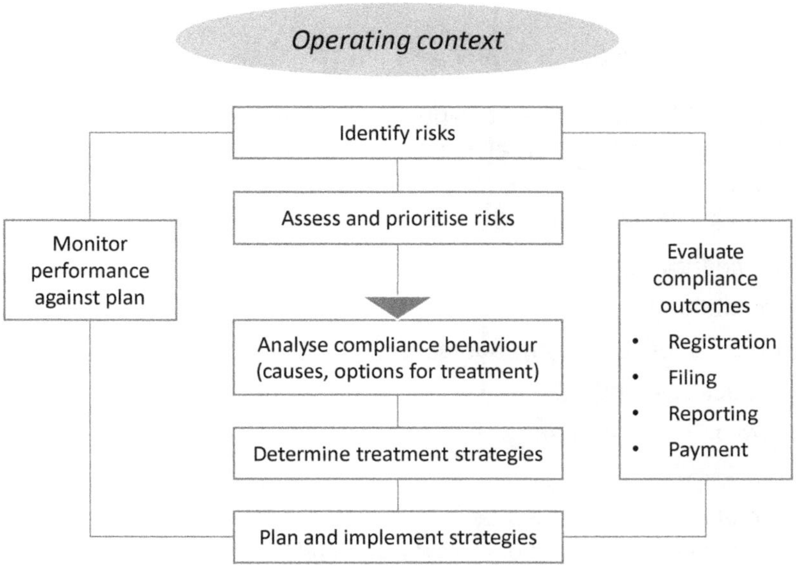

Source: OECD (2004), *Compliance Risk Management: Managing and Improving Tax Compliance*, https://www.oecd.org/content/dam/oecd/en/topics/policy-issues/tax-administration/compliance-risk-management-managing-and-improving-tax-compliance.pdf (accessed 12 September 2024).

With ISORA 2023 capturing a significant amount of new data on compliance risk management approaches, this section examines how tax administrations are organising their processes in this area. It does so by looking at tax administrations approaches towards ***understanding*** and ***managing*** compliance risks, and some of the steps taken by administrations as regards ***preventing*** and ***addressing*** non-compliance.

Understanding tax compliance risks

Around 85% of administrations report having a formal compliance risk management strategy. Almost all of those having in place dedicated approaches for identifying, assessing and prioritising key compliance risks, with close to 30% making compliance risks public and around one quarter publishing outcomes in addressing the risks (see Table 6.1.). This is on the basis that publication can enhance compliance strategies by increasing taxpayer awareness of possible risks and acting as a deterrent to those considering non-compliance. Combined they can also reassure the public that non-compliance is being dealt with. The example in Box 6.1. describes a new automated risk model developed by Australia to identify international risk in the private wealth market.

Table 6.1. Compliance risk management strategy, 2022

Percentage of administrations

Formal compliance risk management strategy exists	If yes, ...								
	Strategy includes formal approach for identifying, assessing and prioritising key compliance risks	If yes, ...							
		Areas covered by the approach...					Risks made public regularly	Results in addressing risks made public regularly
		Return filing	Payment processing	Collection enforcement	Verification / audit	Taxpayer service		
84.5	98.0	89.6	68.8	72.9	100.0	66.7	29.2	27.1

Source: CIAT, IOTA, IMF, OECD, International Survey on Revenue Administration, Table B.20 Compliance risk management: Strategy, https://data.rafit.org/regular.aspx?key=74180916 (accessed on 10 September 2024).

Box 6.1. Australia – International risk in privately held markets

The Australian Taxation Office (ATO) has designed an automated international risk model, to identify international tax risks in the private wealth market. The Private Wealth International Risk Model combines bespoke private wealth risk rules with data matching and trend analysis to identify common risks in privately held businesses, including:

- Related party financing;
- Intangibles migration;
- Mischaracterisation of service arrangements;
- Business restructures; and
- Controlled foreign company risk.

The model allows the ATO to rank taxpayers by international risk, so that resources can be prioritised to focus on the most material cases. It also reduces manual intervention and enables the ATO to identify risks in real time, which mitigates period of review issues (statutory limitations on cases).

Using this new risk model is important to the ATO, because historically tax authorities have focused on identifying the most material international risk in large multi-nationals through Country-by-Country reporting (CbCR) data and publicly available information, which often are not present in privately held groups. As the number and scale of privately held businesses increase globally (largely driven by the scalability of technology-based businesses) this targeted approach allows the ATO to improve the accuracy and efficiency of international risk identification in privately held businesses to complement existing international risk models.

Source: Australia (2024).

Tax gap analysis

The use of tax gap measurements is becoming more common, especially for value added taxes (VAT), as jurisdictions increasingly see the benefits of having high level estimates of non-compliance within the tax system, including identifying compliance risks and understanding drivers of non-compliance.

Tax gap estimation is complex and there are two main approaches:

- **Top-down methodologies** that use aggregated macro-economic data represent a relatively low-cost means of producing such estimates.
- **Bottom-up methodologies** that include information from audits, are more resource intensive but can provide a more accurate picture of lost revenue across segments and tax types.

Two-thirds of the 58 administrations covered in this report indicated that they or another government agency produce periodic tax gap estimates for one or more of the main tax types, with the production of estimates of the VAT tax gap the most prevalent. Around half of jurisdictions that produce assessments make (some of) their estimates publicly available. (See Table 6.2.)

Chapter 11 provides a detailed overview of tax gap estimation by OECD Forum on Tax Administration (FTA) member administrations, including the methodologies used, the different tax gap components and how tax gap analysis is used by tax administrations.

Table 6.2. Tax gap analysis, 2022

Percentage of administrations

Administration or other government agency produces periodic estimates of the tax gap for ...				Tax gap reports published (as a percentage of those that produce estimates)
Personal income tax	Corporate income tax	Value added tax	Other taxes	
38.6	34.5	65.5	32.8	55.3

Source: CIAT, IOTA, IMF, OECD, International Survey on Revenue Administration, Table B.24 Compliance risk management: Tax gap, https://data.rafit.org/regular.aspx?key=74180916 (accessed on 10 September 2024).

Box 6.2. Bulgaria – Measuring the influence of external factors on tax compliance and the tax gap

The National Revenue Agency (NRA) has implemented a project aimed at enhancing the capabilities of the NRA in developing analytical tools and methodologies to determine the extent of tax non-compliance.

The project uses econometric models to understand the key factors that determine taxpayer behaviour and to forecast the evolution of tax non-compliance in Bulgaria. Three models were built focused on the following areas: the shadow economy, Personal Income Tax (PIT) and Value-Added Tax (VAT). The models measured the size of the shadow economy at the country-level and tax gaps for VAT and PIT, as well as assessing their causes.

The models are used by the NRA on regular basis to estimate and forecast the compliance levels, and to choose appropriate measures to increase compliance.

For more information, please see here: https://reform-support.ec.europa.eu/publications-0/strengthening-tax-compliance-assessing-external-context-and-taxpayers-behaviour_en#files (accessed on 10 September 2024).

Source: Bulgaria (2024).

Random audits

Slightly less than two thirds of participating tax administrations report having random audit programmes in place (see Table 6.3.). As well as enhancing any deterrent effect, these programmes also provide a more accurate understanding of compliance risks that can enhance risk-profiling systems. About half of the administrations with established random audit programmes report also using the data to produce tax gap estimates. Those administrations that do not use random audit programmes often cite the significant burden on the taxpayers, particularly low-risk taxpayers who would otherwise not be audited.

Table 6.3. Random audits, 2022

Percentage of administrations

Administration conducts random audits	If yes, purpose of random audits ...					
	Test compliance in targeted sectors	Enhance risk profiling systems	Produce tax gap estimates	Measure behavioural effects of audits	Solely for audit purposes as general deterrent	Other
63.8	70.3	75.7	56.8	37.8	51.4	21.6

Source: CIAT, IOTA, IMF, OECD, International Survey on Revenue Administration, Table B.36 Verification / audit activity: Random audits, https://data.rafit.org/regular.aspx?key=74180918 (accessed on 10 September 2024).

Increasing availability of data

As more and more data is stored electronically, and the transfer, storage and integration of data has become easier through the application of new techniques and processes, there has been a huge increase in the amount of data available to tax administrations for compliance purposes, that can help them to understand risk areas and promote tax compliance. Frequently used data sources include:

- ***Data from devices***: Data can be collected from devices that register transactions such as online cash registers and trip computers for taxis and trucks, and also gate registrations from barriers and weigh bridges.
- ***Data from banks, merchants or payment intermediaries and service providers***: This allows direct verification of income or assets reported by the taxpayer. Some jurisdictions already receive transaction details or transaction totals for taxpayers on a regular basis.
- ***Data from suppliers***: Collecting data from suppliers, either directly or through the taxpayer, allows a more complete picture to be drawn about the activities and income of the taxpayer. This is seen in the increasing use of e-invoicing systems which, as noted in Chapter 4, allows some tax administrations to prefill tax returns.

- ***Data from the customer***: This is easiest in cases where the number of customers is limited and known, but increasingly mechanisms to leverage customer data are being used, for example in the verification of cash receipts.
- ***Unstructured data concerning the taxpayer***: Increasingly electronic traces relevant to business activities and transactions can be found on the internet and in social media.
- ***Data from other government agencies***: Data held by other government agencies for example for licencing, regulatory or social security purposes can be relevant in verifying tax returns or in risk assessments.
- ***Data from international partners***: International exchanges of data from the *International Standards for Automatic Exchange of Information in Tax Matters* (OECD, 2023[3]) and *Country-by-Country Reporting* (OECD, 2015[4]) is massively increasing the quantity of data available on international activity and providing useful information for audit and case selection processes and in some cases for prefilling of tax returns.

Much of this is a result of technological advancements and the digitalisation of the economy, and tax administrations can help to further promote the digitalisation and digital transformation of business operations as can be seen in the example included in Box 6.3.

Box 6.3. Japan – Promotion of the digitalisation of businesses through stakeholders

The National Tax Agency (NTA) has started promoting the digitalisation of general business operations to improve accuracy and processing speeds.

Up until now, the NTA has mainly focused its digitalisation efforts on tax procedures. However, if various day-to-day business processes (for example, billing payments and accounting) were also digitalised, this would improve the overall accuracy of processing and productivity of general business operations.

The NTA has a wide variety of stakeholders, including related private organisations, tax professionals, and local economic organisations. In promoting the digitalisation of businesses, it is essential to work and cooperate with these organisations, related ministries and agencies more than ever.

The NTA will continue to work on the digitalisation of society as a whole through further cooperation and collaboration with related organisations to create momentum for digitalisation among businesses, such as the Joint Declaration on Digitalisation and the Declaration on the Promotion of Cashless Payment, as well as by strengthening cooperation and collaboration with other ministries and agencies to promote awareness of and encourage the use of digital invoices and various subsidies.

Source: Japan (2024).

Table 6.4. shows for which types of income individual payment details are generally reported to the administration. Not surprisingly, almost all administrations receive information on wage and salary payments. This is followed by dividend and interest payments where around 80% of administrations receive information on individual payments. Looking at the jurisdiction level data, a significant number of administrations receive comprehensive information on income payments making pre-filling regimes possible (see Chapter 4) and underreporting by the taxpayer more difficult. (See also Table B.50.)

Table 6.4. Types of income generally subject to reporting of individual payment details, 2022

Percentage of jurisdictions

Wage and salary	Dividends	Interest	Rents	Specified business income	Royalties, patents	Sales / purchases of shares	Sales / purchases of real estate	Other types of income
93.1	79.3	77.6	47.4	54.4	64.9	54.4	50.9	47.4

Source: CIAT, IOTA, IMF, OECD, International Survey on Revenue Administration, Table B.50 Reporting of payment details, https://data.rafit.org/regular.aspx?key=74180917 (accessed on 10 September 2024).

With significant amounts of data being available, tax administrations are investing in systems for importing, storing and managing third-party data. Table 6.5. summarises for which types of third-party data administrations have such systems. Around 80% of administrations are working with customs data, data from social security agencies, and/ or data on property ownership and sales. Close to half of the administrations are also importing, storing and managing data from online vendors.

Table 6.5. Managing third party data, 2022

Percentage of administrations

Systems for importing, storing and managing third-party data available for ...						Quality of the data reported by third parties checked on a systematic basis	If yes, outcomes are routinely reported back to the third parties
Customs data	Data from stock exchanges	Data from the Social Security Agency	Data from online (internet-based) vendors	Data from Utilities (e.g. electricity)	Data on property ownership and sales		
80.7	39.7	79.3	48.3	31.0	79.3	77.6	71.1

Source: CIAT, IOTA, IMF, OECD, International Survey on Revenue Administration, Table B.51 Third-party data, https://data.rafit.org/regular.aspx?key=74180918 (accessed on 10 September 2024).

With ongoing digital transformation, there is also more tax related data becoming available from taxpayer's business systems. This includes, for example, e-invoicing systems and the use of devices that register and transfer data to the administration. As Table 6.6. illustrates, half of the administrations receive data from electronic fiscal devices or cash registers and in two-thirds of those situations, data is transferred automatically. A small number of administrations (around 15%) also receive data from other devices such as taxi meters.

Table 6.6. Electronic invoicing and devices that register transactions, 2022

Percentage of administrations

Certain categories of taxpayers are required to use an electronic invoice mechanism that transfers data to the tax administration	Administration receives data from devices that register transactions	If yes, type of device and data transfer			
		Electronic fiscal devices / cash registers		Other devices (e.g. taxi meters)	
		Data is transferred automatically	Data is transferred on request	Data is transferred automatically	Data is transferred on request
37.9	50.0	62.1	37.9	6.9	24.1

Source: CIAT, IOTA, IMF, OECD, International Survey on Revenue Administration, Tables A.105 Compliance approaches: Electronic invoicing, and A.106 Compliance approaches: Devices that register transactions, https://data.rafit.org/regular.aspx?key=74180897 (accessed on 10 September 2024).

Box 6.4. Examples – Electronic invoicing and devices that register transactions

Lithuania – Smart Electronic Cash Register Subsystem

The State Tax Inspectorate (STI) has implemented a project for the creation and implementation of the Smart Electronic Cash Register Subsystem (i.EKA), one of the seven parts of the intelligent Tax Administration System project in Lithuania. The objectives of the i.EKA project are to reduce the administrative burden on businesses, increase the efficiency of the STI, and reduce the size of the shadow economy by modernising and optimising the use of cash registers through creating and implementing new electronic services:

- Remote registration of cash registers and other points of sale – this allows businesses to automatically fill in an electronic technical passport, remotely perform registration of a means of payment, notify a change of conditions, adjust registration data, and process the digital certificates necessary for the process of recording and transferring transactions.
- Virtual fiscalisation for cash registers and other points of sale – this service enables the automatic transfer of receipt data (for example, receipt amount, VAT rates and amount) from cash registers or other means of payment to the tax authority directly, forming an electronic journal of a cashier's operations.

This has enabled more efficient control of income accounting and real-time reviews of cash register registration data, as well as the ability to generate cross-cutting reports on i.EKA managed data. The data obtained from the cash registers can be used for comparison with the data provided in declarations submitted by taxpayers to assess if there are any risks. Customers of registered businesses can verify the submission of their receipt data to STI and whether the transmitted data is correct. If there are discrepancies, the buyer can submit a report about potential violations.

Saudi Arabia – Electronic Invoicing (Fatoora Project)

Electronic invoicing (e-invoicing) was introduced as part of Saudi Arabia's (KSA) ongoing economic renaissance and digital transformation efforts. As part of this, the Saudi Zakat, Tax, and Customs Authority (ZATCA) introduced the National E-invoicing Project ("Fatoora Project").

The implementation of this Project was divided into two distinct phases:

- Phase 1, from 4 December 2021, focuses on the generation of e-invoices. It also includes provisions regarding the processing of electronic invoices, and the essential task of record-keeping.
- Phase 2, from 1 January 2023, involves the integration of taxpayers' e-invoicing systems with ZATCA's e-invoicing portal (Fatoora). It mandates the transmission of e-invoices and e-notes, along with the requirement to share them with ZATCA.

E-invoicing has had several positive impacts in KSA, being implemented by over 300 000 taxpayers through over 700 listed solution providers to generate, transmit, and store e-invoices.

The key impacts are:

- Manually generated paper-based invoices have been completely eliminated since Phase 1.
- Over 950 million e-invoices have been generated since the launch, with a success rate of 98%.
- Clearance of invoices by Fatoora has been achieved in less than 0.1 seconds through fully automated solutions.

E-invoicing has played a significant role in the government's digital transformation plans detailed in the Kingdom's Vision 2030 strategy. This initiative demonstrates ZATCA's commitment to adopting digital technology, supporting a digital economy, and functioning as a critical facilitator in reaching ZATCA's goal of becoming a "World Class" digital revenue administration organisation.

Sources: Lithuania (2024) and Saudi Arabia (2024).

With increasing amounts of data being handled by tax administrations, the implementation of mechanisms to protect and manage data is now commonplace, and a critical function. These mechanisms support wider data governance processes, and in turn help maintain taxpayer trust in the system as well as meet legal obligations (See Table 6.7.). Moreover, as data systems become more connected, the importance of cyber security is growing. The 2023 edition of this publication contained a few examples from tax administrations in this space – see Tax Administration 2023, Box 10.5. (OECD, 2023[5]).

Table 6.7. Data governance, 2022

Percentage of administrations that have the respective process in place

Comprehensive data management strategy exists	Data quality of reported data is assessed	Data ethics framework in place	User data access and security is controlled	Unauthorised access is automatically detected	Data Privacy Officer is employed	Cyber security unit exists	External parties hired to test the security of systems
66.0	88.0	74.0	100.0	84.3	90.2	90.2	82.0

Note: The table is based on data from 52 jurisdictions that are covered in this report and that are included in the ITTI database.
Source: OECD et al. (2024), Inventory of Tax Technology Initiatives, https://web-archive.oecd.org/temp/2023-03-09/618463-data-management.htmhttps://www.oecd.org/tax/forum-on-tax-administration/tax-technology-tools-and-digital-solutions/, Table DM4 (accessed on 10 September 2024).

Tax compliance and gender

The ISORA 2023 survey also explored whether tax administrations started looking into tax compliance by gender. Identifying whether a gender difference exists in tax compliance, could help administrations to tailor compliance approaches, but also to address underlying causes through tailored taxpayer services and education campaigns.

Only eight administrations reported collecting gender-disaggregated data for individual taxpayers on tax compliance and six of those have undertaken a compliance analysis based on gender. Interestingly, half of those administrations concluded from their analysis that it is not necessary to make changes to the way they administer the tax system.

Table 6.8. Collection of gender-disaggregated tax compliance data for individual taxpayers, 2022

Percentage of administrations

Gender-disaggregated data for individual taxpayers on tax compliance collected	If yes, ...			
	Administration has undertaken a compliance analysis based on gender	If yes, changes made based on this analysis		
		Yes	Not yet	Not necessary
13.8	75.0	16.7	33.3	50.0

Source: CIAT, IOTA, IMF, OECD, International Survey on Revenue Administration, Table B.21 Compliance risk management: Gender-disaggregated data, https://data.rafit.org/regular.aspx?key=74180916 (accessed on 10 September 2024).

Managing tax compliance risks

Data science

Over recent years, the application of advanced analytics to risk management and risk targeting is becoming increasingly common:

- Table 6.9. shows 80% of tax administrations reporting using big data in their work, and of those that use big data nearly all are using it to improve their compliance work.
- Of the 58 tax administrations covered by this report, nearly all report using data science / analytical tools with the remaining administrations in the process of preparing the use of such tools going forward (see Table 6.10.).
- Similarly, the use of artificial intelligence, including machine learning, for risk assessments and detecting fraud is already undertaken or in the process of being implemented by around half of the administrations covered in this publication (see Table 6.9.).

This increasingly sophisticated use of analytics on expanded data sets is leading to a sharpening of risk management and the development of a range of intervention actions, including through automated processes. Additionally, the OECD report *Advanced Analytics for Tax Administration: Putting data to work* (OECD, 2016[6]) provides practical guidance on how tax administrations can use analytics to support compliance and service delivery.

Table 6.9. Use of big data and artificial intelligence for analytical purposes, 2022

Percentage of administrations

Use of big data							Use of artificial intelligence (AI)	
	If yes, purpose of big data use ...						Use of AI in risk assessment processes	Use of AI for detection of tax evasion and fraud
Administration uses big data	Improve compliance	Identify trends	Policy forecasting	Revenue forecasting	Provide new services	Other uses		
80.0	97.5	72.5	47.5	60.0	45.0	17.5	52.9	49.0

Note: The percentages are based on ITTI data from 52 jurisdictions that are covered in this report and that have completed the global survey on digitalisation.
Source: OECD et al. (2024), Inventory of Tax Technology Initiatives, https://web-archive.oecd.org/temp/2023-03-09/618463-data-management.htm, Table DM3 and https://web-archive.oecd.org/temp/2023-03-09/618466-tax-rule-management-and-application.htm, Table TRM3 (accessed on 10 September 2024).

Box 6.5. Examples – Artificial intelligence and data for analytical purposes

Australia – Enhancing capabilities across business, technology and data & analytics domains

The ATO is one of the largest consumers of third-party data in Australia.

To enable the ATO to follow the OECD's Tax Administration 3.0 vision, the ATO has embarked upon a modernisation programme. This programme has successfully delivered upon its initial tranches, underpinned by some innovative capabilities, including:

- Nexus agile delivery methodology: The implementation of a Nexus delivery method under the scaled agile framework, to facilitate improved collaboration between architecture and delivery team members, resulting in increased delivery speed. This has shifted the culture from monolithic system delivery to rapid, iterative value driven releases.

(*Note: The Nexus framework builds on Scrum (an agile team collaboration framework) to enable multiple teams to work together on a single product by minimising cross-team dependencies and integration issues. It focuses on continuous integration and delivery, ensuring that teams contribute to a cohesive and integrated outcome by the end of each sprint.*)

- Uplifted cross-disciplinary capabilities for the future: The ATO has established multi-disciplinary teams, with cross-skilled team members from data consumers, engineers and producers. This has reduced skill dependencies, enabling continuous and timely design.

Pattern based approach to enhance ATO data capabilities: The ATO has implemented a use-case driven approach to deploy patterns in its new capabilities, made up of two key components:

- Solution patterns – Reusable end-to-end solutions for specific data characteristics to achieve a business outcome.
- Component patterns – Reusable, configuration-driven patterns within an application to satisfy common and repeatable requirements e.g., reusable patterns for ingesting streaming data across multiple use cases.

The ATO has seen a reduction in development time starting to emerge at the end of its first delivery tranche, and significant use-cases emerging that are lining up to use its new data patterns, including the administration of highly complex tax affairs using fully automated solutions.

Finland – Status centres

The Finnish Tax Administration has in recent years reformed the way it operates, and as part of this has introduced status centres to measure to what extent its operations are achieving the administration's goals. This is done by comparing and collecting data on activities and targets in one place, allowing for employees to make decisions and set further goals based on the evidence.

Thousands of employees in the tax administration actively use status centres, including for team meetings where successes, lessons and challenges can be identified to inform next steps. Data sharing and communication is key in advancing evidence-based decisions to support the administration's goals and find solutions to any challenges faced.

The status centres have seen trust and interaction within teams and across the administration increase. Having access to all the relevant data and information directs attention to any issues, focusing discussion on solutions and enabling informed goal setting.

France – Using artificial intelligence to fight real-estate property income taxation fraud

The Directorate General of Public Finances (DGFiP) has started using artificial intelligence (AI) to identify tax fraud, with positive results.

In particular, DGFiP uses AI to calculate the level of rents that need to be declared for income tax purposes in relation to both property that is owned and rented out. A model has been built to estimate the rental value of each property, which is based on a machine-learning algorithm that analyses and links the amount of rent declared, the characteristics of the rented properties and the socio-economic data for the neighbourhoods in which the properties are located (median income, household composition, number of social housing units, etc.).

The model is then applied to all the residential premises rented out, and the total estimated rental amount for each landlord is compared with the rent they declare, enabling DGFiP to detect any under-reporting of rental income and potential fraud.

This was the first model to be put into production for targeting tax fraud by private individuals, and the cases selected for audit by the model resulted in additional tax being paid in almost 50% of cases.

Whilst the support of service providers was needed to launch this work, the necessary data-science skills have now been developed within DGFiP to carry out this work.

Japan – Use of artificial intelligence and data analytics in taxation

The NTA is working to improve the efficiency and sophistication of tax collection by using AI. This makes it possible to determine taxpayers with a higher risk of not filing their tax returns correctly and increases revenue by collecting more tax.

The NTA analyses data from a variety of sources, including tax returns and financial statements provided by taxpayers, information provided by third parties, and information from tax audits. This data is then analysed using statistical analysis and machine learning methods to determine which taxpayers are most likely to not file their tax returns. By utilising the results of this analysis, NTA is able to carry out its tax audit and compliance measures more efficiently.

For example, in 2022 AI determined that the average amount of additional tax due per corporate tax and consumption tax audits for small and medium-sized enterprises was 40% higher than the tax actually received. Part of the issue was that regional taxation bureaus struggle to contact taxpayers, even after attempting phone calls or in-person visits. Therefore, AI is used to predict the most preferable method to make contact, ranging from making phone calls to in-person visits and sending letters. This is based off information such as previous contact archives of taxpayers and their tax returns.

Sources: Australia (2024), Finland (2024), France (2024) and Japan (2024).

Table 6.10. Evolution of the application of data science tools, artificial intelligence and robotic process automation between 2018 and 2022

Percentage of administrations

	Data science / analytical tools			Artificial intelligence, including machine learning			Robotic process automation		
Status of implementation and use	2018	2022	Difference in percentage points (p.p.)	2018	2022	Difference in p.p.	2018	2022	Difference in p.p.
Technology implemented and used	71.9	96.6	+24.7	29.8	63.8	+34.0	22.8	58.6	+35.8
Technology in the implementation phase for future use	19.3	3.4	-15.9	15.8	24.1	+8.3	14.0	6.9	-7.1
Technology not used, incl. situations where implementation has not started	8.8	0.0	-8.8	54.4	12.1	-42.3	63.2	34.5	-28.7

Source: CIAT, IOTA, IMF, OECD, International Survey on Revenue Administration, Tables A.108 Innovative technologies: Implementation and usage - Blockchain, artificial intelligence, and cloud computing, and A.109 Innovative technologies: Implementation and usage - Data science, robotic process automation, and APIs, https://data.rafit.org/regular.aspx?key=74180897 (accessed on 10 September 2024).

With the use of analytics becoming a common and integrated part of tax administrations across the world, in developed and developing countries alike, the OECD's Forum on Tax Administration developed the *Analytics Maturity Model* (OECD, 2022[7]) to help tax administrations self-assess their current level of maturity in their analytics usage and capability. This provides insight into their current status by identifying areas of weaknesses as well as strengths. As Figure 6.2. shows, it has been completed by over 40 tax administrations, and the results of this are guiding and supporting administrations in their analytics strategies.

Figure 6.2. Results of the Analytics Maturity Model self-assessments

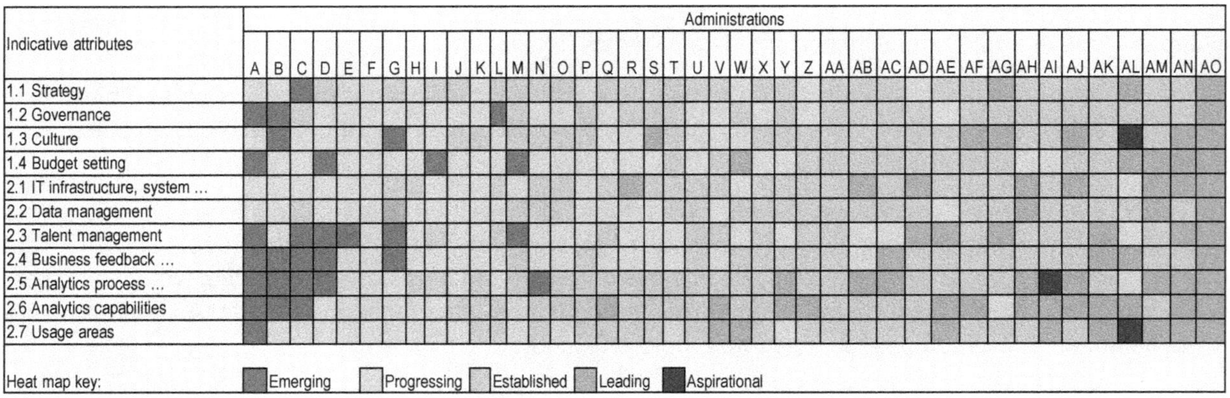

Source: OECD (2022), Analytics Maturity Model, https://www.oecd.org/en/topics/sub-issues/comparative-analysis-of-tax-administrations/tax-maturity-models.html (accessed on 10 September 2024).

Taxpayer programmes

Another approach for targeted risk management is the creation of units looking into the tax affairs of specific taxpayer segments. Two specific areas where tax administrations have found it advantageous to manage specific groups of taxpayers on a segmented basis are large business taxpayers, and high net wealth individuals (HNWIs). The rationale for focusing administration resources on managing these groups revolves around the:

- ***Significance of tax compliance risks***: due to the nature and type of transactions, offshore activities, opportunity and strategies to minimise tax liabilities; and in the case of large business, the differences between financial accounting profits and the profits computed for tax purposes.
- ***Complexity of business and tax dealings***: particularly the breadth of their business interests and in the case of HNWI, the mix of private and tax affairs.
- ***Integrity of the tax system***: the importance of being able to assure stakeholders about the work undertaken with these high-profile groups of taxpayers.

Additionally, in the case of large taxpayers, while being a small number of taxpayers, they are typically responsible for a disproportionate share of tax revenue collected. Even though large taxpayer offices/ programmes manage only 1.7% of corporate taxpayers, on average they account for 44% of all net revenue collected, including withholding payments on behalf of employees (Table 6.11.). Looking at the individual country-level, the data indicates that for most jurisdictions between 30% and 60% of their total net revenue was received from taxpayers covered by their large taxpayer programmes (see Figure 6.3.).

Table 6.11. Importance of large taxpayer offices / programmes (LTO/P), 2022

FTEs in LTO/P as percentage of total FTEs	Corporate taxpayers managed through LTO/P as percentage of active corporate taxpayers	Percentage of net revenue administered under LTO/P in relation to total net revenue collected by the tax administration	FTEs on audit, investigation and other verification function in the LTO/P as percentage of total FTEs in LTO/P	Total value of additional assessments raised through LTO/P as percentage of total value of additional assessments raised from audits
3.9	1.7	43.8	62.1	31.8

Note: The table shows the average percentages across the jurisdictions that were able to provide the information.
Sources: CIAT, IOTA, IMF, OECD, International Survey on Revenue Administration, Tables D.17 Large taxpayer office / program ratios: Full-time equivalents (FTEs), and D.18 Large taxpayer office / program ratios: Corporate taxpayers, additional assessments raised, and net revenue administered, https://data.rafit.org/regular.aspx?key=74180900 (accessed on 10 September 2024).

Figure 6.3. Percentage of revenue administered through large taxpayer offices/programmes, 2022

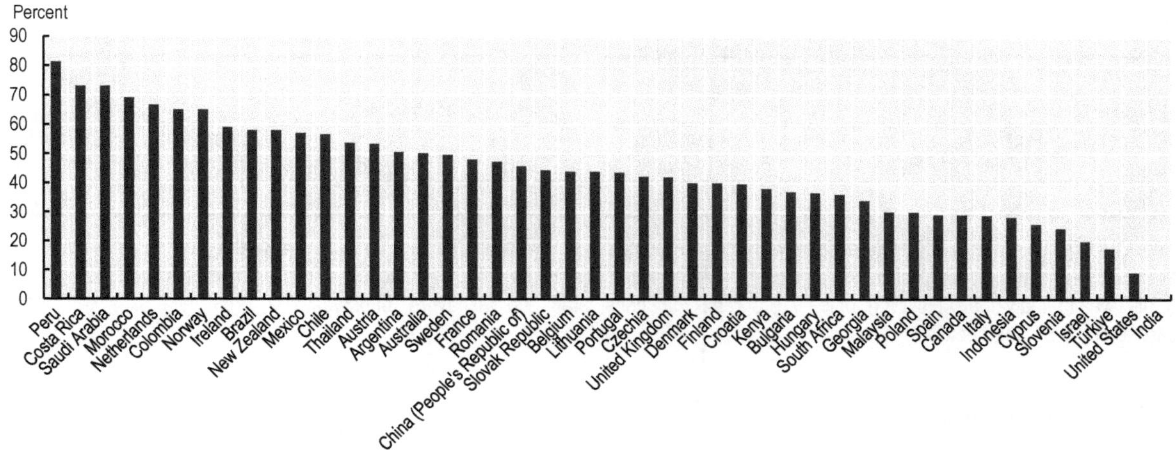

Source: CIAT, IOTA, IMF, OECD, International Survey on Revenue Administration, Table D.18 Large taxpayer office / program ratios: Corporate taxpayers, additional assessments raised, and net revenue administered, https://data.rafit.org/regular.aspx?key=74180900 (accessed on 10 September 2024).

StatLink https://stat.link/3riw1u

While the management of these groups of taxpayers is often undertaken as a programme, in a large number of jurisdictions these programmes are also structural involving a Large Taxpayer Office or HNWI unit. As can be seen in Table 6.12. and Table 6.13., the scope of the work of these units varies considerably, ranging from undertaking traditional audit activity, through to "full service" approaches which may also encompass co-operative compliance programmes (see Chapter 8 for more on this). However, on average more than 60% of tax administration staff in large taxpayer offices or programmes are working on audit, investigation and other verification related issues (see Table 6.11.).

As regards the main criteria for including taxpayers in LTO/P and HNWI programmes, these are (by order of importance):

- ***For large corporate taxpayers***: Turnover/revenue, economic sector, and amount of taxes (see Table B.16); and
- ***For HNWIs***: Assets/wealth, and income (Table B.17).

Table 6.12. Large taxpayer offices / programmes: Existence and functions carried out, 2022

Percentage of administrations

Large taxpayer office / programme exists	If yes, functions carried out ...					
	Registration	Return and payment processing	Services	Audit	Collection of arrears	Dispute resolution
87.9	51.0	62.7	94.1	100.0	62.7	72.5

Source: CIAT, IOTA, IMF, OECD, International Survey on Revenue Administration, Tables A.34 Large taxpayer office / program: Existence and revenue collected, A.35 Large taxpayer office / program: Functions - Registration, return and payment processing, and services, and A.36 Large taxpayer office / program: Functions - Audit, debt collection, dispute resolution, https://data.rafit.org/regular.aspx?key=74180907 (accessed on 10 September 2024).

Table 6.13. HNWI programmes: Existence and functions carried out, 2022

Percentage of administrations

HNWI programme exists	If yes, ...						
	Part of LTO/P	Functions carried out					
		Registration	Return and payment processing	Services	Audit	Collection of arrears	Dispute resolution
39.7	65.2	34.8	43.5	91.3	39.1	39.1	43.5

Source: CIAT, IOTA, IMF, OECD, International Survey on Revenue Administration, Table A.40 High net wealth individuals (HNWIs) office / program: Existence and revenue collected, https://data.rafit.org/regular.aspx?key=74180907 (accessed on 10 September 2024), and Table B.18 High net wealth individuals (HNWIs) office / program: Functions, staff and taxpayers, https://data.rafit.org/regular.aspx?key=74180915 (accessed on 10 September 2024).

Planning for future risks

While it is key for tax administrations to understand current compliance risks and prepare appropriate response strategies, it is equally important to understand and prevent risks which may arise in the future. The increasing availability of data along with the enhanced capacity of tax administrations to handle and analyse that data allows tax administrations to more robustly assess future tax risks.

The ability to identify, understand and manage risks in a rapidly changing environment is a critical element of successful and resilient tax administration. Table 6.9. highlights the large number of tax administrations who engage in forecasting, which is putting them in a position to assess where new compliance risks may arise, and to develop appropriate mitigation strategies. This is leading to the creation of sophisticated risk management programmes, that can embed risk management across the organisation rather than being carried out in silos.

Box 6.6. Finland – Foresight activities

The Finnish Tax Administration conducts foresight activities systematically and as a result, the administration's top management is provided with information on this four times a year to help assess whether the strategy requires updating.

The groups engaged in foresight activities also share futures information for use in other part of the administration to help give a broad perspective on how the operating environment is changing. There are seven groups: customer relations, customer experience and stakeholders; changes in work; technology; user experience; public administration; PESTLE (Political, Economic, Sociological, Technological, Legal, Environmental); and observations from customer service.

To encourage the widespread use of this insight, information is made available in the management's status centre. In addition, there are also monthly coffee sessions focused on current foresight activities and a staff training programme.

As a result, the Tax Administration's foresight activities help foster a collaborative culture and are also widely networked. This collaboration extends to other public authorities and with other countries' tax authorities so that there is a good snapshot of the present situation and future challenges identified.

Source: Finland (2024).

Planning for future risks also involves tax administrations navigating a number of challenges that might, if not addressed, undermine their overall efforts. Complex and evolving laws and regulations, digital transactions, and cross-border activities can make it difficult to identify and mitigate compliance risks effectively. In this respect, ISORA 2023 invited tax administrations to characterise a number of challenges in addressing compliance risks related to international tax issues.

Table 6.14. summarises tax administration's views and shows that human resource (HR) related issues cause most concerns. Recruiting people with the right skills, experience and knowledge to deal with international tax issues is perceived as being very challenging by more than half of the administrations. Retaining those people is also considered very challenging by close to 40% of administrations.

Table 6.14. Challenges in addressing compliance risk related to international tax issues, 2022

Percentage of administrations

	Characterisation of level of challenge		
Challenges	Very challenging	Somewhat challenging	Not challenging
Recruiting people with the right skills, experience and knowledge	55.2	43.1	1.7
Retaining people with the right skills, experience and knowledge	37.9	62.1	0.0
Obtaining data for compliance risk identification, analysis and management	19.0	72.4	8.6
Using data for compliance risk identification, analysis and management	19.0	65.5	15.5
Developing an effective compliance improvement plan	19.0	67.2	13.8
Having the right legislative framework	20.7	65.5	13.8
Developing an effective organisational structure	8.6	79.3	12.1

Source: CIAT, IOTA, IMF, OECD, International Survey on Revenue Administration, Table B.22 Compliance risk management: Characterization of challenges related to international tax issues, https://data.rafit.org/regular.aspx?key=74180916 (accessed on 10 September 2024).

Preventing non-compliance

Tax administrations rely heavily on the positive compliance attitudes of taxpayers in reporting and paying their taxes. This is often termed "voluntary compliance". Compliance attitudes are particularly important where tax administrations rely heavily on taxpayers to undertake full and accurate self-reporting of taxable income and taxable events and to make payments.

As highlighted in Chapter 5, tax compliance can be heavily affected by elements outside of the control of the tax administration, but they can use a variety of service-related approaches to support voluntary compliance and prevent non-compliance. Typically, those approaches take place before tax returns are filed and include:

- Reminding taxpayers of deadlines (filing and paying);
- Facilitating taxpayer access to third-party data already collected, for example, through pre-filing regimes or access to such data through taxpayer portals;
- Running targeted campaigns to encourage compliance; and
- Providing educational and support initiatives.

Streamlining communication with taxpayers can also be fruitful as can be seen in the example in Box 6.7.

Box 6.7. Spain – Simplifying taxpayer communications

One of the main objectives of the Spanish Tax Agency (AEAT) is to promote voluntary compliance from taxpayers. To achieve this goal, AEAT has undertaken a project to simplify the content and structure of its communications with citizens. Updates include:

- The introduction of a header page that outlines in simple language the key information about the purpose of the document, recipient, and actions requested from the taxpayer.
- Reduction in the length of documents to streamline information.
- Simplification of the response forms attached to make it easier for taxpayers to fill out.
- Availability of customer services via telephone (pre-booked appointments only) and webchat.

This project has already produced benefits. There has been a 20.2% increase in responses, reputational benefits for AEAT, and reduced the administrative burden on staff.

Source: Spain (2024).

However, there are also non-service-related approaches that tax administrations have at their disposal to influence compliance. For example, around one-third of administrations indicated that they provide taxpayers with information on predetermined compliance interventions (see Table 6.15.). Knowing that an intervention might come, may encourage taxpayers to pay closer attention to tax compliance issues.

Table 6.15. Selected interventions before returns are filed, 2022

Percentage of administrations that undertake the relevant intervention

Facilitating taxpayer access to 3rd party data already collected	Targeting campaigns to encourage compliance	Reminding taxpayers of filing deadlines	Providing information on predetermined compliance interventions	Other interventions
74.1	81.0	96.6	34.5	36.2

Source: CIAT, IOTA, IMF, OECD, International Survey on Revenue Administration, Table B.26 Compliance risk management: Interventions before return filing, https://data.rafit.org/regular.aspx?key=74180916 (accessed on 10 September 2024).

Administrations also reported the use of letters, emails or social media reminding and encouraging taxpayers to fulfil their tax obligations. This might be done through generic mass communication, or in the form of preventive personalised communication to taxpayers with previous non-compliance as regards certain obligations. The use of telephone calls to taxpayers that are considered high-risk has also been indicated.

As regards large businesses, tax administrations also pointed to the use of co-operative compliance programmes and advanced pricing arrangements as a means for preventing non-compliance. Those approaches are described in more detail in Chapter 8.

Behavioural insights and nudges

Another approach for preventing non-compliance is the use of behavioural insights. Behavioural insights is an interdisciplinary field of research using principles from the behavioural sciences such as psychology, neuroscience, and behavioural economics to understand how individuals absorb, process, and react to information. These principles can be used to design practical policies and interventions based on human behaviour. This can be particularly powerful when combined with insights gathered from the analysis of the increasingly large volumes of data available to tax administration, both internally and externally generated. One example of this are nudge messages during the return filing process, providing taxpayers with an indication where there might be potential issues/ errors in the figures being reported.

Around half of the administrations report employing behavioural researchers (see Table 10.4.) and the 2021 report *Behavioural Insights for Better Tax Administration: A Brief Guide* prepared by the OECD's Forum on Tax Administration Behavioural Insight Community of Interest contains many examples of this in practice (OECD, 2021[8]).

Box 6.8. Examples – Behavioural insights and nudges

Australia – Contemporising Goods and Sales Tax risk models

The Contemporising Goods and Sales Tax Risk Models (CGRM) project has developed near to real-time prompts for Goods and Sales Tax (GST) reporting to prevent compliance issues before they arise, by supporting those who want to do the right thing and helping them to reduce mistakes.

The ATO's data-driven models help reduce the errors and mistakes that taxpayers can make while lodging their Business Activity Statements (BAS) online.

The ATO uses available data to identify where BAS lodged online contain an identifiable or likely reporting error. The ATO then generates nudge messaging recommending that taxpayers check their BAS before they lodge their refund.

This model aligns with a key focus area in the 2023-24 ATO Corporate Plan to improve small business tax performance with a digital-first approach, by providing system-generated tax guidance to minimise errors.

This framework can be expanded in the future to include new tailored nudge messages that assist taxpayers to reduce errors.

This initiative has yielded impressive results in the first two years:

- Year 1 (2021-22): 196 000 nudge messages were sent to 102 000 taxpayers. This early engagement helped taxpayers to correct errors before lodging their BAS and resulted in the self-correction and protection of revenue of AUD 51.1 million.
- Year 2 (2022-23): 543 000 nudge messages were sent to 217 000 taxpayers. This early engagement helped taxpayers to correct errors before lodging their BAS and resulted in the self-correction and protection of revenue of AUD 43.2 million.

China (People's Republic of) – Promoting tax compliance with behavioural insights

New behavioural insight methods have been deployed by the People's Republic of China (hereafter "China") with regards to filing tax returns. The STA has explored sending different types of prompts and reminders to taxpayers in order to increase the number of filed tax returns.

Taking account of China's vast size and regional differences in behaviour, different provinces across China were chosen as initial pilots. Overall, it was found that introducing reminder messages and prompts via text message, phone calls and China's income tax app increased filings by 13%. The STA found that taxpayers in the higher socioeconomic brackets were more likely to be influenced by the prompts and reminders to file their tax returns. It was also found that messages which were more positive in tone (i.e. encouraging people to fill out their tax returns) were more effective than negative in tone messages (i.e. referring to possible consequences and penalties if tax returns were not filed).

Slovak Republic – Online notifications to encourage compliance

The Slovak Republic encourages voluntary compliance from its taxpayers by contacting them using online notifications to remind them of their tax obligations. The notifications vary from reminders to pay taxes and any outstanding payments, to pointing out potential errors in tax returns and giving taxpayers the opportunity to correct these. This applies for both individual taxpayers and businesses.

Notifying taxpayers online of their obligations not only increases voluntary compliance levels with little cost to the tax administration, but also increases the efficiency of the tax administration and enables taxpayers to give any feedback, improving customer service.

Türkiye – Using behavioural insights to increase compliance

Türkiye's tax administration experiences a large volume of demand for its services. In order to ensure rapid responses to taxpayers and reduce the workload of its staff, Türkiye trialled using behavioural insights to send SMS messages to certain groups to increase compliance:

- Personal Income Taxpayers: SMS messages were sent to taxpayers who had not made their income tax payments, reminding them of the declaration period deadline. After the declaration period deadline had passed, taxpayers who had not submitted their declarations were identified and a SMS message was sent to them explaining the subsequent process. Taxpayers who had submitted their declarations but not yet made payments were sent a message explaining how to make payments and reminding them of their outstanding debts.
- Motor Vehicle Taxpayers: SMS messages were sent informing taxpayers that the declaration period had started. Taxpayers who did not made their payments were reminded at regular intervals until the end of the declaration period. After the end of the declaration period, thank you messages were sent to taxpayers who had made their payments.

Sources: Australia (2024), China (People's Republic of) (2024), Slovak Republic (2024) and Türkiye (2024).

Taxpayer rating programmes

There has been an increasing number of administrations reporting the introduction of taxpayer rating programmes to encourage compliance through instilling a sense of responsibility around paying taxes and providing indicators for taxpayers to measure how well they are complying with their obligations. To further incentivise compliance, this is sometimes accompanied with a rewards system for those who comply. Box 6.8. contains the latest developments as regards those programmes.

Box 6.9. Examples – Taxpayer rating programmes

Georgia – Taxpayer Behaviour Rating Programme

To encourage trust and engagement between the tax authority and taxpayers, Georgia has introduced the Taxpayer Behaviour Programme. This evaluates taxpayers' overall compliance with their tax obligations and aims to improve compliance levels through instilling a sense of responsibility to pay tax. It is primarily aimed at VAT and mid-size taxpayers.

The Programme uses four indicators to measure how well taxpayers are complying:

1. Tax registration
2. Timely declaration of income
3. Accuracy and completeness of declared information
4. Budget accountability

Taxpayers are evaluated on a 10-point scale with an initial allocation of maximum points. Points are deducted based on how well taxpayers adhere to the indicators, with explanations available online. Assessments are conducted monthly, and taxpayers can view their assigned ratings on the e-portal, along with a historical overview of ratings across reporting periods. Taxpayers are provided with the opportunity to submit feedback on their assigned behaviour rating through a designated feedback form. Plans are being explored to enable taxpayers to make their ratings visible to specific audiences, and potentially even make them public.

Latvia – Taxpayer Rating System

Latvia has introduced taxpayer ratings for companies, to enable them to track their compliance performance and improve it. Each company can access its rating and an explanation of how it is formed in their Electronic Declaration System profile.

The ratings levels are:

- A - Good performance – reliable taxpayers that could be good cooperation partners.
- B - Needs improvement – taxpayers that generally fulfil their obligations, but there is room for improvement. Taxpayer could be a business partner, but evaluation required in terms of cooperation to determine whether the company has significant tax debts or not.
- C - Violations – excluded from the VAT payer register or economic activity suspended.
- N - Inactive – no economic activity.
- J - Newly-registered – established within the last 6 months.

The indicators which make up the ratings are:

- Registration data: whether bankruptcy proceedings have been initiated, if economic activity has been suspended, exclusion from the VAT register, company officials' tax compliance history.
- Timely submission of declarations and reports.
- Tax payments paid on time and in full; if a debt arises, pays the debt in instalments.
- Penalties: proportion of fines is small compared to total tax payments; does not indicate a serious violation,
- Wage assessment: comparison with the average wage in the industry and region. Unusually low wages indicate undeclared wage risks and can lower the rating.
- Information indicating violations: risks revealed in risk analyses or information received through international exchange of information.

These indicators help companies to understand where and how they can improve their rating. The State Revenue Service (SRS) provides support to companies with higher ratings, whilst restrictions are in place for companies with a C rating.

Lithuania – Using risk profiles to measure compliance risks

The STI launched the internal taxpayer risk profile (RISKIS) and the external tax profile (Client profile), which offer a convenient, quick and thorough assessment of taxpayer behaviour through using risk criterion and aggregated data visualisation.

RISKIS has 36 criteria used to flag taxpayers that may be at risk of not paying their taxes on time. The criteria are divided into five dimensions - registration, filing, behaviour, control, and payment. The results for each criterion are displayed using the traffic light principle: red indicates a high risk, yellow suggests a medium risk, green signifies no risk, and grey means that the taxpayer is not eligible to be evaluated by means of that specific criterion. For each criterion, relevant data is presented, providing factual information on why a particular criterion has been triggered. For example, if a criterion is triggered due to a failure to submit a tax return, the specific return form and time-period will be displayed. Using different graphics and diagrams, users can easily understand where the taxpayer is on the risk profile. RISKIS also provides a graphical web of dependencies.

The Client profile consists of 21 criteria, similar to those used in RISKIS. The key difference is that Client profiles are visible to individual taxpayers, which gives them some idea of the kinds of behaviour that indicate a risk to STI. All companies can access their respective taxpayer profiles and take action to mitigate risks, make necessary changes, and present themselves as less risky entities. Companies can also share their Client profile information with other peers.

Flat numbers of tax debt and tax loans are also displayed on RISKIS and Client profiles. All the data in both RISKIS and Client profiles is updated on a daily basis.

Slovak Republic – Tax Reliability Index

To encourage compliance, the Slovak Republic uses a Tax Reliability Index to assess its taxable entities that have been registered for income tax for at least two years. Taxpayers are assessed on various criteria, including non-payment of tax, late filing of tax returns, and findings from tax inspections. Based on a points system, taxpayers are automatically assigned one of the following grades:

- Highly reliable
- Reliable
- Less reliable
- Not evaluated

Once assigned a grade, this is published online and made public. Taxpayers have the opportunity to challenge their grade. To reward good behaviour and encourage compliance, those in the highly reliable grade are given benefits such as a 50% reduction in the fee for issuing a binding opinion. Alternatively, those in the less reliable category have restrictions placed on them, such as a shorter deadline for the submission of documents required during a tax audit or investigation.

Sources: Georgia (2024), Latvia (2024), Lithuania (2024) and the Slovak Republic (2024).

Addressing non-compliance

Tax administrations determine through a combination of methods and tools whether a taxpayer is non-compliant with their obligations. This may include data matching programmes; data analytics and the use of algorithms, for example, as part of compliance risk models; information sharing between government agencies and jurisdictions; and risk reviews where officials might look into public records and social media (See also Table 6.16.). Box 6.10. contains some of the latest developments in this space.

Table 6.16. Selected interventions after returns are filed but before formal audit action, 2022

Percentage of administrations that undertake the relevant intervention

Identifying inconsistencies through cross-matching of 3rd party data	Identifying anomalies or outliers through data analytics to prompt taxpayer disclosure	Risk reviews	Requesting further information	Other interventions
91.4	81.0	87.9	82.9	41.4

Source: CIAT, IOTA, IMF, OECD, International Survey on Revenue Administration, Table B.27 Compliance risk management: Interventions after return filing, and measurement of intervention effectiveness, https://data.rafit.org/regular.aspx?key=74180916 (accessed on 10 September 2024).

Box 6.10. Examples – Identifying non-compliance

Australia – Automated Network and Grouping Identification Engine

The Automated Network and Grouping Identification Engine (ANGIE) is an automated, rules-based graph database drawing information from a range of internal and external data sources to help ATO staff identify and visualise complex group structures, networks, and understand relationships between entities and group members.

ANGIE replaces legacy systems responsible for linking clients together via known relationships into defined groups (referred to as client groupings). It allocates the groups to populations for the responsible ATO business area to review based on risk priorities, and enables staff to:

- Provide an accurate, dynamic, and customisable view of populations and client groups;
- Identify changes to a client group and/or population including movements in and out of them;
- Visualise and analyse group structures over time and automatically identify significant changes across time periods;
- Engage with the right taxpayers by accurately identifying client groups and effective control;
- Identify potential risks by seeing where income is earned, assets are owned, and structural changes.

The ATO is expanding ANGIE, with a focus on more sophisticated analytics, powerful visualisation tools and a wider range of grouping populations. This will improve performance, reliability, usefulness and visibility across the ATO, ensuring that the ATO can respond to the increasingly complex networks and emerging behaviours.

Belgium – Data Integrated Operational System application

Belgium has introduced the Data Integrated Operational System application to enable employees of the Federal Public Service Finance to execute everyday tasks more efficiently. DIOS is a fully integrated single taxpayer database in which the user can both retrieve all the information they need and perform all the relevant analysis in one place. The functionalities provided include the following:

- The search engines allow for taxpayers to be traced on the basis of incomplete and/or incorrect data (without exact ID identification). A taxpayer can also be traced through other files even if they are not the main subject.
- The network analysis function allows the user to visualise the taxpayer's network.
- The score card analysis tool automatically detects potential 'suspicious' behaviour directly and/or indirectly linked to a taxpayer or licence holder.
- Users can export standard reports to communicate the results of their investigations in a simple and easy to understand way.
- Various data mining projects have been integrated into the project to improve and optimise the use of business intelligence.

Canada – Foreign Source Matching Programme

The Canada Revenue Agency (CRA) has implemented the use of the Common Reporting Standard (CRS) and Foreign Account Tax Compliance Act (FATCA) data in its Foreign Source Matching (FSM) programme.

FSM focuses on individual Canadian residents with potential unreported income from foreign countries, by comparing the foreign source data with what was reported on their income tax return.

A pilot was conducted in 2023 to expand the FSM workload by using the CRS and FATCA data feeds, and involved the review of potentially unreported income from 27 jurisdictions. The pilot had approximately 2 000 FATCA and CRS forms linked to taxpayers who may not have reported the interest and dividend income indicated on the forms. The pilot yielded positive results and had a good return on investment.

The FSM program will continue to work with the FATCA and CRS data feeds and monitor the success of these files and identify potential for program growth if applicable.

Italy – Using predictive models to aid compliance work

To aid with its compliance work, the Italian Revenue Agency has developed a predictive model which ranks taxpayers according to how well they comply with their obligations. The model uses historical tax audit data on taxpayers, and produces a set of scores that can be used to prioritise cases for additional checks and audits.

The process for selecting taxpayers for audit has different phases:

1. Risk analysis to detect suspicious behaviours and identify high risk cases for further analysis.
2. Investigation into these high-risk cases, including sending questionnaires to customers or contacting them for clarification on any uncertainties.
3. If the investigation finds tax violations, the tax administration will formally request the taxpayer to pay an amount based on the violation.
4. Taxpayers can choose whether to pay the amount or to start a tax litigation.

The methodology is based on modelling each phase of the process through a suitable probability distribution. These different models are then combined to predict a score expressing the overall profitability of the investigation of each selected taxpayer.

Sources: Australia (2024), Belgium (2024), Canada (2024) and Italy (2024).

Based on those methods and tools, a tax administration might request further information (see Table 6.16.) or provide a taxpayer the opportunity of voluntary disclosure. Where deemed necessary, a "compliance action" will be launched to determine whether taxpayers have properly reported their tax liability.

The increasing availability of data and the introduction of sophisticated analytical models and artificial intelligence are allowing administrations to better identify returns and claims or transactions which might require further review or be fraudulent. Furthermore, these models, many of which can operate in real-time, are allowing administrations to conduct automated electronic checks on all returns or on transactions of a particular type.

The use of automated electronic checks or using rules-based approaches to treat some defined risks (for example, automatically denying a claim, issuing a letter or matching a transaction) is providing administrations with more effective and efficient ways to undertake some of this work. As Table 6.17.

indicates, around 80% of administrations are using electronic compliance checks as part of the return filing process, with:

- Around 60% of those doing this during the process of completing the return or while submitting it, for example, via prompts and real-time nudging indicating that information might be missing or deductions to high; and
- Almost 85% using electronic checks post return submission.

Table 6.17. Electronic compliance checks, 2022

Percentage of administrations that undertake the relevant approach

Electronic compliance checks used as part of the returns filing process	If yes, checks are made ...		
	During process of completing the return	On submitting the return	Post submission of return
79.3	60.9	63.0	84.8

Source: CIAT, IOTA, IMF, OECD, International Survey on Revenue Administration, Table A.86 Verification / audit activity: Electronic compliance checks, https://data.rafit.org/regular.aspx?key=74180894 (accessed on 10 September 2024).

The type of compliance action that will be taken may vary depending on the severity of each case and as shown in Table 6.18., close to 90% of administration have (or are in the process of developing) a formal framework for compliance interventions which incorporates traditional tax audit within a framework based on classes of interventions that provide for a consistent, appropriate response to risk and taxpayer compliance behaviour.

In this respect, more than 85% of administrations reported providing a proportionate response to non-compliance, for example, applying graduated fines and penalties that reflect the degree of taxpayer co-operation and/ or compliance history. In addition, around 80% of administrations indicated that taxpayers can benefit if they make early disclosure of errors or omissions and if they fully co-operate. (See Table 6.18.)

Table 6.18. General approaches towards compliance, 2022

Percentage of administrations that have the relevant approach

Providing a proportionate response to non-compliance	Providing opportunities to voluntarily correct mistakes or omissions in tax returns	Ensuring taxpayers benefit under early disclosure of errors or omissions and full co-operation	Reminding and encouraging taxpayers to fulfil tax obligations	Formal framework for compliance interventions exists or is being developed
86.2	98.3	82.8	94.8	89.7

Source: CIAT, IOTA, IMF, OECD, International Survey on Revenue Administration, Table B.25 Compliance risk management: Compliance intervention framework, https://data.rafit.org/regular.aspx?key=74180916 (accessed on 10 September 2024).

Box 6.11. Examples – Automated compliance

France – The optical extraction of estate declarations project

The Optical Extraction of Estate Declarations project, initiated by DGFiP, represents significant progress in enhancing the administrative processing of succession forms for tax purposes. This initiative combines advanced Optical Character Recognition (OCR) with the latest generative artificial intelligence technologies to extract and analyse financial data from these documents.

Succession forms, which detail the assets and liabilities of a deceased individual, are complex because they contain diverse information that ranges from personal details of the deceased to specific financial products that may have tax implications. The ability to accurately decipher and categorise this information is crucial for the correct assessment and collection of estate taxes.

The project's OCR technology is tailored to navigate through the dense and often handwritten text found in succession forms. It extracts the information needed for tax calculation, addressing one of the major bottlenecks in the field of taxation: the classification and analysis of financial assets.

Generative AI further enhances this process by interpreting various writing styles and legal terminologies. It recognises and understands the specific terms that define familial relationships and the legal context of succession, facilitating the accurate mapping of inheritance chains and the determination of each heir's tax responsibilities.

This initiative has significantly improved DGFiP's capability to enforce tax laws and regulations more effectively. By digitising and structuring the wealth of data contained in succession forms, the risk of evasion and error has reduced, thereby promoting a more compliant and efficient tax system.

Singapore – Missing Trader Fraud buffer model

Missing Trader Fraud (MTF) poses a significant risk to public revenue. MTF is a form of VAT/Goods and Sales (GST) Tax fraud where a fraudulent supplier collects VAT/GST from customers for the sales made, but does not remit this VAT/GST to the tax authority. Meanwhile, GST-registered customers down the supply chain continue to claim refunds from the tax authority for the VAT/GST paid on their purchases.

Using artificial intelligence to tackle GST fraud, the Inland Revenue Authority of Singapore (IRAS) has developed an auto-machine learning solution, the MTF Buffer Model, to pre-emptively detect intermediary (buffer) entities engaging in MTF activity. This enables IRAS to intervene early and disrupt the supply chain before they can perpetrate MTF further. This approach challenges the notion that MTF can only be detected at the "end" of the MTF chain when exporters attempt to make the fraudulent GST refund claim.

As the Model targets intermediary or buffer entities set up to obscure the MTF supply chain, IRAS is able to identify the complicit entities and uncover the entire MTF chain in a much shorter time. IRAS has experimented with an auto-machine learning tool, DataRobot, to test and evaluate the performance of various models using different algorithms to identify one with optimal results. To date, the model has yielded encouraging results and is assessed to be three times more effective in detecting buffer entities compared to traditional approaches.

Sources: France (2024) and Singapore (2024).

Following the identification of inconsistencies or anomalies and when further engagement with the taxpayer did not address the potential issue of non-compliance or error, tax administrations may launch an audit action. The scope and depth of the audit can depend on the potential issue and the findings during the pre-audit engagement with the taxpayer. Table 6.19. shows that the vast majority of administrations have different audit actions at their disposal.

Table 6.19. Post-filing enforcement actions, 2022

Percentage of administrations that undertake the relevant action

Desk audits	Single issue audits	Limited scope audits	Comprehensive audits	Avoidance and evasion investigations
91.4	93.1	93.1	94.8	91.4

Source: CIAT, IOTA, IMF, OECD, International Survey on Revenue Administration, Table B.28 Compliance risk management: Post-filing enforcement actions, https://data.rafit.org/regular.aspx?key=74180916 (accessed on 10 September 2024).

Box 6.12. Examples – Post-filing enforcement actions

India – Mitigation of risk in High-Risk Refund claim

In order to reduce the number of incorrect refund claims, the data mining and intelligence information system of the Indian Department of Revenue analyses the data using High-Risk Refund (HRR) rules and shares the outcome with the Central Processing Centre (CPC), which processes the Income Tax returns. After this, the CPC puts the processing of a refund on hold until the taxpayer confirms their claim of a refund as being correct or the taxpayer revises their return. As a result, a large number of taxpayers reduced the amount of their refund claims.

However, over time various issues have arisen with this approach such as delays in the processing of returns, increased interest payments by the Government as a result of delayed refunds and interest outgo from the Government on delayed payments etc. In addition, new legislation that allowed for more deduction meant that a new approach needed to be adopted.

Under the new approach the HRR rules are applied but when a taxpayer does not respond to a request for more information, after a defined time-period, the claim is shared with Jurisdictional Assessing Officers (JAO). The JAO then assesses if a refund is released, or the case is considered for further scrutiny.

Latvia – Simplified instructions

From 2023, Latvia has simplified how it conducts its tax inspections by reducing the different types of inspections to just one – tax control. This makes it easier to work with taxpayers and increase compliance levels.

This type of inspection first checks specific discrepancies, then gives taxpayers an opportunity to explain the discrepancy and correct it. If the tax control detects uncorrected inconsistencies, the taxpayer will be informed about paying back the amount of the inconsistency and the appropriate late fee. This is known as a tax control bill.

A penalty is applied for illegal manipulations of cash registers and fines are also applied if significant compliance violations are discovered.

There is also the option to sign a voluntary tax payment agreement in the early stages of inspection, which can reduce fines by up to 85% or in some cases eliminate them altogether.

Sources: India (2024) and Latvia (2024).

Administrative sanctions for taxpayer non-disclosure

In cases of non-disclosure of information or misreporting, tax administrations typically have a range of sanctions at their disposal. Those sanctions are intended to act as a deterrent to non-compliant behaviour; to enforce compliance with a specific provision of the law (for example, the filing of a tax return); and to punish those who offend.

As shown in Table 6.20., almost all administrations apply administrative sanctions for taxpayer non-disclosure. Those that do, typically apply a common administration penalty framework that exists across the major tax types. Around 80% of administrations take into consideration the taxpayer's culpability and a similar percentage of administration is empowered to remit or reduce penalties under certain circumstances. Furthermore, one-quarter of administrations are empowered to make public details of taxpayers subject to administrative penalties imposed for non-disclosure.

Table 6.20. Administrative sanctions for taxpayer non-disclosure, 2022

Percentage of administrations

Administration applies administrative sanctions for taxpayer non-disclosure	If yes, selected features of approach ...			
	Common administrative penalty framework for non-disclosure across the major tax types exists	Penalties imposed generally take account of taxpayers' culpability (i.e. degree of blame)	Administration is empowered to remit / reduce penalties in appropriate circumstances	Administration is empowered to make public details of some / all taxpayers subject to administrative penalties imposed for non-disclosure
96.6	92.9	78.6	82.1	25.0

Source: CIAT, IOTA, IMF, OECD, International Survey on Revenue Administration, Table B.38 Administrative sanctions for taxpayer non-disclosure: Application and selected features, https://data.rafit.org/regular.aspx?key=74180918 (accessed on 10 September 2024).

Using the ISORA 2023 data, this first part of Chapter 6 provided a comprehensive overview of tax administrations' approaches to compliance risk management. It examined their work on understanding and managing tax compliance risks, and how data and data science support those processes, before looking at measures taken to prevent and address non-compliance.

In relation to preventing and addressing non-compliance, it is important to note that many of the other Chapters also include information on the work tax administrations are doing to positively influence tax compliance, for example, pre-filling regimes (Chapter 4), taxpayer services (Chapter 5), or mechanisms to prevent disputes (Chapter 7). Despite the extensive data from the periodic ISORA 2023 survey, it is essential to be aware that this is only a glimpse of the work tax administrations are doing to ensure compliance.

The next part of this Chapter will provide some insights into the compliance actions that tax administrations take and how this has evolved over the past few years.

Measuring the effectiveness of interventions

Measuring the effectiveness of tax compliance interventions is important for several reasons, including optimising resource allocation, improving cost effectiveness, and designing more effective and targeted interventions.

As can be seen in Table 6.21., around 70% of administrations measure the effectiveness of interventions that are undertaken before an audit. Approaches include the use of statistical models to monitor the effect of interventions, such as adjustment rates, additional return filings; the use of behavioural science, for example, nudging letters with control groups; and measuring the number of cases that have been moved to audit.

In addition, a significant number of administrations has put in place indicators that allow them to understand the effectiveness of audit work, mostly looking at audits that yield in a positive result (93%) followed by additional assessments raised (88%) and audit coverage (74%). Other indicators that have been reported include the number of disputes lost following an audit, positive changes in taxpayer behaviour following an audit or other intervention, and the impact on voluntary compliance of other taxpayers operating in the same sector.

The following sections look at some performance indicators regarding audits and tax crime investigations.

Table 6.21. Measuring effectiveness of interventions, 2022

Percentage of administrations

Measurement of effectiveness of interventions before return filing and after return filing (but before audit)	Indicators to measure effectiveness of enforcement actions				Standards for auditor productivity exist
	Audit coverage	Value of additional assessments raised through audit	Percentage of audits that yield a positive result	Other indicators	
70.7	74.1	87.9	93.1	44.8	67.2

Source: CIAT, IOTA, IMF, OECD, International Survey on Revenue Administration, Tables B.27 Compliance risk management: Interventions after return filing, and measurement of intervention effectiveness, and B.29 Compliance risk management: Enforcement effectiveness indicators, https://data.rafit.org/regular.aspx?key=74180916 (accessed on 10 September 2024).

Audits

On average, audit adjustment rates have remained stable over the period 2018 to 2022 (see Table 6.22.). However, as shown in Figure 6.4., the rates vary significantly across the administrations covered by this report.

The importance of audits can also be seen when looking at the additional assessments raised. On average, the additional assessments raised from audits are between 3.4% and 4.4% of total revenue collections. This has been relatively flat over the years 2018 to 2020 but declined in 2021 and 2022 (see Table 6.22.). Looking at the jurisdiction level data, it can be seen that there are significant differences across the 54 administrations that were able to provide data (see Figure 6.5.).

Table 6.22. Audit adjustment rates and additional assessments raised, 2018-22

	2018	2019	2020	2021	2022
Audit adjustment rates – in percent (39 jurisdictions)	57.3	58.7	57.7	61.3	60.9
Additional assessments raised through audits as a percentage of tax collections (48 jurisdictions)	4.1	4.1	4.4	3.8	3.4

Note: The table shows the average audit adjustment rates and additional assessments raised through audits (excluding electronic compliance checks) for those jurisdictions that were able to provide the information for the years 2018 to 2022. The number of jurisdictions for which data was available is shown in parentheses.
Source: CIAT, IOTA, IMF, OECD, International Survey on Revenue Administration, Table D.46 Audit ratios: Hit rate and additional assessments raised, https://data.rafit.org/regular.aspx?key=74180903 (accessed on 10 September 2024).

Breaking this down by tax type, it shows that the ratio of additional assessments raised to tax collected is the greatest for corporate income tax (CIT). On average, CIT additional assessment raised as a percentage of CIT collected around is around 6%, and the percentage for value added tax is around 3.5%. Both percentages for those business taxes are well above the percentages for personal income tax (1.6%) and employer withholding taxes (1.0%). (See Figure 6.6.)

In many jurisdictions, the additional assessments raised through large taxpayer offices or programmes (LTO/P) make-up a significant share of the total additional assessments raised from audits (see Figure 6.7.). On average, LTO/Ps contribute around 30% of the total additional assessments raised from audits (see Table 6.11.).

Figure 6.4. Audit adjustment rates, 2022

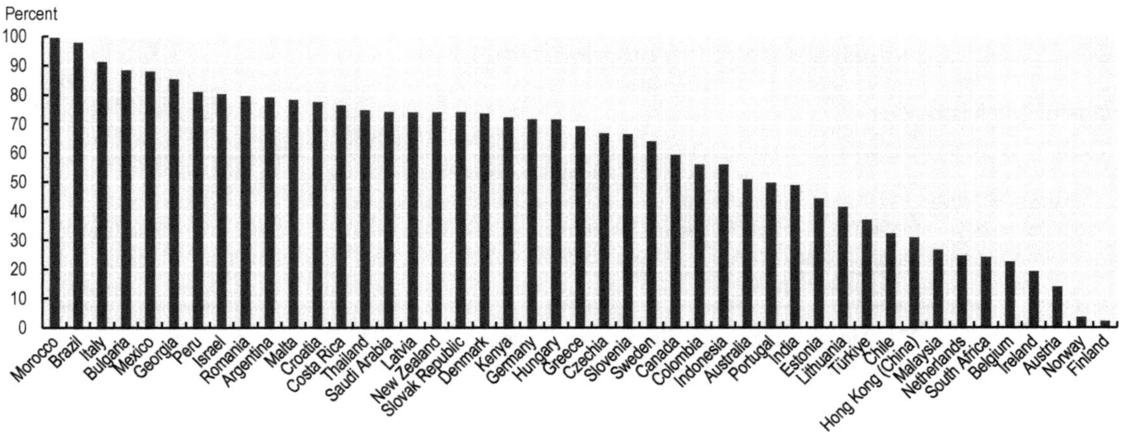

Source: CIAT, IOTA, IMF, OECD, International Survey on Revenue Administration, Table D.46 Audit ratios: Hit rate and additional assessments raised, https://data.rafit.org/regular.aspx?key=74180903 (accessed on 10 September 2024).

StatLink https://stat.link/7pcx5a

Figure 6.5. Additional assessments raised through audit as percentage of tax collections, 2022

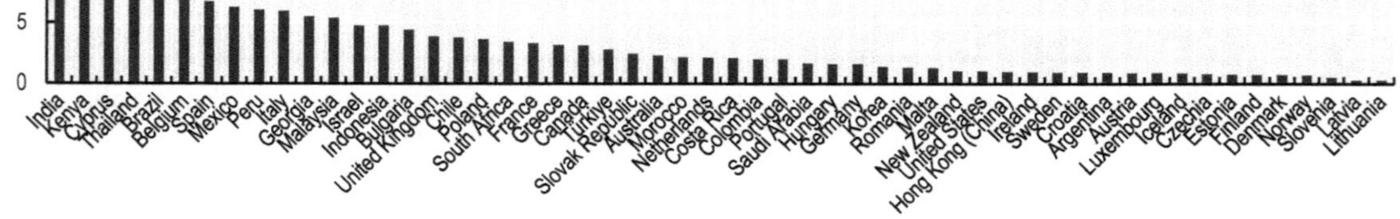

Source: CIAT, IOTA, IMF, OECD, International Survey on Revenue Administration, Table D.46 Audit ratios: Hit rate and additional assessments raised, https://data.rafit.org/regular.aspx?key=74180903 (accessed on 10 September 2024).

StatLink https://stat.link/brdmk1

Figure 6.6. Additional assessments raised through audit as percentage of tax collected by tax type, 2022

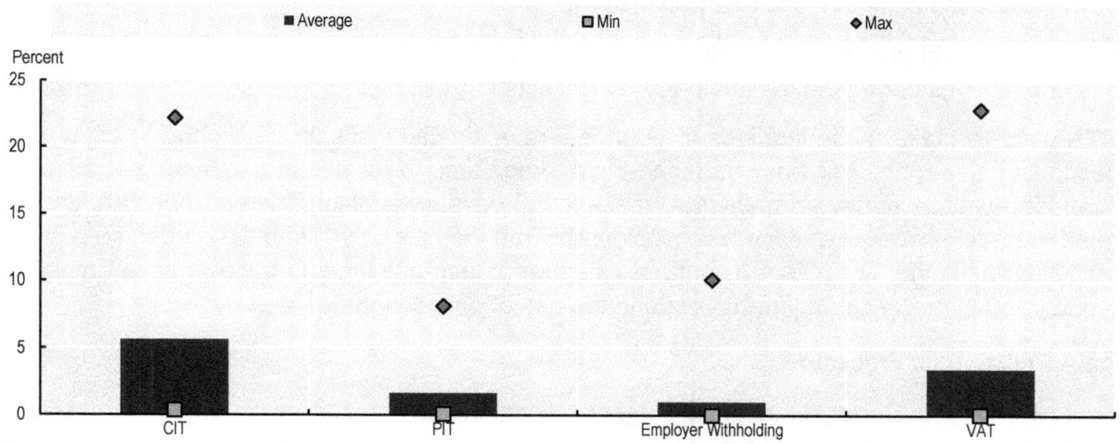

Note: CIT data for India and Kenya has been excluded from the calculations as it would distort the average ratios.
Source: CIAT, IOTA, IMF, OECD, International Survey on Revenue Administration, Tables D.47 Audit ratios: Additional assessments raised by tax type - CIT and PIT, and D.48 Audit ratios: Additional assessments raised by tax type - PAYE and VAT, https://data.rafit.org/regular.aspx?key=74180903 (accessed on 10 September 2024).

StatLink https://stat.link/hl9at5

Figure 6.7. Additional assessments raised from audits undertaken by LTO/P as a percentage of additional assessments raised from all audits, 2022

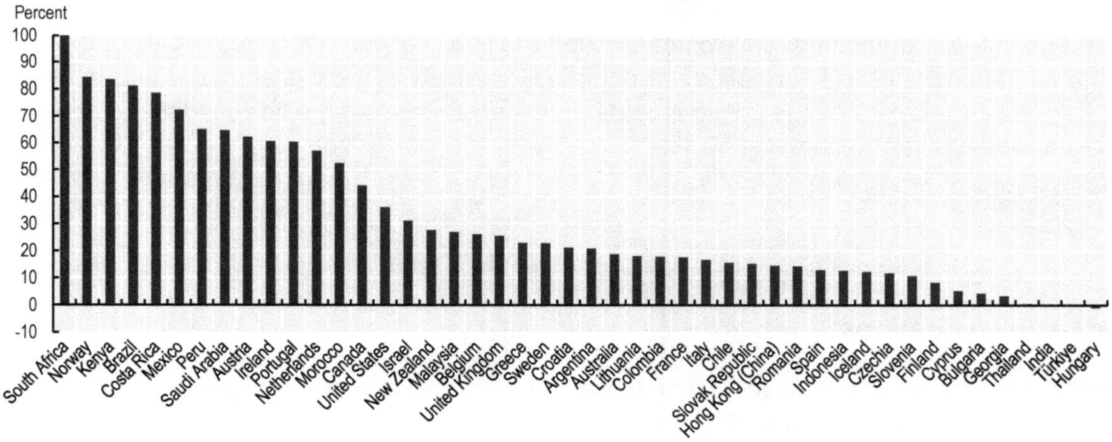

Source: CIAT, IOTA, IMF, OECD, International Survey on Revenue Administration, Table D.18 Large taxpayer office / program ratios: Corporate taxpayers, additional assessments raised, and net revenue administered, https://data.rafit.org/regular.aspx?key=74180900 (accessed on 10 September 2024).

StatLink https://stat.link/n0rek1

Box 6.13. Examples – Audits

Japan – Digitalisation of inquiries to financial institutions

The NTA issues approximately six million inquiries a year to financial institutions for information on deposits and savings during the tax audit and tax collection processes.

The NTA used to make these inquiries through letters or on-site visits, but switched to using online inquiries in October 2021. This has shortened the average time to receive a response from a financial institution for a written inquiry from several weeks to 2.3 days. In addition, the elimination of the need for written or on-site correspondence has considerably reduced the administrative burden on both NTA and financial institutions. The NTA will continue its efforts to increase the number of financial institutions that can support this service and further expand the use of online inquiries.

Portugal – Digital Audit Procedure

The audit procedure in Portugal has undergone significant digital transformation aimed at transitioning to a paperless environment. These changes entail the complete digitisation of documentation associated with the tax audit procedure. By embracing digital methodologies, the efficiency of the tax and customs audit procedure has been improved, facilitating enhanced traceability and control across its entire lifecycle.

Furthermore, this has also improved the sustainability of the Portuguese Tax and Customs Authority. By reducing reliance on paper and therefore reducing the physical archive storage, this initiative has yielded substantial cost reductions while advancing environmental conservation efforts.

This project has also brought benefits for the taxpayer, as it enables:

- Enhanced transparency: The audit procedure is meticulously documented and made available step-by-step within the dedicated taxpayer's area on the Tax and Customs Authority website. This heightened transparency fosters increased trust and accountability throughout the process.
- Streamlined communication: Communication channels between the Tax and Customs Authority and taxpayers have been refined to operate exclusively in the digital realm. This streamlined approach accelerates the speed in audit procedures, promoting efficiency and quickening the resolution of tax matters.

Sources: Japan (2024) and Portugal (2024).

Tax crime investigations

As mentioned in Chapter 2, slightly more than half of the tax administrations covered in this publication are involved in conducting tax crime investigations, and the ISORA survey asked them to provide information regarding the number of cases referred for prosecution.

Table 6.23. shows the total number of cases referred for prosecution during the fiscal year for the 30 administrations that have responsibility for conducting tax crime investigations and that were able to provide the data for the years 2018 to 2022. While the number of cases referred for prosecution was similar in 2018 and 2019, a significant reduction in the total number of cases referred for prosecution is visible since 2020.

This is also reflected in the jurisdiction level data, which shows that around 75% of administrations that have responsibility for conducting tax crime investigations referred a declining number of cases for prosecution over the past years (see Table A.88).

Table 6.23. Evolution of tax crime investigation cases referred for prosecution between 2018 and 2022

Year	No. of cases referred for prosecution during the fiscal year	Change in percent (compared to previous year)
2018	41 081	
2019	39 768	-3.2
2020	33 210	-16.5
2021	29 918	-9.9
2022	23 523	-21.4

Note: Only includes data for administrations that have responsibility for tax crime investigation and were able to provide the information for the years 2018 to 2022.
Source: CIAT, IOTA, IMF, OECD, International Survey on Revenue Administration, Table A.88 Tax crime investigations: Number of cases, https://data.rafit.org/regular.aspx?key=74180895 (accessed on 10 September 2024).

Compliance burdens

The core task of a tax administration is to raise revenue to fund government services and to do so in a way which does not impose unnecessary burdens on taxpayers. Minimising burdens is central to achieving the core task as they can impact the willingness or, in some cases, the ability of taxpayers to comply with their obligations. Excessive burdens can also incur significant opportunity costs for taxpayers, potentially reducing economic growth.

That tax administrations are aware of the importance of minimising compliance burdens is evident from the improvements being made to taxpayer-facing processes, such as electronic filing and payment, pre-filling regimes, new and enhanced communication channels, and an increase in self-service options. The numerous examples included in this and previous editions of the Tax Administration Series represent a small part of the many things tax administrations do in this respect.

To support ongoing improvements and better understand where burdens occur more than one-third of administrations have started evaluating taxpayer compliance burdens and most of those do it on an annual basis. In addition, Table 6.24. shows that:

- ***Administrations measure perceptions of compliance burdens***: While time and money spent to comply with tax obligations are generally considered essential indicators for measuring compliance burdens, taxpayers are also looking at the cognitive load and emotional burden. It is against this that approximately 85% of administrations that evaluate burdens are also assessing perceptions of compliance burdens.
- ***Compliance burdens are monitored for different segments***: Recognising that burdens are distinct for different taxpayer segments, more than 80% of administrations are taking a segmented approach to measuring compliance burdens.
- ***Formal strategies are put in place***: With the evaluation of compliance burdens being the first step, more than 70% of administrations that conduct those evaluations have put in place a formal strategy to reduce compliance burdens.

Table 6.24. Evaluating taxpayer compliance burden, 2022

Percentage of administrations

Taxpayer compliance burden evaluated	If yes, ...						
	Evaluation frequency			Perceptions of compliance burdens measured	Evaluation undertaken by an external party	Compliance burden monitored for different taxpayer segments	Formal strategy to reduce compliance burdens exists
	Annual	Once every two years	Less frequently				
36.8	57.1	14.3	28.6	85.7	61.9	81.0	71.4

Source: CIAT, IOTA, IMF, OECD, International Survey on Revenue Administration, Table B.52 Taxpayer compliance burden, https://data.rafit.org/regular.aspx?key=74180919 (accessed on 10 September 2024).

References

OECD (2023), *International Standards for Automatic Exchange of Information in Tax Matters: Crypto-Asset Reporting Framework and 2023 update to the Common Reporting Standard*, OECD Publishing, Paris, https://doi.org/10.1787/896d79d1-en. [3]

OECD (2023), *Tax Administration 2023: Comparative Information on OECD and other Advanced and Emerging Economies*, OECD Publishing, Paris, https://doi.org/10.1787/900b6382-en. [5]

OECD (2022), *Analytics Maturity Model*, OECD, Paris, https://www.oecd.org/en/topics/sub-issues/comparative-analysis-of-tax-administrations/tax-maturity-models.html (accessed on 10 September 2024). [7]

OECD (2021), *Behavioural Insights for Better Tax Administration: A Brief Guide*, OECD Publishing, Paris, https://doi.org/10.1787/582c283e-en. [8]

OECD (2017), *The Changing Tax Compliance Environment and the Role of Audit*, OECD Publishing, Paris, https://doi.org/10.1787/9789264282186-en. [2]

OECD (2016), *Advanced Analytics for Better Tax Administration: Putting Data to Work*, OECD Publishing, Paris, https://doi.org/10.1787/9789264256453-en. [6]

OECD (2015), *Transfer Pricing Documentation and Country-by-Country Reporting, Action 13 - 2015 Final Report*, OECD/G20 Base Erosion and Profit Shifting Project, OECD Publishing, Paris, https://doi.org/10.1787/9789264241480-en. [4]

OECD (2004), *Compliance Risk Management: Managing and Improving Tax Compliance*, OECD, Paris, https://www.oecd.org/content/dam/oecd/en/topics/policy-issues/tax-administration/compliance-risk-management-managing-and-improving-tax-compliance.pdf (accessed on 12 September 2024). [1]

OECD et al. (2024), *Inventory of Tax Technology Initiatives*, https://web-archive.oecd.org/tax/forum-on-tax-administration/tax-technology-tools-and-digital-solutions/index.htm (accessed on 10 September 2024). [9]

7 Collection

This chapter comments on tax administration performance in managing the collection of outstanding taxes, and describes the features of a modern tax debt collection function. It goes on to provide an overview of the collection powers available to tax administrations and their usage. Finally, it showcases examples of approaches applied by administrations to prevent debt being incurred.

Introduction

The collection function involves engaging with, and potentially taking enforcement action, against those who do not file a return on time and/ or do not make a payment when it is due. Even with the growth in pre-filled or no-return approaches over past years (see Chapter 4), the filing of a tax return or declaration is still required in many jurisdictions participating in this publication. Although 2022 on-time filing rates averaged between 76% and 87%, at least 100 million returns were not filed on time that year (see Tables 4.8. as well as A.47, A.51, A.55, and A.60). It is important therefore that administrations continue to focus efforts on improving the timely collection of late and outstanding returns.

Looking at the collection of late payments, all but one administration participating in the survey report that staff resources are being devoted to taking action to secure the payment of overdue tax payments (the Chilean tax administration reported not being responsible for debt collection; see Table A.19). Information provided by administrations attribute on average around 11% of total staff numbers to the collection function (see Chapter 10).

This chapter:

- Takes a brief look at the features of a modern tax debt collection function and the elements of a successful tax debt management strategy;
- Comments on tax administration performance in managing the collection of outstanding debt;
- Looks at debt collection powers and their usage; and
- Provides examples of preventive approaches to debt being incurred.

Features of a debt collection function

To maintain high levels of voluntary compliance and confidence in the tax system, administrations must ensure that their debt collection approaches are both “fit for purpose” and meet taxpayer’s expectations of how the system will be administered. This means not only taking firm action against taxpayers that knowingly do not comply, but also using more customer service style approaches where taxpayers want to meet their obligations, but for reasons such as short-term cash-flow issues, are not able to do so.

Increasingly, tax administrations are taking an end-to-end or systems view of their processes and researching the reasons why returns may not be filed or payments made. They are also using information about the taxpayer’s previous history, to identify patterns and/or anomalies. Box 7.1. highlights some developments in this area.

Box 7.1. Examples – Improving debt collection

Canada – Collections Verification Workload Management System

The Collections Verification Workload Management System (CVWMS) platform marks a major milestone in the Canada Revenue Agency (CRA) transformation.

With work underway, the primary focus is on creating a case management system that empowers collections and compliance programmes to streamline processes and enhance operations. The CVWMS is adopting a horizontal approach to value delivery, in which new system functionality will be developed for many workloads concurrently. Taking a horizontal approach allows the CRA to enhance data management standards, enabling the production of relevant and timely business intelligence.

CVWMS has already yielded significant achievements. It has successfully reduced administrative burdens, increased resilience and agility, and optimised data management and standards. The platform's integration with other agency systems has facilitated efficient business rules management and led to an increase in quality assurance. Benefits realised from onboarded users include:

- A reduction in the amount of time it takes to perform an account summary
- A reduction in the time it takes to create and assign accounts to officers
- Improved reporting capabilities
- Quicker access to information
- Quicker recovery of lost revenue
- Better service to Canadians

This system has proven to be a robust platform that will continue to deliver tangible results.

Georgia – Tax Debt Management Reform

In 2022, Georgia piloted the Tax Debt Management Reform programme to increase taxpayer compliance. This has been refined with a number of recent improvements to achieve results, for example:

- New criteria have been developed to identify taxpayers with outstanding debts. From this group, taxpayers are automatically picked out by the system where action is required, and these are passed to the relevant staff in the Georgian tax administration. Taxpayers with growing or recent debts are prioritised.
- New software has been introduced to aid employees in their work, through an electronic case management system.

These changes have had positive results. The proportion of recognised tax debt in relation to total tax revenues is now less than 20%, and there has been an increase in the voluntary payment rate of debts. There has also been growing interest amongst taxpayers in entering into agreements for the deferral of debt payments, with a sizeable number of these agreements being automatically initiated without the need for human intervention.

Sources: Canada (2024) and Georgia (2024).

The 2014 report *Working Smarter in Tax Debt Management* (OECD, 2014[1]) provided an overview of the modern tax debt collection function, describing the essential features as:

- ***Advanced analytics*** – that make it possible to use all the information tax administrations have about taxpayers to accurately target debtors with the right intervention at the right time.
- ***Treatment strategies*** – the collection function needs a range of interventions, from those designed to minimise the risk of people becoming indebted, to support taxpayers to make payments and to take appropriate enforcement measures where appropriate.
- ***Outbound call centres*** – which make it possible to efficiently pursue a large number of debts.
- ***Organisation*** – debt collection is a specialist function and is usually organised as such. The right performance measures and a continuous improvement approach help drive desired outcomes.
- ***Cross border debts*** – the proper and timely use of international assistance is crucial, particularly the "Assistance in Collection Articles" in agreements between jurisdictions.

The 2019 report *Successful Tax Debt Management: Measuring Maturity and Supporting Change* (OECD, 2019[2]) provides further insights into the elements of a successful tax debt management strategy, setting out four strategic principles that tax administrations may wish to consider when setting their strategy for tax debt management. These principles focus on the timing of interventions in the tax debt cycle, from consideration of measures to prevent tax debt arising in the first place, via early and continuous engagement with taxpayers before enforcement measures, to effective and proportionate enforcement and realistic write-off strategies. The underlying premise for these principles is that focusing on tackling debt early, and ideally before it has arisen, is the best means to minimise outstanding tax debt. The report also contains a compendium of successful tax debt management initiatives and an overview of a *Tax Debt Management Maturity Model* which was subsequently published as a self-standing document (OECD, 2019[3]).

Performance in collecting outstanding debt

The total amount of outstanding arrears at fiscal year-end remains very large, in the region of EUR 2.7 trillion. For survey and comparative analysis purposes, "total arrears at year-end" is defined as the total amount of tax debt and debt on other revenue for which the tax administration is responsible that is overdue for payment at the end of the fiscal year. This includes any interest and penalties. The term also includes arrears whose collection has been deferred (for example, as a result of payment arrangements).

The total amount of "collectable arrears" at fiscal year-end was around EUR 810 billion. Collectable arrears is defined as the total arrears figure less (i) any disputed amounts for which collection action has been suspended pending the outcome, (ii) amounts that are not legally recoverable, and (iii) arrears which are unable to be collected, for example, where the debtor has no funds or other assets.

As a result, and despite efforts to make data comparable, care needs to be taken when comparing specific data points as the administration of taxation systems and administrative practices differ between jurisdictions.

In 2022, the average ratio for total year-end arrears to net revenue collected was 29% (see Table D.41). As in past years, it remains heavily influenced by the very large ratios of a small number of jurisdictions that show ratios above 50%. If these jurisdictions are removed, the average reduces to around 13% of net revenue (see Figure 7.1. and Figure 7.2. as well as Table D.41). *(Note: The percentages mentioned in this paragraph are different from those in Table 7.1. as the table shows average arrears ratios only for those jurisdictions that were able to provide the information for the years 2018 to 2022.)*

Table 7.1. Changes in average arrears ratios, 2018-22

Arrears ratio	2018	2019	2020	2021	2022	Change in percent between 2018-22
Total year-end arrears as percentage of net revenue collected (50 jurisdictions)	28.2	27.9	34.7	30.2	27.7	-1.7
Total year-end collectable arrears as percentage of total year-end arrears (41 jurisdictions)	49.6	50.5	53.2	53.4	51.8	+4.4

Note: The table shows average arrears ratios for those jurisdictions that were able to provide the information for the years 2018 to 2022. The number of jurisdictions for which data was available is shown in parentheses. Data for Bulgaria was excluded from the calculation of the average for the 'total year-end arrears as a percentage of net revenue collected' as its data for the years is not comparable (see Table A.74).
Source: CIAT, IOTA, IMF, OECD, International Survey on Revenue Administration, Table D.41 Arrears ratios: Closing stock and collectable arrears, https://data.rafit.org/regular.aspx?key=74180902 (accessed on 10 September 2024).

When looking at the data over the five-year period from 2018 to 2022, a decrease in the average ratio of total year-end arrears to net revenue collected is visible for the last two years. This follows the significant increase of the ratio during 2020 – the first year of the pandemic – where the ratio increased on average by more than 20% at a time where many governments took action to support individuals and businesses as part of the pandemic by extending payment terms, or suspending collection of outstanding debt (CIAT/IOTA/OECD, 2020[4]). Following the latest available data, the average ratio of total year-end arrears to net revenue collected is now back to pre-pandemic levels. (See Table 7.1.)

The change in the average ratio, is also generally reflected in the jurisdiction level data: Between 2019 and 2020 the "total arrears to net revenue collected" ratio increased in 86% of jurisdictions, whereas between 2020 and 2022 the ratio decreased in 77% of jurisdictions (see Table D.41).

Figure 7.1. Total year-end arrears as a percentage of total net revenue (for administrations with a ratio above 50%), 2022

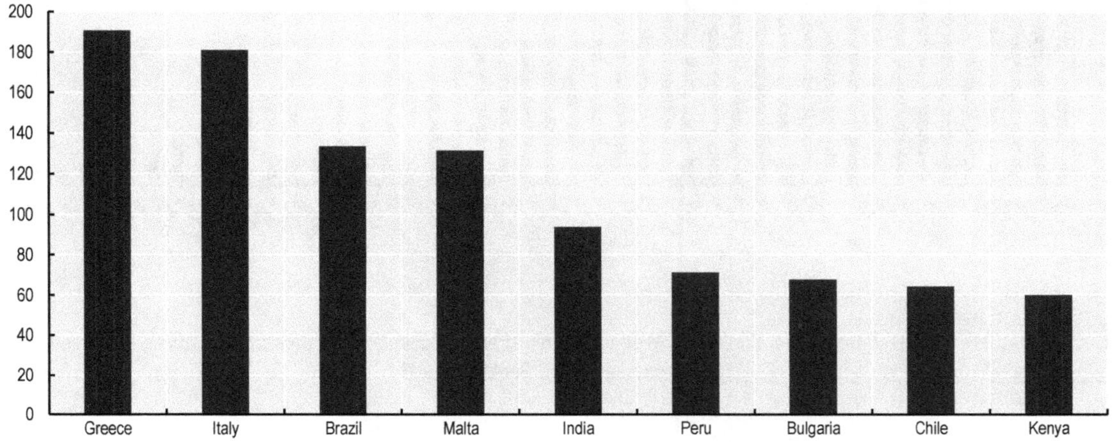

Source: CIAT, IOTA, IMF, OECD, International Survey on Revenue Administration, Table D.41 Arrears ratios: Closing stock and collectable arrears, https://data.rafit.org/regular.aspx?key=74180902 (accessed on 10 September 2024).

StatLink https://stat.link/6xhzg0

Figure 7.2. Total year-end arrears as a percentage of total net revenue (for administrations with a ratio below 50%), 2022

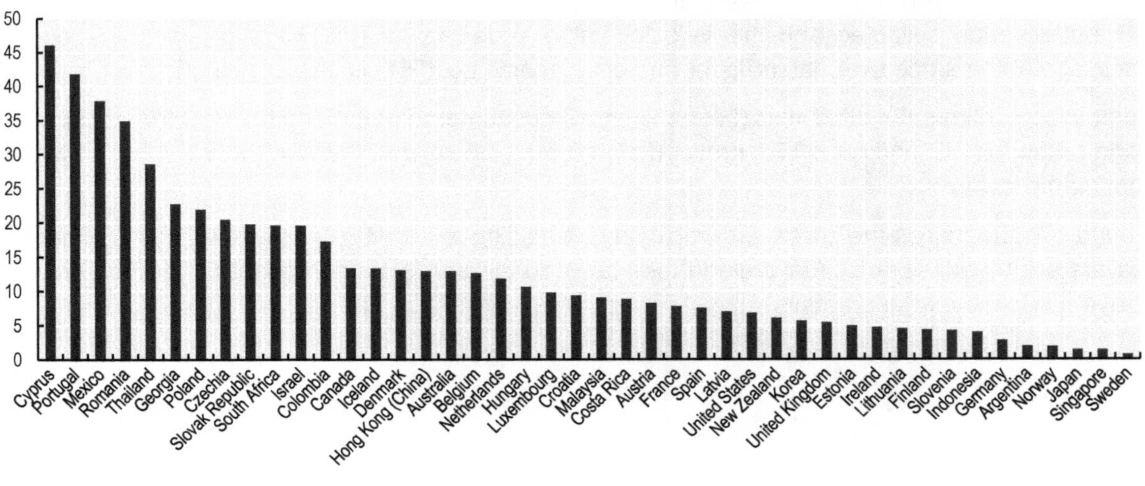

Source: CIAT, IOTA, IMF, OECD, International Survey on Revenue Administration, Table D.41 Arrears ratios: Closing stock and collectable arrears, https://data.rafit.org/regular.aspx?key=74180902 (accessed on 10 September 2024).

StatLink https://stat.link/zd9kvi

Looking at collectable tax arrears, the 2022 data shows that on average around half of the total arrears are considered collectable. That is an increase of 4% compared to 2018. (See Table 7.1.) However, Figure 7.3. illustrates well the differences between jurisdictions: in some jurisdictions almost all arrears are considered collectable, while in others almost all arrears are considered not collectable.

Figure 7.3. Total year-end collectible arrears as percentage of total year-end arrears, 2022

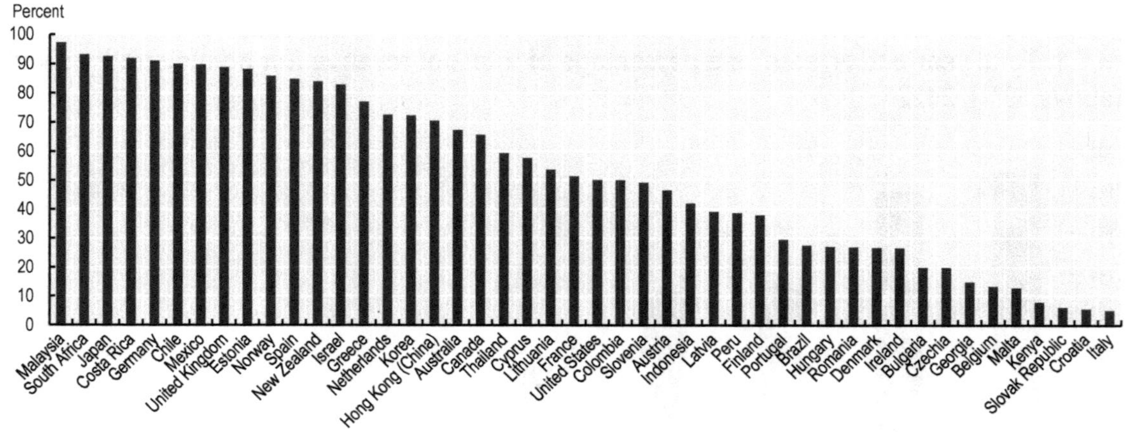

Source: CIAT, IOTA, IMF, OECD, International Survey on Revenue Administration, Table D.41 Arrears ratios: Closing stock and collectable arrears, https://data.rafit.org/regular.aspx?key=74180902 (accessed on 10 September 2024).

StatLink https://stat.link/cid3bt

Figure 7.4. shows the change of total year-end arrears between 2021 and 2022. In absolute numbers, the total year-end arrears increased in 34 out of 53 jurisdictions that were able to provide the information. (Note: This does not contradict the above observation that arrears ratios are decreasing. While in absolute numbers, arrears are going up in many jurisdictions, the 'total arrears to net revenue collected' ratio is decreasing as total revenue collections have increased even more.)

In looking at the amount of arrears for the main tax types (see Table 7.2.), it seems that individuals are more likely to pay on time than businesses. In 2022, the average ratio of corporate income tax (CIT) arrears to CIT net revenue collected and the ratio for value added taxes (VAT) are around 20% and 24%, respectively. At the same time, the ratio for personal income tax (PIT) is much lower at 15%.

The data also confirms the difficulties that businesses encountered at the beginning of the pandemic. The average ratios for CIT and for VAT increased significantly between 2019 and 2020 but are now back to pre-pandemic levels.

At around 6%, the ratio is the lowest for employer withholding taxes (WHT). However, this is expected, as employers are responsible for forwarding those taxes to the administration on behalf of their employees and have no right over the amounts.

Figure 7.4. Movement of total arrears between 2021 and 2022

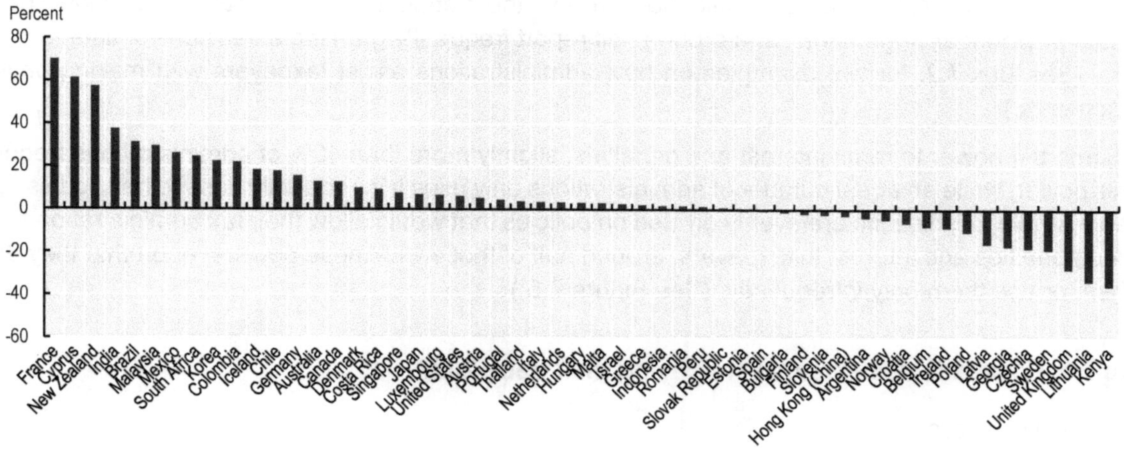

Source: CIAT, IOTA, IMF, OECD, International Survey on Revenue Administration, Table D.42 Arrears ratios: Year-on-year change, https://data.rafit.org/regular.aspx?key=74180902 (accessed on 10 September 2024).

StatLink https://stat.link/4w8h5e

Table 7.2. Evolution of average ratio of year-end arrears to net revenue collected by tax type between 2018 and 2022

Tax type	2018	2019	2020	2021	2022
CIT arrears as percentage of CIT collected (40 jurisdictions)	23.7	26.4	30.1	23.9	19.9
PIT arrears as percentage of PIT collected (41 jurisdictions)	16.5	14.4	15.8	15.3	15.5
Employer WHT arrears as percentage of PIT collected (34 jurisdictions)	7.2	6.5	7.2	6.9	6.2
VAT arrears as percentage of VAT collected (39 jurisdictions)	23.8	23.5	30.2	25.1	23.6

Note: The table shows the average ratios for jurisdictions that were able to provide the information for the years 2018 to 2022. The number of jurisdictions for which data was available is shown in parentheses. Data for Bulgaria was excluded from the calculation of the average for the total year-end arrears as a percentage of net revenue collected as its data for the years was not comparable (see Table A.74). Further, because they would distort the averages, data for Brazil and Greece was excluded in the calculation of the average for CIT and data for Malta was excluded in the calculation of the average for VAT.
Source: CIAT, IOTA, IMF, OECD, International Survey on Revenue Administration, Tables D.44 Arrears in relation to collection by tax type: CIT and PIT, and D.45 Arrears in relation to collection by tax type: PAYE and VAT, https://data.rafit.org/regular.aspx?key=74180902 (accessed on 10 September 2024).

Collection powers and their usage

The legislative framework includes provisions that enable tax officials to undertake certain actions in relation to the management of debt, the collection of amounts overdue and the enforcement of actions that can be taken against delinquent debtors. Figures 7.5. to 7.7. summarise this information for all 58 jurisdictions in the series, looking at:

- Powers administrations can use to assist taxpayers paying their debt;
- Powers administrations have to collect outstanding amounts; and
- Powers administrations have to enforce debt payment by triggering certain pressure points.

Powers to assist taxpayers paying their debt

As shown in Figure 7.5., most administrations report the frequent use of powers that allow them to formulate payment arrangements, and around half report frequently granting extensions of time to pay tax arrears. (See Box 7.2. for two examples on how administrations assist taxpayers with making payment arrangements.)

As regards the power to remit interest and penalties, slightly more than 40% of administrations frequently use this power, while an equal number of administrations only uses it infrequently despite having this option available. While jurisdictions are evenly divided on policies that would allow their tax administration to offer reduced penalties and interest to taxpayers, around half of those with these powers report that they do not use them or use them only infrequently. (See Figure 7.5.)

Figure 7.5. Powers to assist taxpayers paying their debt, 2022

Percentage of jurisdictions

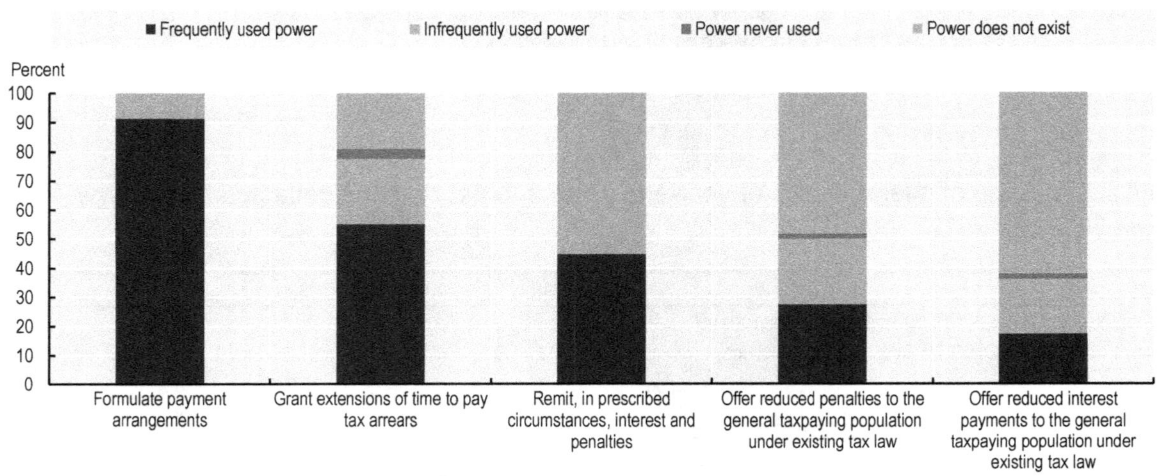

Source: CIAT, IOTA, IMF, OECD, International Survey on Revenue Administration, Tables B.31 Tax arrears: Collection powers and their usage - Part 1, B.32 Tax arrears collection powers and their usage - Part 2, B.33 Tax arrears collection powers and their usage - Part 3, and B.34 Tax arrears collection powers and their usage - Part 4, https://data.rafit.org/regular.aspx?key=74180917 (accessed on 10 September 2024).

StatLink https://stat.link/urn4t8

Box 7.2. Examples – Assisting taxpayers paying their debt

Canada – Payment Arrangement Calculator

Taxpayers who cannot pay their debt immediately now have the ability to enter into payment agreements without speaking to the Canada Revenue Agency (CRA).

First introduced to the public on the website Canada.ca in June 2017, the Payment Arrangement Calculator (PAC) functioned as a standalone tool guiding taxpayers in calculating a frequency of payments for their outstanding CRA debt. Taxpayers would log into the secure portals (My Account or My Business account) and manually input the information provided by the PAC into the Pre-Authorized Debits (PAD) payment option to enter into an agreement to pay their debt over time.

In February 2023, PAC functionalities were integrated within the PAD payment process as an enhancement to payments options within My Account and My Business Account. This initiative allows taxpayers to:

- Modify the amount to be paid;
- View the current prescribed interest rate;
- Select the start date, frequency and number of payments;
- Include interest in their calculated payments.

This allows for less traffic on CRA general enquiry lines for payment arrangements, and also meets the demands of many Canadians who prefer the fast and efficient option of making online payments.

United Kingdom – Self-Serve Time to Pay

The United Kingdom's HM Revenue & Customs' (HMRC's) vision for the future of tax administrations is designed to improve its resilience, effectiveness, and support for taxpayers, ensuring it is as easy as possible for customers experiencing financial difficulties to pay any tax that may be owed.

In line with this, HMRC has introduced a new service for customers – Self-Serve Time to Pay (SSTTP), which works by providing eligible customers with the ability to make payments up front and set up a payment plan via direct debit. A Manual Affordability Assessment has been added to this, which allows a customer to input their income and expenditure information to receive a payment plan which is affordable to them. If taxpayers cannot set up a payment plan through the online portal, they can get assistance via webchat.

This aims to reduce reliance on telephone services and increase the digitalisation of tax services. Since going live, over 22 500 repayment plans have been set up with a cumulative value of over GBP 190 million.

Sources: Canada (2024) and United Kingdom (2024).

Powers to collect outstanding amounts

Administrations report extensive use of offsetting tax arrears against other tax overpayments, using garnishee orders over salaries and property, and collecting via third parties, such as banks and employers. As regards the use of powers to collect disputed taxes while a case is under judicial or administrative review and powers to collect through agreements with other tax administrations, approximately half of administrations that have those powers report non-use or infrequent use. (See Figure 7.6.)

Box 7.3. contains an example of cross-national collaboration to improve debt collection.

Box 7.3. Belgium – Project BENE

A common challenge faced by the Belgian and Dutch tax administrations is how to deal with tax debtors living in the other country. This means that the Belgian and Dutch tax administrations are limited in their national collection and recovery options when confronted with debtors living or registered abroad. Normally, they would have to request mutual assistance to recover the tax, which is costly and time intensive.

In order to overcome this situation in a more cost-effective way, a cross-national project involving both tax administrations was implemented in 2023, called Project BENE. This project targets taxpayers living in the Netherlands and owing debts to the Belgian tax administration; and, reciprocally, taxpayers living in Belgium owing debts to the Dutch tax administration.

The aim is to both increase payment compliance and decrease the need to formally request mutual recovery assistance, using reminder letters. A first reminder letter is sent by the administration where the debt is due. If after 30 days no payment or response is received, a second reminder letter is sent by the administration where the debtor resides. Only if both letters remain unanswered is mutual assistance requested.

Source: Belgium (2024).

Figure 7.6. Powers to collect outstanding amounts, 2022

Percentage of jurisdictions

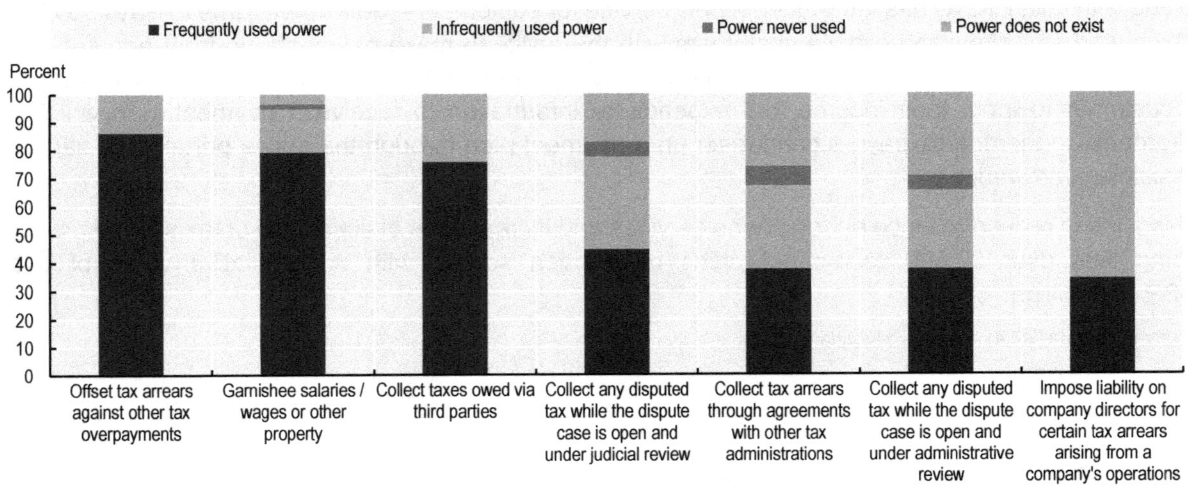

Source: CIAT, IOTA, IMF, OECD, International Survey on Revenue Administration, Tables B.31 Tax arrears: Collection powers and their usage - Part 1, B.32 Tax arrears collection powers and their usage - Part 2, B.33 Tax arrears collection powers and their usage - Part 3, and B.34 Tax arrears collection powers and their usage - Part 4, https://data.rafit.org/regular.aspx?key=74180917 (accessed on 10 September 2024).

StatLink https://stat.link/6l14da

Powers to enforce debt payment

Given that the powers in Figure 7.7. can have severe consequences (for example, temporarily closing a business, publishing names of debtor taxpayers, restricting travel, etc.) it is not surprising that in the majority of jurisdictions the administration does not have many of those powers, or does not use them or uses them only infrequently. The exception is the requirement of having a tax clearance certificate when bidding for government contracts, which is less severe in its nature but very effective, and therefore used frequently by more than 75% of administrations.

Figure 7.7. Powers to enforce debt payment, 2022

Percentage of jurisdictions

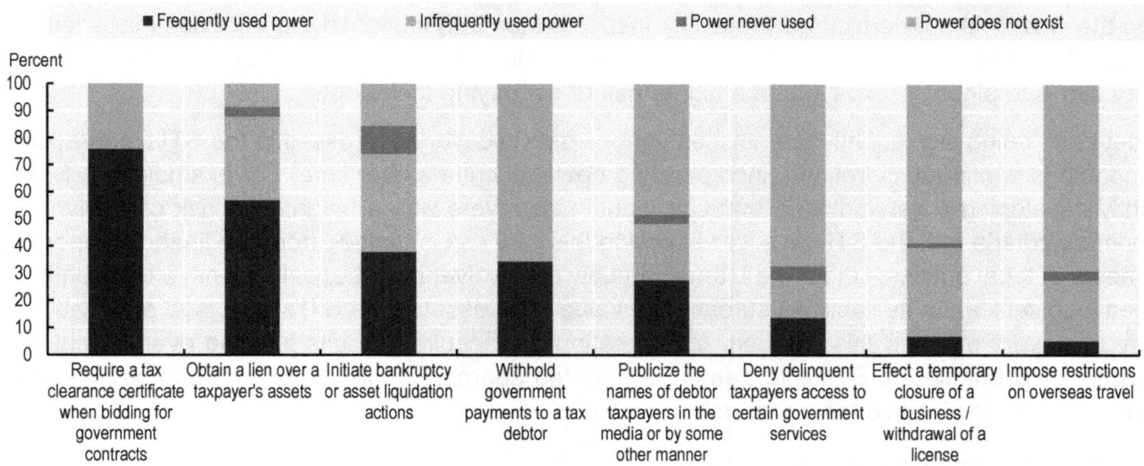

Source: CIAT, IOTA, IMF, OECD, International Survey on Revenue Administration, Tables B.31 Tax arrears: Collection powers and their usage - Part 1, B.32 Tax arrears collection powers and their usage - Part 2, B.33 Tax arrears collection powers and their usage - Part 3, and B.34 Tax arrears collection powers and their usage - Part 4, https://data.rafit.org/regular.aspx?key=74180917 (accessed on 10 September 2024).

StatLink https://stat.link/o1ap4r

Preventive approaches

The range of actions undertaken by tax administrations to prevent debt from arising and to collect outstanding arrears continues to evolve. Box 7.4. illustrates the approaches taken by some administrations. Advances in predictive modelling and experimental techniques as reported in the OECD report *Advanced Analytics for Better Tax Administration* (OECD, 2016[5]) and in the compendium of successful tax debt management practices contained in the OECD report *Successful Tax Debt Management: Measuring Maturity and Supporting Change* (OECD, 2019[2]) are helping many administrations better match interventions with taxpayer specific risk. The approaches used fall into one of the following categories:

- **Predictive analytics**, which tries to understand the likelihood of certain outcomes and, as regards debt collection, includes modelling the risk that an individual or company will fail to pay as well as models that attempt to assess the likelihood of insolvency or other payment problems; and
- **Prescriptive analytics**, which is about predicting the likely impact of actions on taxpayer behaviour, so that tax administrations can select the right course of action for any chosen taxpayer or group of taxpayers. (OECD, 2016[5])

Many administrations are blending both practices and have trialled a variety of approaches aimed at changing "taxpayer behaviour". As noted in Chapter 6, around half of the administrations report employing behavioural researchers, and the use of behavioural insight practices has the potential to transform the approach to tax debt as administrations move away from the 'one-size-fits-all' approaches (where it is cost-effective to do so) and instead try to identify:

- Which cases should be subject to an intervention;
- When to intervene (for example, even before a return or payment might be due); and
- Which type of action would achieve the best cost-benefit outcome.

Box 7.4. Examples – Preventive approaches

Lithuania – Debtor risk

During the Covid-19 pandemic, the State Tax Inspectorate (STI) launched the debt risk management module, integrating it into the Tax Accounting Information System (TAIS) of the STI. The module's primary aim is to pinpoint taxpayers at a higher risk of not paying their debts.

This debt risk rating significantly streamlines various debt recovery processes in the STI's operations. The module is continuously refined, incorporating new risk criteria over time. For example, the STI is currently developing a new criterion that can identify taxpayers with a heightened risk of insolvency. The primary criteria that the STI uses for assessing this new risk is derived from the financial reporting documents of legal entities. Under the Lithuanian Law on Insolvency of Legal Persons, a legal entity is deemed insolvent when its liabilities surpass the value of its assets. The STI's goal is to automatically identify taxpayers meeting this criterion. Incorporating the acquired results into the overall debt risk assessment will enable the STI to implement a targeted approach to its debtors, to comprehensively determine the most effective tactics for debt recovery.

Spain – Preventive approaches in compliance

Spain has introduced preventive actions to guard against the risk of not being able to recover tax due. Three initiatives have been introduced:

- Using data analysis techniques to better identify and measure recovery risks. To better understand the recovery risks, numerous indicators are examined such as asset stripping, recovery history and activity history in terms of filing tax returns etc.
- Improving cooperation between control and recovery units, such as through facilitating the exchange of analysis information between teams.
- Improving IT tools to facilitate preventive recovery.

The aim of these interventions is to provide a thorough, automatic and analytical evaluation of the risk that a taxable person will not pay their debt, and be able to act promptly on these risks if necessary.

Sources: Lithuania (2024) and Spain (2024).

References

CIAT/IOTA/OECD (2020), “Tax administration responses to COVID-19: Measures taken to support taxpayers”, *OECD Policy Responses to Coronavirus (COVID-19)*, OECD Publishing, Paris, https://doi.org/10.1787/adc84188-en. [4]

OECD (2019), *Successful Tax Debt Management: Measuring Maturity and Supporting Change*, OECD Publishing, Paris, https://doi.org/10.1787/e8fdb816-en. [2]

OECD (2019), *Tax Debt Management Maturity Model*, OECD, Paris, https://www.oecd.org/en/topics/sub-issues/comparative-analysis-of-tax-administrations/tax-maturity-models.html (accessed on 10 September 2024). [3]

OECD (2016), *Advanced Analytics for Better Tax Administration: Putting Data to Work*, OECD Publishing, Paris, https://doi.org/10.1787/9789264256453-en. [5]

OECD (2014), *Working Smarter in Tax Debt Management*, OECD Publishing, Paris, https://doi.org/10.1787/9789264223257-en. [1]

8 Disputes

Dispute prevention and resolution are essential to help preserve trust in the tax systems. This chapter explores the strategies put in place by tax administrations to resolve and prevent disputes fairly and efficiently.

Introduction

Taxpayer rights and obligations are frequently set out in law or taxpayer charters (see also Chapter 9, Table 9.4.). Underpinning these rights and obligations is effective access to processes that allow taxpayers to challenge assessments and decisions. This safeguards taxpayer rights and ensures that appropriate checks and balances exist on the exercising of tax powers by administrations. At the same time, tax administrations and taxpayers should also strive to work together to prevent disputes from arising in the first place, thus reducing burdens and uncertainty for both parties.

This chapter examines the dispute resolution and review strategies in the jurisdictions covered by this report, as well as their performance in this area. This is an important function of tax administrations, and on average around 5% of total staff numbers are dedicated to the management of disputes, including litigation, dispute resolution, appeals, objections and rulings (see Chapter 10).

Dispute resolution review mechanisms

All 58 jurisdictions covered in this report provide taxpayers with the right to challenge assessments. Almost all administrations report having an internal review mechanism in place, and a large majority of administrations provide taxpayers with the option to seek an independent review by an external body, which can help improve legal certainty for taxpayers while avoiding potentially lengthy and costly legal proceedings. For those administrations that offer both review mechanisms, approximately 80% require taxpayers to seek an internal review before their case can be reviewed by an external body. (See Table 8.1.)

Table 8.1. Dispute resolution: Available review mechanisms, 2022

Percentage of administrations

Mechanisms available for taxpayers to challenge assessments			Taxpayers must first pursue internal review where an internal review is permissible
Internal review by tax administration	Independent review by external body	Independent review by a higher appellate court	
98.3	93.1	100.0	80.7

Source: CIAT, IOTA, IMF, OECD, International Survey on Revenue Administration, Tables A.89 Dispute resolution: Review mechanisms, and A.90 Dispute resolution: Review procedure, https://data.rafit.org/regular.aspx?key=74180895 (accessed on 10 September 2024).

Performance in dispute resolution

While tax administrations cannot generally control the timing of judicial processes, many of them are working on improving dispute resolution processes to make them quicker. These might include mediation or other non-judicial routes. The examples included in Box 8.1. illustrate how administrations are improving their case management systems.

Box 8.1. Examples – Dispute resolution case management

Brazil – Classification and labelling of processes and allegations

Brazil has taken measures to reduce the backlog of cases and average time for judgements to be taken. The tax administrative litigation area of the Federal Revenue Service is responsible for managing activities related to trials, including management of the national collection of cases and their selection and distribution to judges. Included in the work plan to increase productivity without increasing the number of judges is the initiative: "Classification and Labelling of Processes and Allegations".

This initiative encompassed several actions, including:

- The preparation of tables of possible allegations to be reported by the taxpayer in their appeal;
- The identification of the allegations contained in the appeal;
- The selection and distribution of case groups to judges based on the allegations presented.

Furthermore, there has been progress in terms of:

- Strategic decision making;
- The creation of more homogeneous process groupings to optimise judgments;
- The rapid identification of groups of processes in special situations, for example, when publishing a judicial decision with repercussions for administrative judgments;
- The formation of a consistent database for machine learning to use artificial intelligence algorithms;
- The classification of processes has also made it possible to do work focused on identifying the causes of exonerations in order to support projects to improve assessments and make procedural changes in judgment activities;

The initiatives proved to be effective, with a 94% increase in resolved cases for 2023 compared to 2022.

Saudi Arabia – Smarter case management using artificial intelligence

The Al-Njaz project provides a smart intelligence solution for legal and tax-related processes regarding the core activities of the Saudi General Secretariat of Tax Committees (GSTC), from case registry up to judicial decisions. It is aimed at leveraging various artificial intelligence techniques for improved decision-making, to prevent discrepancies, ensure compliance with regulations, and analyse historical cases.

Twenty business challenges were identified, that are addressed through use cases grouped into four themes:

- Data Arrangement: This relies on classification techniques to detect duplicate cases, identify similarities and perform consistency checks on the cases. It aims to improve case processing and avoid discrepancies in the rulings of similar cases.
- Compliance Analysis: Focuses on GSTC standards in terms of case requirements. It relies on advanced data science techniques to run verification checks on a document's structure and its related content.
- Purpose of Decision Intelligence: This supports an analyst's decisions throughout the case analysis and decision-making process by using advanced data science techniques such as regression models. Tasks such as decision drafting, quality assurance and quality control (QA/QC) on mandatory data fields are included in this theme.
- AI Analytics: This involves leveraging determinist calculation capabilities to better understand trends and insights to ensure coherence and alignment across various historic decisions and enable future forecasts.

Sources: Brazil (2024) and Saudi Arabia (2024).

Tables 8.2. and 8.3. compare the change between 2018 and 2022 in the number of review cases initiated and on hand at fiscal year-end, for both internal and external reviews. The reductions in the number of cases initiated, see Table 8.2., that were reported by the majority of administrations during the COVID-19 pandemic cannot be observed anymore. Between 2021 and 2022, a slight majority of administrations reporting an increase in the number of cases initiated.

In relation to the number of cases on hand at fiscal year-end, see Table 8.3., the majority of administrations reported decreasing numbers between 2021 and 2022, both for cases under internal and external review. As regards tax cases external review, this continues a trend that can be observed for the last three years.

Table 8.2. Dispute resolution: Change in number of cases initiated during the year, 2018-22

Percentage of administrations that reported an increase or decrease in the number of cases initiated

Movement	Tax cases initiated under internal review procedure				Tax cases initiated under independent review by external bodies			
	Change between				Change between			
	2018-19	2019-20	2020-21	2021-22	2018-19	2019-20	2020-21	2021-22
Increase	51.0	39.2	56.9	51.0	44.4	27.0	44.4	55.3
Decrease	49.0	60.8	43.1	49.0	55.6	72.7	55.6	44.7

Sources: CIAT, IOTA, IMF, OECD, International Survey on Revenue Administration, Tables A.91 Dispute resolution: Number of cases - Tax cases under internal procedures, and A.92 Dispute resolution: Number of cases - Tax cases under independent review by external bodies, https://data.rafit.org/regular.aspx?key=74180895 (accessed on 10 September 2024).

Table 8.3. Dispute resolution: Change in number of cases on hand at fiscal year-end, 2018-22

Percentage of administrations that reported an increase or decrease in the number of cases on hand

Movement	Tax cases on hand under internal review procedure				Tax cases on hand under independent review by external bodies			
	Change between				Change between			
	2018-19	2019-20	2020-21	2021-22	2018-19	2019-20	2020-21	2021-22
Increase	63.3	44.9	54.0	42.0	51.2	33.3	35.7	37.2
Decrease	36.7	55.1	46.0	58.0	48.8	66.7	64.3	62.8

Sources: CIAT, IOTA, IMF, OECD, International Survey on Revenue Administration, Tables A.91 Dispute resolution: Number of cases - Tax cases under internal procedures, and A.92 Dispute resolution: Number of cases - Tax cases under independent review by external bodies, https://data.rafit.org/regular.aspx?key=74180895 (accessed on 10 September 2024).

Figure 8.1. and Figure 8.2. take a more detailed look at the jurisdiction level data and show the change between 2021 and 2022 in the number of review cases on hand at fiscal year-end, for both internal and external reviews. What is interesting to note are the significant increases in the number of internal review cases reported by a few jurisdictions.

At the same time, it should be pointed out that the volume of cases per jurisdiction varies significantly and where the number of cases is very low there can be significant fluctuations between years. This becomes more evident when looking at Figure 8.3., which highlights the wide differences between jurisdictions in the use of internal review procedures. Looking at Table 8.4., which shows the average number of internal review cases initiated over the period 2018 to 2022, it can be observed that the average has been stable around 7.5 internal review cases initiated per 1 000 active PIT and CIT taxpayers (with a slightly higher number in 2021).

Figure 8.1. Internal review procedures: Change between 2021 and 2022 in the number of cases on hand at fiscal year-end

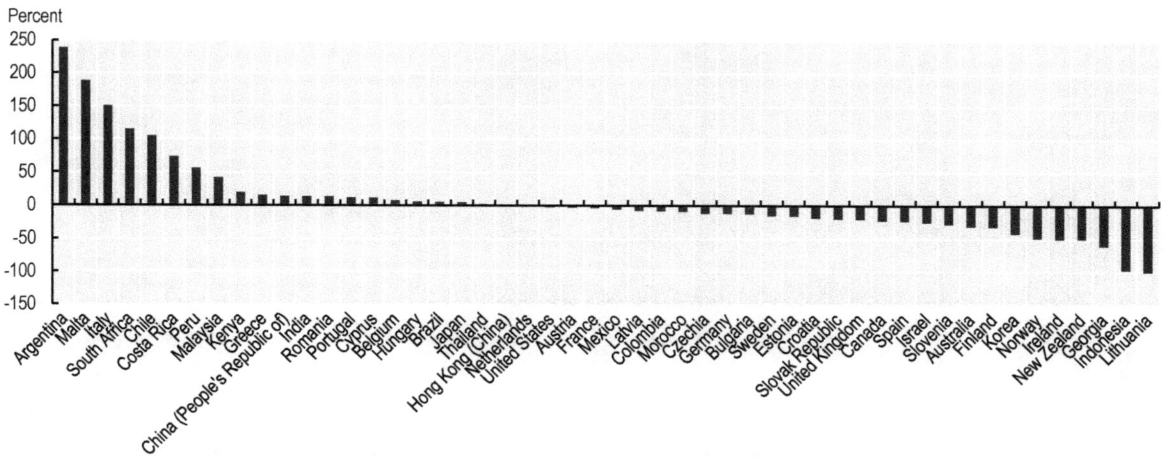

Source: CIAT, IOTA, IMF, OECD, International Survey on Revenue Administration, Table A.91 Dispute resolution: Number of cases - Tax cases under internal procedures, https://data.rafit.org/regular.aspx?key=74180895 (accessed on 10 September 2024).

StatLink https://stat.link/j60iqn

Figure 8.2. Independent review by external bodies: Change between 2021 and 2022 in the number of cases on hand at fiscal year-end

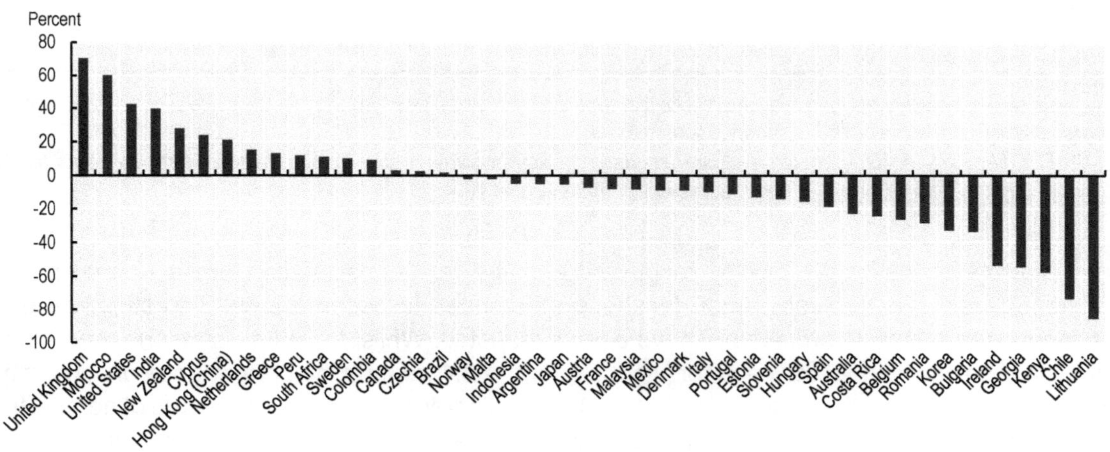

Sources: CIAT, IOTA, IMF, OECD, International Survey on Revenue Administration, Table A.92 Dispute resolution: Number of cases - Tax cases under independent review by external bodies, https://data.rafit.org/regular.aspx?key=74180895 (accessed on 10 September 2024).

StatLink https://stat.link/syrh1d

Figure 8.3. Number of internal review cases initiated per 1 000 active PIT and CIT taxpayers, 2022

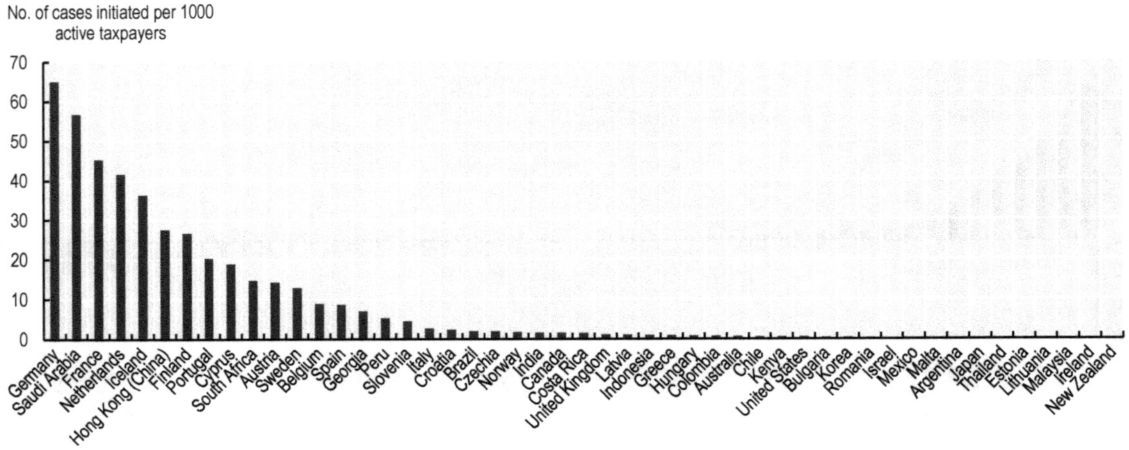

Note: For Saudi Arabia, the "No. of internal cases initiated during the FY per 1 000 active taxpayers" was put in relation to active VAT taxpayers.
Source: CIAT, IOTA, IMF, OECD, International Survey on Revenue Administration, Table D.49 Administrative review cases and litigation, https://data.rafit.org/regular.aspx?key=74180903 (accessed on 10 September 2024).

StatLink https://stat.link/mqaskp

Table 8.4. Average number of internal review cases initiated per 1 000 active PIT and CIT taxpayers, 2018-22

	2018	2019	2020	2021	2022
Average number of internal review cases initiated per 1 000 active PIT and CIT taxpayers (40 jurisdictions)	7.2	7.7	7.3	8.4	7.5

Note: The table shows the averages for those jurisdictions that were able to provide the information for the years 2018 to 2022. The number of jurisdictions for which data was available is shown in parentheses.
Source: CIAT, IOTA, IMF, OECD, International Survey on Revenue Administration, Table D.49 Administrative review cases and litigation, https://data.rafit.org/regular.aspx?key=74180903 (accessed on 10 September 2024).

Different interpretations of tax law by taxpayers and the tax administration are a normal part of tax administration, and it is not uncommon for these differences to become subject to litigation, once the internal and external review procedures have been exhausted. Whilst tax administrations report that most disputes are resolved without the need for litigation, Figure 8.4. reports the performance of administrations for cases decided upon by the courts. It shows significant differences in the success rate of administrations, although for some jurisdictions the number of cases decided is very low, meaning results can fluctuate significantly between years.

Figure 8.4. Percentage of cases resolved in favour of the administration, 2022

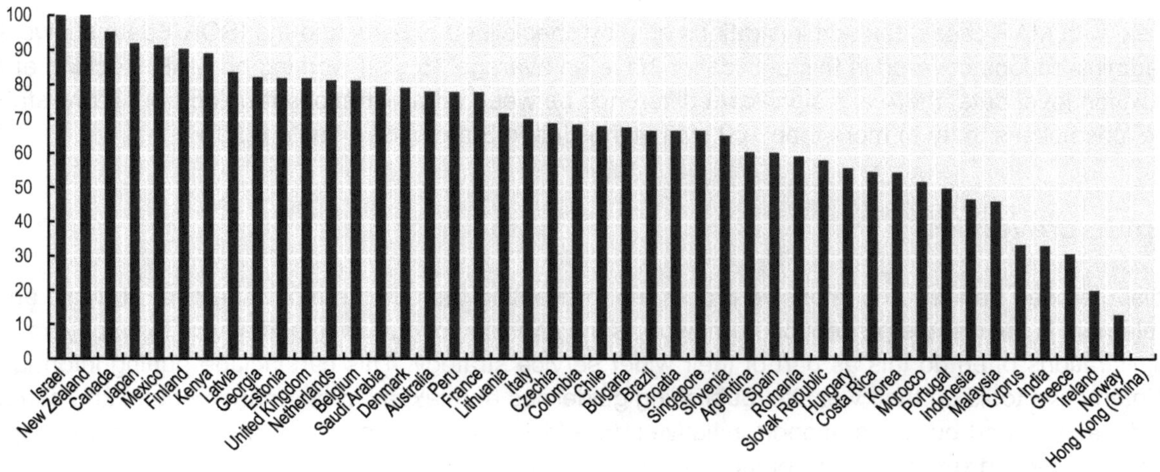

Note: Cases resolved in favour of the administration means those cases where the administration has been successful in more than 50% of the issues contested in each case. For Argentina see the note in Table A.93.
Source: CIAT, IOTA, IMF, OECD, International Survey on Revenue Administration, Table D.49 Administrative review cases and litigation, https://data.rafit.org/regular.aspx?key=74180903 (accessed on 10 September 2024).

StatLink https://stat.link/dzoyiu

Resolving international tax disputes

Cross-border business and international labour mobility are increasingly common. This inevitably leads to disputes over which jurisdictions have the right to tax certain types of income. Tax treaties between jurisdictions, also known as double taxation agreements, aim to remove double taxation by setting out mutually agreed rules on the allocation of taxing rights. To address situations where parties involved disagree on the application or interpretation of those rules, many tax treaties include a provision for a Mutual Agreement Procedure ("MAP") to resolve such disputes, separate from the standard legal remedies available under domestic law.

MAP is crucial for the correct application and interpretation of tax treaties. It ensures that taxpayers who are entitled to treaty benefits are not subjected to taxation that is not in line with the treaty's terms. It is therefore important to ensure that access to the MAP is readily available and that MAP cases are resolved and implemented promptly and within a reasonable timeframe.

Following the publication of the report *Making Dispute Resolution Mechanisms More Effective, Action 14 - 2015 Final Report* (OECD, 2015[1]), which contains a BEPS minimum standard on the resolution of treaty-related disputes, OECD/G20 BEPS Inclusive Framework members agreed to:

- a peer review process to evaluate the implementation of this standard;
- to publish the MAP profile for each jurisdiction; and
- to report and publish MAP statistics under the MAP Statistics Reporting Framework.

The results of this work, including the MAP profiles and statistics, can be found on the OECD website on *Dispute resolution in cross-border taxation* (OECD, 2024[2]).

In addition to this, the OECD with the Forum on Tax Administration (FTA), has developed tools to assist jurisdictions and taxpayers in navigating the MAP process:

- the *Manual on Effective Mutual Agreement Procedures* (OECD, 2007[3]); and

- the *Manual on the Handling of Multilateral Mutual Agreement Procedures and Advance Pricing Arrangements: Enhancing Tax Certainty* (OECD, 2023[4]).

To deal with MAP cases, tax administrations employ specialised experts and the ISORA data shows that the administrations covered in this publication have on average 15 staff working on MAP. Looking at the jurisdiction level data, there is a significant difference between administrations ranging from a few staff in some jurisdictions to up to more than 100 staff in the United States. (See Table B.23.)

Dispute prevention

As disputes can be resource intensive processes, preventing them is the most effective strategy, and a key element in the dispute prevention framework is the provision of guidance and advice to taxpayers. Tax administrations often do this as part of their wider service strategy. This can include putting information and interactive tools on their website, publishing guidelines and taxpayer information briefs, and carrying out educational and business support initiatives. In addition, many administrations offer specific dispute prevention mechanisms and some of those approaches are described in this section.

Rulings

As part of tax administrations' commitment to give taxpayers certainty of treatment, it is now common practice for administrations to set out how they will interpret the laws they administer, and how they will interpret the tax law in particular situations. This takes place through rulings:

- A ***public ruling*** is a published statement of how an administration will interpret provisions of the tax law in particular situations. They are generally published to clarify application of the law, especially where a large number of taxpayers may be impacted by particular provisions and/or where a provision has caused confusion or uncertainty. Typically, a public ruling is binding on the tax administration if the ruling applies to the taxpayer and the taxpayer relies upon it.
- A ***private ruling*** relates to a specific request from a taxpayer (or their tax representative) seeking greater certainty as to how the law would be applied by the tax administration in relation to a proposed or completed transaction(s). The objective of private rulings is to provide additional support and certainty to taxpayers on the tax consequences of more complex transactions.

Table 8.5. Rulings on the application of tax laws, 2022

Percentage of administrations

Public rulings		Private rulings			
			If yes,		
Provided	If yes, binding on the administration	Provided	Binding on the administration	Subject to fees	Required to be issued within a set time frame
84.2	89.6	86.0	91.8	49.0	79.6

Source: CIAT, IOTA, IMF, OECD, International Survey on Revenue Administration, Table B.48 Rulings on the application of tax laws, https://data.rafit.org/regular.aspx?key=74180919 (accessed on 10 September 2024).

Around 85% of administrations reported that they provide public rulings. Interestingly, 10% of those indicated that the public rulings were not binding upon them. A similar number of administrations reported issuing private taxpayer rulings, and again in around 10% of administrations the private rulings are not binding on the tax administration. Eighty percent of tax administrations providing private rulings reported the existence of time limits for the making of rulings, and half of the administrations noted that private rulings are subject to fees. (See Table 8.5.)

Box 8.2. India – Boards of Advance Rulings

India have introduced Boards of Advance Rulings (BARs) to provide tax certainty to non-resident investors. These Boards use email and video conferences to conduct their hearings and provide advance ruling to non-residents on the tax obligations of potential investments.

The receipt of applications, processing of applications, and hearings are all dealt with electronically, ensuring transparency and convenience for the applicant. The BAR has the full powers of India's civil court, and it is possible to appeal its rulings before the Honourable High Court.

Source: India (2024).

Advanced pricing arrangements

Bilateral and Multilateral Advance Pricing Arrangements ("APAs") are binding arrangements between two or more tax administrations and the taxpayers in relation to a specific issue for a prescribed period. In a growing number of cases, these collaborative APAs have successfully contributed to providing advance tax certainty to both taxpayers and tax administrations, ensuring predictability in the tax treatment of international transactions and reducing potential tax disputes.

To support administrations and taxpayers, the FTA MAP Forum has developed the *Bilateral Advance Pricing Arrangement Manual* (OECD, 2022[5]) which is intended as a guide for streamlining the Bilateral APA process to facilitate a cooperative and collaborative process. In addition, the *Manual on the Handling of Multilateral Mutual Agreement Procedures and Advance Pricing Arrangements: Enhancing Tax Certainty* (OECD, 2023[4]) offers guidance to tax administrations and taxpayers on Multilateral APAs from both legal and procedural perspectives.

Close to 90% of administrations covered in this publication reported that they enter into APAs, and to support this process they have on average 17 staff specialised in APAs. However, there is a significant difference at jurisdiction level. (See Table B.23.)

Box 8.3. Chile – Advance Transfer Pricing agreements menu

To streamline tax compliance and enhance information security in the process of applying for Advance Pricing Agreements (APAs), the Internal Revenue Service (SII) has introduced a new online system.

This secure platform simplifies the submission and renewal of APAs requests and provides various additional tools. These include the option for pre-filing meetings, access to the regulations on APAs and Transfer Pricing, statistical insights into request processing and subscribed agreements, a Frequently Asked Question section, video resources, and a comprehensive step-by-step guide for uploading files within the system.

To further enhance user support, an email inbox has been set up to address any queries related to this topic.

Access to this digital platform is available on the official website. This user-friendly interface aims to ensure transparency and efficiency throughout the process.

This system has not only simplified tax procedures but also fostered a collaborative and transparent environment between taxpayers and the competent authority.

Source: Chile (2024).

Co-operative compliance programmes

Over the last few years, there has been an increasing focus on the use of co-operative arrangements to manage compliance and enhance tax certainty. These programmes often involve a more transparent relationship between tax administrations and taxpayers, and can involve more proactive approaches to resolving material tax risks. The concept of co-operative compliance has been the subject of several OECD reports, most recently *Co-operative Tax Compliance: Building Better Tax Control Frameworks* (OECD, 2016[6]).

As the operation of a co-operative compliance programme is resource intensive due to the high level of engagement between tax administration officials and taxpayers, traditionally those programmes were reserved for large companies, and close to 75% of administrations reported having such programmes for large taxpayers. However, technological advances in risk assessment processes have led to a number of administrations reporting the application of this concept to other taxpayer groups, such as High Net Wealth Individual (HNWI) taxpayers (see Table 8.6.).

Table 8.6. Existence of formal co-operative compliance approaches for different taxpayer segments, 2022

Percentage of administrations that have such approaches

Large taxpayers	HNWI taxpayers	Other taxpayers
74.1	24.1	39.7

Source: CIAT, IOTA, IMF, OECD, International Survey on Revenue Administration, Table A.107 Cooperative compliance approaches, https://data.rafit.org/regular.aspx?key=74180897 (accessed on 14 June 2024).

International Compliance Assurance Programme

The International Compliance Assurance Programme (ICAP) is a voluntary programme for a multilateral co-operative risk assessment and assurance process. It is designed to provide multinational enterprise groups (MNE groups) with increased tax certainty with respect to certain of their activities and transactions as long as they are willing to engage actively, openly and in a fully transparent manner. ICAP does not provide an MNE group with the legal certainty that may be achieved, for example, through an APA. However, it does give assurance when tax administrations participating in an MNE group's risk assessment consider covered risks to be low risk.[1] (OECD, 2021[7])

Joint audits

Another tool that can assist in preventing disputes is a joint audit where officials from two or more administrations join to form a single audit team which will examine issues or transactions of taxpayer(s) with cross-border business activities and in which the jurisdictions have a common or complementary interest. By collaborating it may be possible for the participating tax administrations to detect and address differences or potential disputes at an early stage. (OECD, 2019[8])

Notes

[1] See https://www.oecd.org/en/about/programmes/icap.html for more information (accessed on 10 September 2024).

References

OECD (2024), *Dispute resolution in cross-border taxation*, https://www.oecd.org/en/topics/dispute-resolution-in-cross-border-taxation.html (accessed on 10 September 2024). [2]

OECD (2023), *Manual on the Handling of Multilateral Mutual Agreement Procedures and Advance Pricing Arrangements: Enhancing Tax Certainty*, OECD Forum on Tax Administration, OECD Publishing, Paris, https://doi.org/10.1787/f0cad7f3-en. [4]

OECD (2022), *Bilateral Advance Pricing Arrangement Manual*, OECD Forum on Tax Administration, OECD Publishing, Paris, https://doi.org/10.1787/4aa570e1-en. [5]

OECD (2021), *International Compliance Assurance Programme: Handbook for tax administrations and MNE*, OECD Publishing, Paris, https://doi.org/10.1787/a44d51e2-en. [7]

OECD (2019), *Joint Audit 2019 – Enhancing Tax Co-operation and Improving Tax Certainty: Forum on Tax Administration*, OECD Publishing, Paris, https://doi.org/10.1787/17bfa30d-en. [8]

OECD (2016), *Co-operative Tax Compliance: Building Better Tax Control Frameworks*, OECD Publishing, Paris, https://doi.org/10.1787/9789264253384-en. [6]

OECD (2015), *Making Dispute Resolution Mechanisms More Effective, Action 14 - 2015 Final Report, OECD/G20 Base Erosion and Profit Shifting Project*, OECD Publishing, Paris, https://doi.org/10.1787/9789264241633-en. [1]

OECD (2007), *Manual on Effective Mutual Agreement Procedures (MEMAP)*, OECD, Paris, https://doi.org/10.1787/2bb3ab55-en. [3]

9 Institutional setups and governance

This chapter examines the institutional setups and governance arrangements in tax administrations.

Introduction

Like all government bodies, tax administrations are ultimately accountable to the citizens they serve. They must operate and be seen to operate in a fair and impartial manner. This includes being subject to a range of checks and balances to ensure transparency in their operations and proper accountability for their overall management of the tax system.

The framework within which this accountability operates varies between jurisdictions and is a result of various factors, including the institutional arrangements and government structures in place. Differences will also be conditioned by the legislative, regulatory and judicial regime and shaped by the cultural, historical and political background. There is no single approach that will work for all tax administrations.

This chapter examines the institutional setups and governance arrangements in tax administrations by looking at (i) institutional arrangements, (ii) the autonomy of operations, (iii) control and other oversight features, and (iv) the relationship between the tax administration and the taxpayer.

Institutional arrangements

The institutional arrangements for tax administrations are typically grouped around two general categories. Tax administrations are either set-up as (i) directorate(s) or unit(s) within the Ministry of Finance (MOF) or its equivalent, or as (ii) unified semi-autonomous bodies. These can be broken down further into four sub-categories:

- A *single directorate* or unit within the MOF or its equivalent.
- *Multiple directorates* or units within the MOF or its equivalent.
- A *unified semi-autonomous body*, where tax administration and support functions are the responsibility of a Commissioner or Director General who reports to a government minister.
- A *unified semi-autonomous body with a board*, where tax administration and support functions are the responsibility of a Commissioner or Director General who reports to an oversight body/board of management that may include external members. The management board may either be decision-making or advisory.

There are some exceptions to the above categories. For example, in Germany, the responsibility of collecting taxes is largely devolved to regional (i.e. Länder) administrations, while a relatively small central body exercises a high-level coordination role. In addition, in Greece, the Independent Authority for Public Revenue enjoys operational independence, administrative and financial autonomy and is only subject to parliamentary scrutiny.

Figure 9.1. provides an overview of the institutional frameworks for the tax administrations covered by this report. As can be seen, around 60% of administrations are set-up as unified semi-autonomous bodies, with around one-third of those having a board. Eight of administrations describe their boards as being decision-making boards and three describe them as being advisory boards.

There does not appear to be any consensus around board size nor the representation of private section representatives (see Table B.1):

- The average number of board members was around 8.5, ranging from 4 in Peru to 15 in Canada.
- Close to two-thirds of the administrations report having private sector representatives on their board, with some boards made-up entirely from the private sector.

Greece, which falls in the category of "other institutional arrangement" (see above), also has a management board with five members, who may or may not come from the private sector.

Figure 9.1. Institutional frameworks, 2022

Percentage of administrations

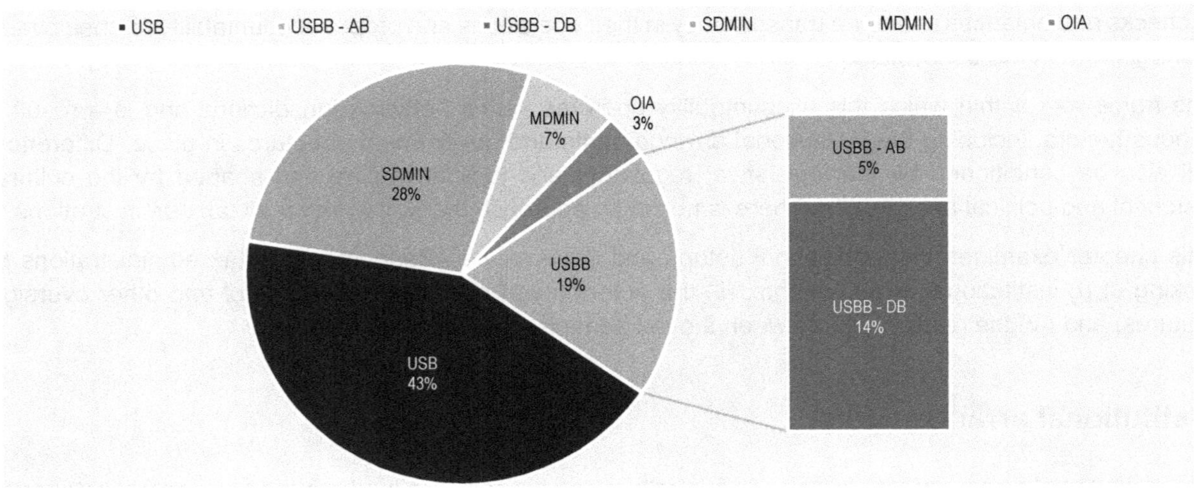

Notes: USB – Unified semi-autonomous Body; USBB – Unified semi-autonomous body with board (AB – Advisory board; DB – Decision-making board); SDMIN – Single directorate in ministry; MDMIN – Multiple directorates in ministry; Other – Other institutional arrangement.
Source: CIAT, IOTA, IMF, OECD, International Survey on Revenue Administration, Table B.1 Institutional framework and management autonomy, https://data.rafit.org/regular.aspx?key=74180913 (accessed on 10 September 2024).

StatLink https://stat.link/hmkjxa

Box 9.1. Canada – The Board of Management

The Canada Revenue Agency (CRA) Board of Management (Board) oversees the organisation and administration of the CRA, and the management of its resources, services, property, personnel, and contracts. The intention was to provide a degree of independence from the federal government reflecting the CRA's service to sub-national governments with the opportunity to innovate beyond the administrative practices of the core civil service.

The Board:

- Meets six times a year, and is accountable to Parliament (through the Minister) on matters related to the general administration and enforcement of program legislation.
- Comprises of fifteen individuals (directors). This includes the Chair, Commissioner (Ex officio), and representatives of every province and a territory in Canada who bring an external and diverse business perspective from the private, or not-for-profit sectors to the work of the CRA.
- Undertakes its oversight role in co-operation with Agency management to ensure that the CRA is efficiently and effectively managed by bringing a forward-looking, strategic perspective to the CRA's operations.
- Provides a challenge function, ensuring the CRA is properly managing and exercising its authorities by reviewing performance reports, financial statements, and performance dashboards.

As the Commissioner and CRA Officials are responsible for the day-to-day management of the CRA, the Board may not direct the Commissioner or other CRA Officials in the exercise of statutory power and other program legislation administration. The Board is also not authorized to receive personal/business information regarding program legislation.

For further information, please see https://www.canada.ca/en/revenue-agency/corporate/about-canada-revenue-agency-cra/board-management.html (accessed on 10 September 2024).

Source: Canada (2024).

Autonomy of operations

The range of autonomy given to a tax administration depends on a variety of factors. These include the general arrangement of government functions and powers, the establishment of a jurisdiction's public sector administration practices, as well as the institutional model adopted for tax administration. For government, the return to granting greater autonomy can be the prospect of increased efficiency and effectiveness, particularly in periods of change. With few exceptions, most tax administrations report that they operate with a degree of autonomy that allows them to appropriately manage their administrative functions (see Table 9.1.).

Table 9.1. Authority delegated to tax administrations, 2022

Percentage of administrations that have the selected authority

Design internal structure	Exercise discretion over operating budget	Exercise discretion over capital budget	Set performance standards
84.5	79.3	69.0	96.6

Source: CIAT, IOTA, IMF, OECD, International Survey on Revenue Administration, Table B.1 Institutional framework and management autonomy, https://data.rafit.org/regular.aspx?key=74180913 (accessed on 10 September 2024).

Autonomy can take many forms, but at its core involves the government setting objectives for the tax system (including tax legislation) as well as an accountability framework, while providing tax administrations with flexibility in the following areas to decide how to deliver those objectives:

- ***Budget expenditure management***, including discretion to allocate/adjust budgeted administrative funds across functions to take account of changed circumstances or to meet new emerging priorities. Around 80% of administrations reported exercising discretion over their operating budget, and around 70% over their capital budget.
- ***Organisation***, determining the internal organisational structure of the tax administration operations, including geographical location of tax offices. Close to 85% of administrations reported having the authority to design their internal structure.
- ***Planning***, having responsibility for formulating strategic and operational plans. Almost all administrations reported preparing strategic plans as well as annual business/ operational plans (see Table 9.3.)
- ***Performance standards***, having discretion to set (in association with central bodies) administrative performance standards. Almost all administrations have that authority.
- ***Personnel recruitment, development and remuneration***, having the ability to set qualification standards for categories of recruits, recruit and dismiss staff (in accordance with public sector policies); negotiate remuneration levels in accordance with broader public sector-wide

arrangements; and establish and operate training and development programmes. See Chapter 10, Table 10.9. for more detail on this.

- ***Information and communication technology (ICT)***, having the authority to administer its own in-house ICT systems, or to outsource the provision of such services.

Control and other oversight features

Internal controls

Administrations generally have robust internal controls built into their ICT framework to detect and prevent internal fraud, as well as internal audit functions as reported by 97% of administrations. This is supported through clear human resource policies to deal with employee misconduct. In this respect, 97% of the administrations covered by this publication report having a public service-wide code of conduct, and close to 90% report having their own code of conduct.

Further, close to two-thirds of the administrations indicated having in place an integrity strategy, which typically includes internal awareness campaigns and, in many cases, also agreements with relevant stakeholders. Around half of the administrations also conducts regular surveys to assess perceptions of the administration's commitment to integrity. (See Table 9.2.)

Table 9.2. Internal control features, 2022

Percentage of administrations that have the selected features

<table>
<tr><th rowspan="3">Formal internal assurance mechanisms (internal audit)</th><th colspan="4">Integrity strategy</th><th colspan="2">Code of conduct</th></tr>
<tr><th rowspan="2">Formal integrity strategy</th><th colspan="2">If yes, integrity strategy includes...</th><th rowspan="2">Regular surveys conducted to assess perceptions of administration's commitment to integrity</th><th rowspan="2">Public service-wide code of conduct</th><th rowspan="2">Own code of conduct</th></tr>
<tr><th>Agreements with relevant stakeholders</th><th>Awareness campaigns</th></tr>
<tr><td>96.6</td><td>63.8</td><td>73.0</td><td>97.3</td><td>53.4</td><td>96.6</td><td>87.9</td></tr>
</table>

Source: CIAT, IOTA, IMF, OECD, International Survey on Revenue Administration, Table B.3 Selected governance practices: Audit, code of conduct and integrity, https://data.rafit.org/regular.aspx?key=74180913 (accessed on 10 September 2024).

Box 9.2. Examples – Tax administrations and ethics

Finland – Responsibility and ethical principles in the use of artificial intelligence

The use of Artificial Intelligence (AI) is increasing everywhere in society, including the activities of public authorities. AI enables authorities to provide a better service and operate more efficiently. However, there are also ethical questions relating to the responsible and safe use of AI in official tasks, so that the security of citizens and public officials alike is taken into account and decision-making is transparent.

The Finnish Tax Administration has implemented ethical principles for the use of AI, as follows:

- The AI uses only reliable data.
- A human is always responsible for AI operations.
- AI always follows laws and regulations.
- The Tax Administration takes part in public discussion on responsible and ethical AI applications.

A group of experts from the Tax Administration's different units promote responsible AI use and assesses AI solutions from the perspective of the ethical principles. The group has approximately ten members and meets whenever necessary, usually monthly. The group consists of specialists in communication, law, taxation, technical platforms and analytics. Other experts may also be called in when new expertise is needed.

The Tax Administration promotes responsible AI use by training staff, assessing and providing tools for AI use, and evaluating the solutions in use. The Tax Administration's expert group monitors the development of the EU's AI legislation and adjusts its activities and instructions accordingly.

Spain – Ethics Advisory Committee

The Spanish Tax Agency (AEAT) has launched the Ethics Advisory Committee. Following the guidelines of the AEAT Strategic Plan 2020-2023, this Committee was created to support and assist the AEAT Management Board in ethical issues and corporate conduct.

The Committee adds strategic value in promoting good practices through an official forum, in which ethical issues and dilemmas relevant to AEAT are discussed. It plays a key role in the internal socialisation of the code of principles and conduct in AEAT through the preparation of a catalogue collating good practices in ethics, integrity and transparency, as well as responses to the most relevant issues.

The Committee is made up of eight members: a chair, a secretary and six members. It is chaired either by the Director General of AEAT or a member of the Management Board designated by the Director General.

The Advisory Committee's role is to warn of reputational risks and advise on possible complaints that can be assessed from an ethical perspective.

Sources: Finland (2024) and Spain (2024).

External control and other oversight features

As regards external controls, a significant number of administrations (83%) are subject to a degree of oversight by a public accounts committee (or equivalent) that assesses their results as well as a budgetary review process that monitors their spending. Results are typically reviewed and verified by a national audit function. Parliamentary committees will also usually have the capacity to review performance against output metrics, as well as more strategic goals.

Table 9.3. External control and other oversight features, 2022

Percentage of administrations that have the selected features

Use of external auditor	Annual report		Formal set of service delivery standards		Strategic plan		Annual business/ operational plan	
	Prepared	If yes, published	Prepared	If yes, published	Prepared	If yes, published	Prepared	If yes, published
82.8	94.8	90.9	84.5	61.2	98.3	78.9	94.8	54.5

Source: CIAT, IOTA, IMF, OECD, International Survey on Revenue Administration, Tables B.3 Selected governance practices: Audit, code of conduct and integrity, and B.4 Selected governance practices: Plans, reports and standards; and organizational chart, https://data.rafit.org/regular.aspx?key=74180913 (accessed on 10 September 2024).

Common other oversight features of tax administrations include:

- ***Publication of an annual report***: Around 95% produce an annual report, and 90% of those also publish it. (See Table 9.3.)
- ***Periodic assessments against agreed metrics*** (for example, revenue collections, debt levels, number of compliance interventions, customer service levels): 85% of administrations prepare a formal set of service delivery standards and around 60% of those make the set of delivery standards public. (See Table 9.3.)
- ***Systems of risk oversight***: Slightly more than 80% of administrations have in place formal approaches in place for identifying, assessing and prioritising key compliance risks. However, only 29% make the identified risks public regularly and 27% regularly publish reports of outcomes in addressing key compliance risks. (See Chapter 6, Table 6.1.)
- ***An agreed set of strategic goals and objectives*** to guide administrations' performance. High-level outcome measures and indicators used by tax administrations generally encompass the following:
  - i) taxpayers' satisfaction with the services provided and overall perceptions as being an efficient, fair and effective administration (see also Chapter 5, Table 5.3.);
  - ii) taxpayers' compliance;
  - iii) taxpayer service delivery, such as availability of services and responses to outages;
  - iv) organisational efficiency; and
  - v) employee engagement and satisfaction (see also Chapter 10, Table 10.12.).
- ***Board or executive committee*** to review, assess, and challenge strategic direction (around 20% of tax administrations have a board, see Figure 9.1.).

Annex 9.A. contains a list of selected links to annual reports, strategic plans and organisational charts published by tax administrations participating in this publication.

Control and other oversight features: A high-level picture

Taking the data from the ISORA 2023 survey, Figure 9.2. presents a high-level picture of control and oversight features in tax administration. It does not name individual tax administrations but rather combines a set of data points providing an overall view for three areas:

- ***Preparation of documents***: The preparation of strategic and operations-related documents that can provide guidance, enhance decision-making and assist in resource allocation. Reassuring the public that those documents are prepared, even if they are not published, can enhance community confidence and trust in the tax administration. The data taken into account includes the preparation of (i) a strategic plan; (ii) an annual business / operational plan; (iii) an annual report; (iv) a formal set of service delivery standards; (v) a formal compliance risk management strategy and the existence of a formal approach for identifying, assessing and prioritising key compliance risks; (vi) tax gap estimates; (vii) taxpayer satisfaction surveys; and (viii) an integrity strategy and surveys to assess perceptions of the administration's commitment to integrity.
- ***Publication of documents***: While public knowledge of the preparation of such documents can be helpful, their publication can be a much stronger message to stakeholders. In this respect, the high-level picture takes into account the publication of the afore mentioned documents, or (i) in the case of the compliance risk management strategy, whether the administration makes public regularly the risks and the results in addressing those risks; and (ii) as regards the taxpayer satisfaction surveys, whether the administration makes public the results of the surveys.
- ***Existence of oversight features***: As regards oversights features, the data points considered include the existence of (i) a Board; (ii) an external auditor; (iii) a formal internal assurance

mechanism (internal audit); (iv) a code of conduct; and (v) specific mechanisms for dealing with taxpayer complaints.

The scoring and weighing of the data points took account of the different nature and level of detail of the underlying ISORA questions. Whilst the various aspects of control and oversight features that were explored in ISORA 2023 should not be considered exhaustive and do not have equal weight or significance, their occurrence or lack thereof can provide some indication of the capability of tax administrations in that area.

For each of the three areas, the figure shows the range of administrations that are between the lower and upper quartile (illustrated by the "boxes"), with the median represented by the horizontal lines drawn through the boxes. The lines extending the boxes vertically (the "whiskers") indicate the range of administrations that are in the upper and lower quartiles.

Figure 9.2. shows that most tax administrations covered by this publication are subject to a good degree of oversight and control, and also prepare a significant number of strategic and operational documents. For both of those areas, the median is around 80% with some administrations also scoring 100%.

However, this is very much different as regards the publication of strategic and operational documents where the median drops to below 60% and only a few administrations score above 80%, indicating that there is room for more transparency which may help further enhancing community confidence and trust in tax administration.

Figure 9.2. Control and other oversight features: A high-level picture, 2022

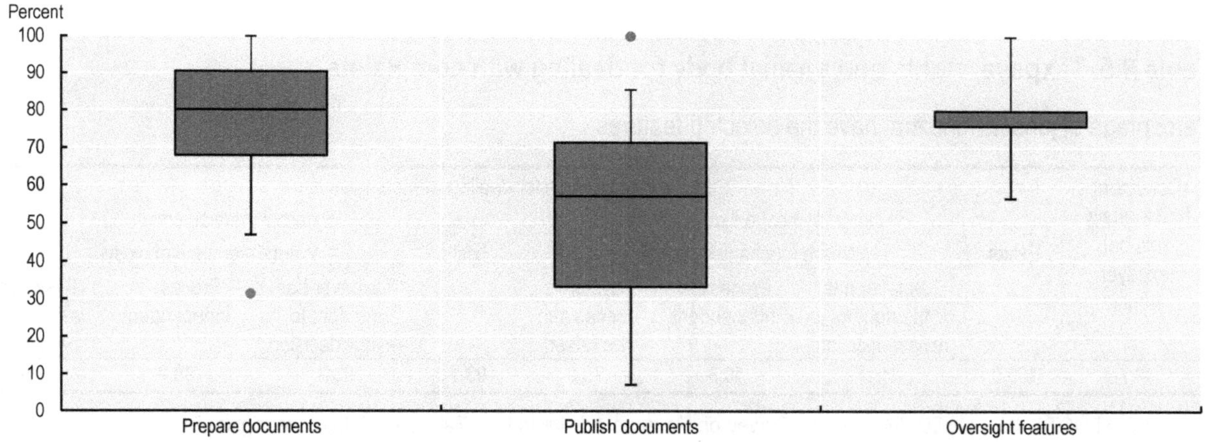

Source: OECD Secretariat calculations based on CIAT, IOTA, IMF, OECD, International Survey on Revenue Administration, https://data.rafit.org/regular.aspx?key=74180914 (accessed on 10 September 2024)

StatLink https://stat.link/gfl798

The relationship between the tax administration and the taxpayer

An important part of the governance of tax administrations is the definition of taxpayer rights and obligations. This can help place the governance framework within broader societal expectations for government services and provide a benchmark for press and civil society. Table 9.4. sets out some of the most commonly reported rights and obligations, and Box 9.2. provides examples on this.

Public reporting of performance against elements of taxpayer rights (such as complaints handling, quality of service, etc.) can help in giving visibility and credibility to such arrangements. This is often done through the publication of annual reports.

Table 9.4. Taxpayer's rights and obligations

Right	Obligation
To be informed, assisted, and heard	To be honest
Of appeal	To be co-operative
To pay no more than the correct amount of tax	To provide accurate information and documents on time
Certainty	To keep records
Privacy	To pay taxes on time
Confidentiality and secrecy	

As Table 9.5. shows, the vast majority of jurisdictions have legislation or administrative procedures in place governing taxpayers' rights and obligations, with the majority of jurisdictions setting out the rights in law or other statutes and the remaining in administrative or other type of documents (see Table B.43). While the codified approach to taxpayer rights has the force of law and in some circumstances may be more robust, the administrative approach tends to be more flexible and service orientated.

In all jurisdictions there is also a special mechanism for dealing with taxpayers' complaints. All administrations have an internal mechanism for dealing with complaints and in half of the administrations this process is independent. In addition, in more than 90% of the jurisdictions there is also a mechanism that is external to the administration. As regards both internal and external mechanisms, in around 80% of jurisdictions the process allows for systemic issues to be raised. (See Table 9.5.)

Table 9.5. Taxpayer rights and special body for dealing with complaints

Percentage of jurisdictions that have the selected features

<table>
<tr><th rowspan="4">Document that formally sets out taxpayer rights</th><th colspan="8">Specific mechanisms for dealing with complaints</th></tr>
<tr><th colspan="4">Internal mechanism</th><th colspan="4">External mechanism</th></tr>
<tr><th rowspan="2">Exists</th><th colspan="3">Where mechanism exists...</th><th rowspan="2">Exists</th><th colspan="3">Where mechanism exists...</th></tr>
<tr><th>Taxpayer has the right to review decision</th><th>Process is independent</th><th>Systemic issues can be raised</th><th>Taxpayer has the right to review decision</th><th>Process is independent</th><th>Systemic issues can be raised</th></tr>
<tr><td>89.7</td><td>100.0</td><td>84.5</td><td>50.9</td><td>75.9</td><td>93.1</td><td>83.3</td><td>88.9</td><td>81.5</td></tr>
</table>

Source: CIAT, IOTA, IMF, OECD, International Survey on Revenue Administration, Tables B.43 Taxpayer rights: Documentation, and B.44 Taxpayer rights: Complaints mechanisms, https://data.rafit.org/regular.aspx?key=74180919 (accessed on 10 September 2024).

Box 9.3. Examples – The relationship between the tax administration and the taxpayer

Australia

The relationship between the tax collector and taxpayer in Australia is set out in the Australian Taxation Office (ATO) Charter (the Charter). The Charter explains what the taxpayer can expect from the ATO and what the ATO is committed to follow in all its dealings with the taxpayer. It sets out:

- the way the ATO conducts itself when dealing with a taxpayer;
- what the taxpayer can expect from the ATO;

- what the taxpayer can do if they are not satisfied.

For further information see also: https://www.ato.gov.au/about-ato/commitments-and-reporting/ato-charter/our-charter (accessed on 10 September 2024).

Where taxpayers remain unsatisfied with the ATO's response, complaints can be taken to the Inspector General of Taxation and Taxation Ombudsman (IGTO). The office of the IGTO is an independent statutory body, separate from the ATO and its governing board. As well as dealing with individual complaints, it will also conduct broader reviews into the administration of taxation, including the identification of systemic issues, and make recommendations to the ATO and to Government.

Canada

There are 16 rights that describe the treatment a taxpayer is entitled to when dealing with the CRA. Additionally, there are five small business commitments. The Taxpayer Bill of Rights builds upon the CRA's mission, vision, and values.

Taxpayer Bill of Rights

1. You have the right to receive entitlements and to pay no more and no less than what is required by law.
2. You have the right to service in both official languages.
3. You have the right to privacy and confidentiality.
4. You have the right to a formal review and a subsequent appeal.
5. You have the right to be treated professionally, courteously, and fairly.
6. You have the right to complete, accurate, clear, and timely information.
7. You have the right, unless otherwise provided by law, not to pay income tax amounts in dispute before you have had an impartial review.
8. You have the right to have the law applied consistently.
9. You have the right to lodge a service complaint and to be provided with an explanation of our findings.
10. You have the right to have the costs of compliance taken into account when administering tax legislation.
11. You have the right to expect us to be accountable.
12. You have the right to relief from penalties and interest under tax legislation because of extraordinary circumstances.
13. You have the right to expect us to publish our service standards and report annually.
14. You have the right to expect us to warn you about questionable tax schemes in a timely manner.
15. You have the right to be represented by a person of your choice.
16. You have the right to lodge a service complaint and request a formal review without fear of reprisal.

For more information see: https://www.canada.ca/en/revenue-agency/corporate/about-canada-revenue-agency-cra/taxpayer-bill-rights.html (accessed on 10 September 2024).

Commitment to small business

As an additional measure within the Taxpayer Bill of Rights:

1. The CRA is committed to administering the tax system in a way that minimizes the costs of compliance for small businesses.

2. The CRA is committed to working with all governments to streamline service, minimize cost, and reduce the compliance burden.
3. The CRA is committed to providing service offerings that meet the needs of small businesses.
4. The CRA is committed to conducting outreach activities that help small businesses comply with the legislation we administer.
5. The CRA is committed to explaining how we conduct our business with small businesses.

Taxpayers' Ombudsperson

Taxpayers can resolve service-related issues with the CRA through the office of the Taxpayers' Ombudsperson. The office identifies and reviews systemic and emerging issues, and will generally review a complaint only after all CRA internal complaint resolution mechanisms have been exhausted. These exclude non-service-related issues, court matters, and complaints that have been addressed by the minister's office.

United States

Taxpayers rights are set out in various parts of tax legislation. In 2014 they were brought together in "Bill of rights" published by the Internal Revenue Service (IRS). These set out ten rights:

1. The Right to Be Informed
2. The Right to Quality Service
3. The Right to Pay No More than the Correct Amount of Tax
4. The Right to Challenge the IRS's Position and Be Heard
5. The Right to Appeal an IRS Decision in an Independent Forum
6. The Right to Finality
7. The Right to Privacy
8. The Right to Confidentiality
9. The Right to Retain Representation
10. The Right to a Fair and Just Tax System

For further information see also: https://www.irs.gov/taxpayer-bill-of-rights (accessed on 10 September 2024).

When complaints and concerns are not resolved through the internal processes of the IRS, taxpayers can go to the Taxpayer Advocate Service (TAS). TAS is an independent organisation within the IRS which is available to both individuals and business. TAS provides taxpayers access to various resources, including information on the Taxpayer Bill of Rights. When a taxpayer qualifies for help, they will be assigned to one advocate. The service is always free.

TAS will also review large-scale or systemic problems in tax law or tax administration. Examples of systemic issues are those which:

- Apply to multiple taxpayers;
- Involve IRS systems, policies, and procedures;
- Involve protecting taxpayer rights, reducing burdens, ensuring fair treatment, or providing essential taxpayer services.

For more information see: https://www.taxpayeradvocate.irs.gov/ (accessed on 10 September 2024).

Sources: Australia (2024), Canada (2024) and United States (2024).

Annex 9.A. Selected links to documents published by tax administrations

This section contains selected links to a number of documents (annual reports, strategic plans and organisational charts) published by tax administrations participating in this publication.

Annex Table 9.A.1. Links to selected tax administration annual reports

Jurisdiction	Links (accessed on 10 September 2024)
Australia	https://www.ato.gov.au/about-ato/commitments-and-reporting/annual-report-and-other-reporting-to-parliament/annual-report
Belgium	https://finances.belgium.be/fr/sur_le_spf/rapports-annuels
Bulgaria	https://nra.bg/wps/portal/nra/za-nap/osnovni-dokumenti/Godishni-otcheti-za-deynostta-na-NAP
Canada	https://www.canada.ca/en/revenue-agency/corporate/about-canada-revenue-agency-cra/departmental-performance-reports.html
Chile	https://www.sii.cl/cuenta_publica/CP2023.pdf
Cyprus	https://www.mof.gov.cy/mof/tax/taxdep.nsf/All/1BF0DAFC814512A6C225822C004877FF
Finland	https://vero.fi/en/About-us/finnish-tax-administration/finnish-tax-administrations-year/earlier-annual-reports/
France	https://www.economie.gouv.fr/dgfip/rapports-dactivite-dgfip
Georgia	https://www.rs.ge/AboutUs-en?cat=5&tab=1
Greece	https://www.aade.gr/apologistikes-ektheseis
Hong Kong (China)	https://www.ird.gov.hk/eng/ppr/are.htm
Hungary	https://nav.gov.hu/kiadvanyok/evkonyvek
Iceland	https://www.skatturinn.is/um-rsk/embaettid/arsskyrslur/
Indonesia	https://pajak.go.id/id/tahunan-page
Ireland	https://www.revenue.ie/en/corporate/press-office/annual-report/index.aspx
Japan	https://www.nta.go.jp/about/introduction/torikumi/report/report.htm
Latvia	https://www.vid.gov.lv/en/annual-reports-state-revenue-service
Luxembourg	https://aed.gouvernement.lu/fr/publications/RA.html and https://impotsdirects.public.lu/fr/profil/rapports.html
Malaysia	https://www.hasil.gov.my/en/about-hasil/corporate-profile/annual-report/
Malta	https://cfr.gov.mt/en/Documents/MTCA%20AR%202023%20SPREADS%2031%20COMP%202.pdf
Morocco	https://www.tax.gov.ma/wps/portal/DGI/Nous-connaitre/Rapports-d_activite
Netherlands	https://www.rijksoverheid.nl/documenten/rapporten/2023/05/24/1-jaarrapportage-2022-belastingdienst
New Zealand	https://www.ird.govt.nz/about-us/publications/annual-corporate-reports/annual-report
Norway	https://www.skatteetaten.no/om-skatteetaten/analyse-og-rapporter/arsrapporter/
Peru	https://www.sunat.gob.pe/cuentassunat/planestrategico/informeGestion.html
Portugal	https://info.portaldasfinancas.gov.pt/pt/at/Instrumentos_Gestao/Relatorio_atividades/Pages/default.aspx
Romania	https://www.anaf.ro/anaf/internet/ANAF/despre_anaf/strategii_anaf/rapoarte_studii
Saudi Arabia	https://zatca.gov.sa/ar/HelpCenter/Documents/ZATCA_REPORT_2022.pdf
Singapore	https://www.iras.gov.sg/who-we-are/what-we-do/annual-reports-and-publications/annual-reports
Slovak Republic	https://www.financnasprava.sk/sk/financna-sprava/vyrocne-spravy
South Africa	https://www.sars.gov.za/about/annual-reports-strategic-plans/
Spain	https://sede.agenciatributaria.gob.es/Sede/informacion-institucional/memorias.html
Sweden	https://www.skatteverket.se/download/18.48cfd212185efbb440b2db9/1676993313236/arsredovisning-skatteverket-2022-skv165-utgava31.pdf
Switzerland	https://www.estv.admin.ch/estv/de/home/die-estv/estv-ueber-uns/estv-taetigkeitsbericht.html
Thailand	https://rd.go.th/22590.html

Jurisdiction	Links (accessed on 10 September 2024)
Türkiye	https://www.gib.gov.tr/kurumsal/stratejik-yonetim/faaliyet-raporlari
United Kingdom	https://www.gov.uk/government/collections/hmrcs-annual-report-and-accounts

Annex Table 9.A.2. Links to tax administration strategic plans

Jurisdiction	Links (accessed on 10 September 2024)
Belgium	https://finances.belgium.be/fr/sur_le_spf/strat%C3%A9gie/plan_strategique_et_plan_operationnel
Bulgaria	https://nra.bg/wps/portal/nra/za-nap/osnovni-dokumenti/Strategicheski-planove-za-deynostta
Canada	https://www.canada.ca/en/revenue-agency/corporate/about-canada-revenue-agency-cra/summary-corporate-business-plan.html
Colombia	https://www.dian.gov.co/dian/entidad/PlanEvalInstitucional/6-Plan-Estrategico-2023.pdf
Cyprus	https://www.mof.gov.cy/mof/tax/taxdep.nsf/All/463072B158C68A59C2258308001CF6AC
Denmark	https://sktst.dk/om-os/vores-byggesten#strategiske
Estonia	https://www.emta.ee/en/business-client/board-news-and-contact/estonian-tax-and-customs-board/introduction-and-structure
Georgia	https://www.rs.ge/AboutUs-en?cat=1&tab=1
Greece	https://www.aade.gr/aade/epiheirisiaka-shedia-stohothesia/epiheirisiaka-shedia/stratigiko-shedio-aade-2020-2024
Indonesia	https://pajak.go.id/id/sasaran-dan-rencana-strategis-2020-2024-direktorat-jenderal-pajak
Ireland	https://www.revenue.ie/en/corporate/documents/governance/sos-2023-2025.pdf
Italy	https://www.agenziaentrate.gov.it/portale/documents/20143/4461603/PIAO+2022-2024.pdf
Kenya	https://kra.go.ke/images/publications/KRA-8TH-CORPORATE-PLAN-.pdf
Latvia	https://www.vid.gov.lv/en/strategy
Lithuania	https://www.vmi.lt/evmi/en/polaris-2021-2025
Malaysia	https://www.hasil.gov.my/en/about-hasil/corporate-profile/irbm-corporate-plan/
Malta	https://cfr.gov.mt/en/cfr/Documents/MTCA%20Strategic%20Plan%202023_2025.pdf
Netherlands	https://www.rijksoverheid.nl/documenten/jaarplannen/2022/01/31/meerjarenvisie-belastingdienst-2020-2025
New Zealand	https://www.ird.govt.nz/about-us/publications/annual-corporate-reports/statement-of-intent
Norway	https://www.skatteetaten.no/strategi/
Peru	https://www.sunat.gob.pe/cuentassunat/planestrategico/pei.html
Poland	https://www.gov.pl/web/kas/strategia-kas
Portugal	https://info.portaldasfinancas.gov.pt/pt/at/Instrumentos_Gestao/plano_estrategico/Pages/default.aspx
Romania	https://static.anaf.ro/static/33/Anaf/20210316192634_strategia_anaf_2021-2024.pdf
Slovenia	https://www.gov.si/assets/organi-v-sestavi/FURS/Strateski-dokumenti/Strategija-Financne-uprave-RS-2021-2025.pdf
South Africa	https://www.sars.gov.za/about/annual-reports-strategic-plans/
Spain	https://sede.agenciatributaria.gob.es/Sede/planificacion/plan-estrategico-agencia-tributaria-2020-2023/plan-estrategico-agencia-tributaria-2020-2023.html
Sweden	https://www.skatteverket.se/download/18.5b35a6251761e6914208c33/1613125015264/Skatteverkets%20strategiska%20riktning.pdf
Thailand	https://rd.go.th/62801.html
Türkiye	https://www.gib.gov.tr/stratejik_planlar
United Kingdom	https://www.gov.uk/government/publications/tax-administration-strategy
United States	https://www.irs.gov/about-irs/irs-inflation-reduction-act-strategic-operating-plan

Annex Table 9.A.3. Links to tax administration organisational charts

Jurisdiction	Links (accessed on 10 September 2024)
Argentina	https://www.afip.gob.ar/institucional/documentos/Organigrama-hasta-Direccion.pdf
Australia	https://www.ato.gov.au/about-ato/who-we-are/executive-and-governance/organisational-chart

Jurisdiction	Links (accessed on 10 September 2024)
Austria	https://www.bmf.gv.at/en/the-ministry/internal-organisation/Tax-Authority-Austria.html
Belgium	https://financien.belgium.be/en/about_fps/structure_and_services/organogram
Brazil	https://www.gov.br/receitafederal/pt-br/acesso-a-informacao/institucional/estrutura-organizacional
Canada	https://www.canada.ca/en/revenue-agency/corporate/about-canada-revenue-agency-cra/ministerial-transition-2023/organization.html
Chile	https://www.sii.cl/sobre_el_sii/organigrama/organigrama.html
China (People's Republic of)	https://www.chinatax.gov.cn/chinatax/n810209/index.html
Colombia	https://www.dian.gov.co/dian/entidad/Paginas/Organigrama.aspx
Croatia	https://www.porezna-uprava.hr/HR_o_nama/Stranice/organizacija.aspx
Cyprus	https://www.mof.gov.cy/mof/tax/taxdep.nsf/page05_gr/page05_gr?opendocument
Denmark	https://skm.dk/ministeriet/om-skatteministeriet/skatteministeriets-koncern
Estonia	https://www.emta.ee/en/business-client/board-news-and-contact/estonian-tax-and-customs-board/introduction-and-structure
France	https://www.economie.gouv.fr/dgfip/lorganigramme-dgfip
Estonia	https://www.financnisprava.cz/cs/financni-sprava/financni-sprava-cr/organizacni-struktura
Greece	https://www.aade.gr/menoy/aade/organogramma
Hong Kong (China)	https://www.ird.gov.hk/eng/abo/org.htm
Hungary	https://nav.gov.hu/en/about_us/management
Iceland	https://www.skatturinn.is/um-rsk/embaettid/skipurit-rikisskattstjora/nr/251
Indonesia	https://pajak.go.id/index.php/id/struktur-organisasi
Israel	https://www.gov.il/BlobFolder/aboutoffice/about-israel-taxes-authority/he/about_structure-misim-170821.pdf
Italy	https://www.agenziaentrate.gov.it/portale/web/guest/agenzia/chi-siamo/organigramma-centrale
Latvia	https://www.vid.gov.lv/en/structure
Lithuania	https://www.vmi.lt/evmi/en/vmi-prie-fm-struktura
Luxembourg	https://aed.gouvernement.lu/fr/organigramme.html and https://impotsdirects.public.lu/fr/profil/organigramme.html
Malta	https://cfr.gov.mt/en/cfr/Pages/Organigram.aspx
Morocco	https://www.tax.gov.ma/wps/portal/DGI/Nous-connaitre/Notre-organisation/Organigramme-central
Netherlands	https://over-ons.belastingdienst.nl/wp-content/uploads/2023/04/Organogram-Belastingdienst-1-1-2023.pdf
Norway	https://www.skatteetaten.no/om-skatteetaten/om-oss/organisasjon-og-ledelse/organisasjonen/
Peru	https://www.sunat.gob.pe/institucional/quienessomos/igo/dofp/2022/organigrama.pdf
Portugal	https://info.portaldasfinancas.gov.pt/pt/at/Documents/AT_Organograma_sintetico.pdf
Romania	https://www.anaf.ro/anaf/internet/ANAF/despre_anaf/organizare/organigrama
Singapore	https://www.iras.gov.sg/who-we-are/our-organisation/organisation-structure
Slovenia	https://www.gov.si/assets/organigrami/organi-v-sestavi/Organigram-Financni-Urad-RS.pdf
Spain	https://sede.agenciatributaria.gob.es/Sede/gobierno-abierto/transparencia/organigrama.html
Sweden	https://www.skatteverket.se/omoss/organisation.4.7b610ded10741da92fa80001414.html
Switzerland	https://www.estv.admin.ch/estv/en/home/fta/about-us/organigram.html
Thailand	https://rd.go.th/324.html
Türkiye	https://www.gib.gov.tr/kurumsal/organizasyon-semasi
United States	https://www.irs.gov/pub/newsroom/marketing/internet/irs-organization-chart.pdf

10 Budget and workforce

This chapter looks at the resources devoted to tax administrations and provides information on their workforce. It sets out how administrations are responding to new challenges and maintaining their capability while managing a workforce that has to adapt to a changing work environment.

Introduction

Central to a tax administration meeting its role in collecting revenue and providing services to citizens and businesses, is sufficient financial resources and a skilled workforce that can deliver quality outputs efficiently and effectively. This chapter examines the financial resources available to tax administrations, and how they are spent. It also provides information on tax administrations' workforce, and how tax administrations are managing their people.

Budget

Operating expenditures

The overall level of resources devoted to tax administration is an important and topical issue for most governments, external stakeholders, and of course tax administrations themselves. While the budgetary approaches differ, in most jurisdictions the budget allocated is tied to the delivery of performance outputs which are outlined in an annual business plan.

When looking at the budget figures, around 80% of tax administrations report an increase in their operational expenditure between the years 2021 and 2022. This is slightly more administrations reporting an increasing budget than during the previous periods (see Table 10.1.).

Table 10.1. Changes in operating expenditures, 2018-22

Percentage of administrations

Change	From 2018 to 2019	From 2019 to 2020	From 2020 to 2021	From 2021 to 2022
Increase in operating expenditure	75.5	71.7	77.4	80.8
Decrease in operating expenditure	24.5	28.3	22.6	19.2

Note: The table is based on the data from 53 jurisdictions covered in this publication that were able to provide the information for the years 2018 to 2022.
Source: CIAT, IOTA, IMF, OECD, International Survey on Revenue Administration, Table A.16 Tax administration expenditures: Operating and salary expenditure, https://data.rafit.org/regular.aspx?key=74180905 (accessed on 10 September 2024).

However, this data should be treated with caution. While on paper a significant number of administrations saw increases in their budget, this may be a result of added responsibilities that come with additional budget as well as additional funding for investments in technology and new services to respond to taxpayer demands. It also does not take into account increases as a result of inflation, and that a significant part of the budget is needed for salary costs, accounting for on average 72% of operating budgets annually (see also Figure 10.1.). Any increases in budgets can be rapidly consumed by salary increases, which may be a contractual obligation.

Components of tax administration operating expenditure

As stated above, the largest reported component of tax administration operating budgets is staff costs, with salary alone accounting for on average 72% of operating budgets annually, even though there are some differences among jurisdictions (see Figure 10.1.).

Figure 10.1. Salary cost as a percentage of total operating expenditure, 2022

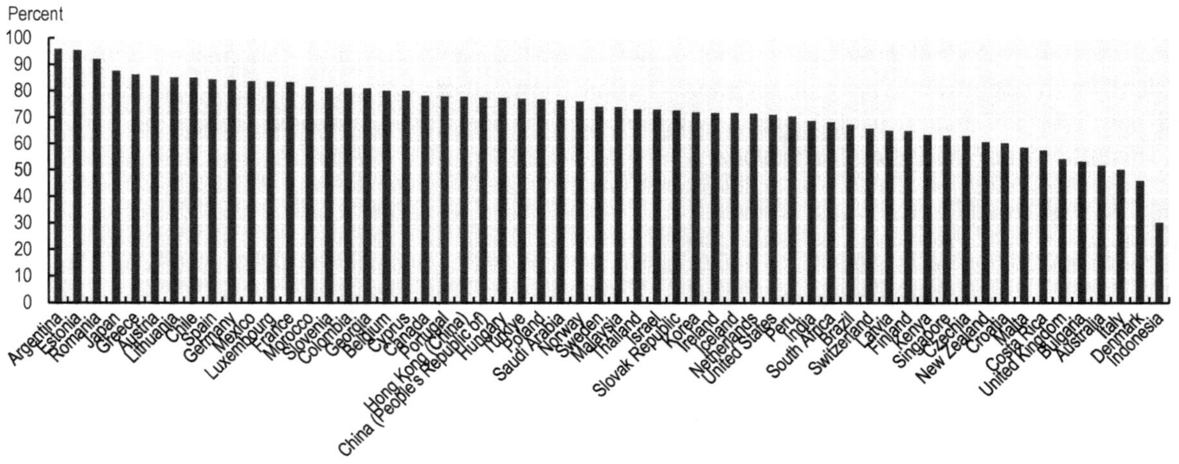

Source: CIAT, IOTA, IMF, OECD, International Survey on Revenue Administration, Table D.6 Resource ratios: Cost, https://data.rafit.org/regular.aspx?key=74180898 (accessed on 10 September 2024)

StatLink https://stat.link/1ar49m

Another important component is the operating cost for information and communication technology (ICT). Given the importance of ICT to tax administration's operating models, they are constantly working on new approaches to ICT development such as the example provided by Australia (see Box 10.1).

Box 10.1. Australia – New approaches in information technology development

The Australian Taxation Office (ATO) has established a Developer Services Branch and is working directly with its internal developer community through a working group to come up with new approaches in information technology (IT) development.

The working group is a small, selected group of developers who represent their areas across IT. This group aims to ensure ATO developers have a say on issues that will impact their work. To date this has seen the group advise on issues such as:

- Process automation through the Automation Strategy
- Test data management
- Modernising standard operating environments
- Developer tooling upgrades

Key outcomes from the group since its formation have been an increased satisfaction and awareness within the developer community of developer services, as well as a strong real time feedback channel with internal development users. This community is now providing peer assistance across business areas for common concerns or queries, strengthening the relationships between delivery groups and increasing the adoption of common guidance and patterns. This guidance is created by subject matter experts as well as end users.

Source: Australia (2024).

On average ICT expenditure accounts for about 11% of operating expenditure. However, reported levels of ICT expenditure vary enormously between administrations. For those administrations able to provide ICT-related cost, around 40% reported an annual operating ICT expenditure exceeding 10% of the administration's total operating expenditure in 2022 and another 30% reported figures between 5% and 10% (see Table D.6).

While some of this variation can be explained by the different sourcing and business approaches, some cannot and point, at least on the surface, to expenditure levels that maybe somewhat below the support needed to provide the rapidly changing electronic and digital services administrations are increasingly being called upon to deliver. In parallel to this, administrations report that they are investing more in their cybersecurity practices, which are needed to protect the integrity of their system and maintain taxpayer trust. Box 10.5. of the 2023 edition of this series highlighted some examples (OECD, 2023[1]).

The averages for both items (salary and ICT) have remained stable over the past years as can be seen in Table 10.2.

Table 10.2. Average salary and ITC cost as percentage of operating expenditure, 2018-22

Percentage of administrations

Cost components	2018	2019	2020	2021	2022
Salary cost as percentage of operating expenditure (56 jurisdictions)	73.2	73.0	73.6	72.9	72.6
ICT operating cost as percentage of operating expenditure (51 jurisdictions)	10.8	11.4	11.3	11.2	11.1

Note: The table is based on the data from jurisdictions covered in this publication that were able to provide the information for the years 2018 to 2022. The number of jurisdictions for which data was available is shown in parentheses.
Source: CIAT, IOTA, IMF, OECD, International Survey on Revenue Administration, Table D.6 Resource ratios: Cost, https://data.rafit.org/regular.aspx?key=74180898 (accessed on 10 September 2024).

Cost of collection

It has become a fairly common practice for tax administrations to compute and publish (for example, in their annual reports) a "cost of collection" ratio as a surrogate measure of their efficiency / effectiveness. The ratio is computed by comparing the annual expenditure of a tax administration, with the net revenue collected over the course of a fiscal year. Given the many similarities in the taxes administered by tax administrations, there has been a natural tendency by observers to make comparisons of "cost of collection" ratios across jurisdictions. Such comparisons have to be treated with a high degree of caution, for reasons explained in Box 10.2.

In practice there are a number of factors that may influence the cost/revenue relationship, but which have nothing to do with relative efficiency or effectiveness. Examples of such factors and variables include macroeconomic changes as well as differences in revenue types administered. These factors are further elaborated in Box 10.2.

Despite those factors, the "cost of collection" ratio is included in this report for two reasons:

1. The "cost of collection" ratio is useful for administrations to track as a domestic measure as it allows them to see the trend over time of their work to collect revenue and, as pointed out in Box 10.2., they may be able to account for the main factors that can influence the ratio; and
2. The inclusion of the "cost of collection" ratio and the accompanying comments set out in Box 10.2. can serve as a prominent reminder to stakeholders of the difficulties and challenges in using the easily calculated "cost of collection" ratio for international comparison.

Table 10.3. illustrates the change in the "cost of collection" ratios between 2018 and 2022 for the administrations included in this report. It shows that around three-quarters of the administrations had decreasing ratios between 2021 and 2022, which is very similar to the previous period. This is in contrast to the approximately 80% of administrations which had increasing ratios over the period 2019 to 2020, most likely a result of declining revenue collections during the COVID-19 pandemic.

Table 10.3. Changes in "cost of collection" ratios, 2018-22

Percentage of administrations

Change	From 2018 to 2019	From 2019 to 2020	From 2020 to 2021	From 2021 to 2022
Increase in cost of collection	43.4	83.0	22.6	24.5
Decrease in cost of collection	56.6	17.0	77.4	75.5

Note: The table is based on the data from 53 jurisdictions covered in this publication that were able to provide the information for the years 2018 to 2022.
Source: CIAT, IOTA, IMF, OECD, International Survey on Revenue Administration, Table D.6 Resource ratios: Cost, https://data.rafit.org/regular.aspx?key=74180898 (accessed on 10 September 2024).

Figure 10.2. looks at the movement in the "cost of collection" ratios over the five-year period from 2018 to 2022 from a jurisdiction-level perspective. However, as mentioned in Box 10.2., the chart and the underlying figures have to be interpreted with great care.

Figure 10.2. Movement in "cost of collection" ratios between 2018 and 2022

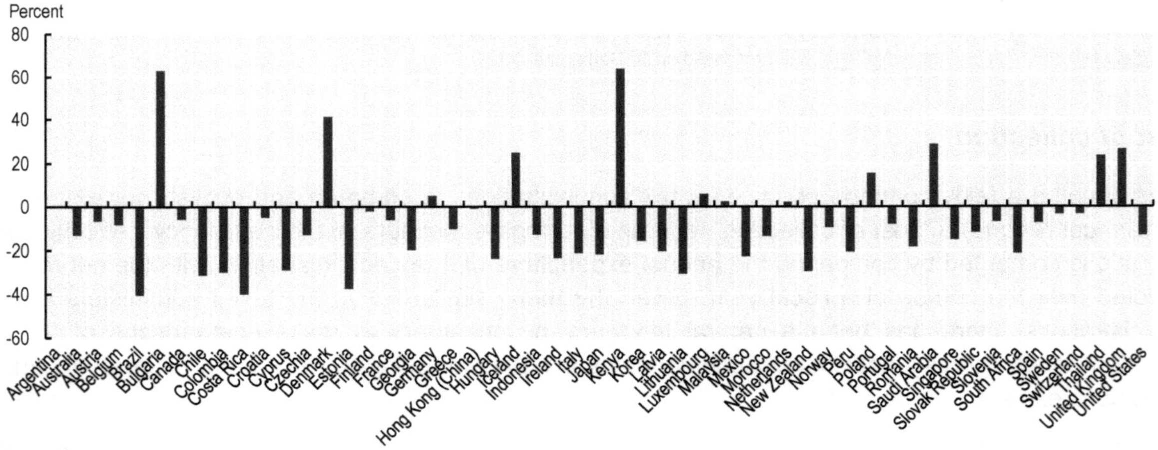

Note: When interpreting this chart the factors mentioned in Box 10.2. should be taken into account. Data for India, Israel and Türkiye have been excluded, see notes in Table A.16 Tax administration expenditures: Operating and salary expenditure.
Source: CIAT, IOTA, IMF, OECD, International Survey on Revenue Administration, Table D.6 Resource ratios: Cost, https://data.rafit.org/regular.aspx?key=74180898 (accessed on 10 September 2024).

StatLink https://stat.link/udzneb

Box 10.2. Difficulties and challenges in using the "cost of collection" ratio as an indicator of efficiency and/or effectiveness

Observed over time, a downward trend in the "cost of collection" ratio can appear to constitute evidence of a reduction in relative costs (i.e. improved efficiency) and/or improved tax compliance (i.e. improved effectiveness). However, experience has also shown that there are many factors that can influence the ratio which are **not** related to changes in a tax administrations' efficiency and/or effectiveness and which render this statistic highly unreliable in the international context:

- **Changes in tax policy**: Tax policy changes are an important factor in determining the cost/revenue relationship. In theory, a policy decision to increase the overall tax burden should, all other things being equal, improve the ratio by a corresponding amount, but this has nothing to do with improved operational efficiency or effectiveness.
- **Macroeconomic changes**: Significant changes in rates of economic growth etc. or inflation over time are likely to impact on the overall revenue collected by the tax administration and the cost/revenue relationship.
- **Abnormal expenditure of the tax administration**: From time to time, a tax administration may be required to undertake an abnormal level of investment (for example, the building of a new information technology infrastructure or the acquisition of more expensive new accommodation). Such investments are likely to increase overall operating costs over the medium term, and short of offsetting efficiencies which may take longer to realise, will impact on the cost/ revenue relationship.
- **Changes in the scope of revenues collected**: From time to time, governments decide to shift responsibility for the collection of particular revenues from one agency to another which may impact the cost/revenue relationship.

From a fully domestic perspective, an administration may be able to account for those factors by making corresponding adjustments to its cost or collected revenue. This can make tracking the "cost of collection" ratio a helpful measure to see the trend over time of the administration's work to collect revenue. If it were gathered by tax type, it may also help inform policy choices around how particular taxes may be administered and collected.

However, its usefulness with respect to international comparison is very limited. While administrations may be able to account for the above factors from a domestic perspective, it will be difficult to do this at an international level as such analysis would have to consider:

- **Differences in tax rates and structure**: Rates of tax and the actual structure of taxes will all have a bearing on aggregate revenue and, to a lesser extent, cost considerations. For example, comparisons of the ratio involving high-tax jurisdictions and low-tax jurisdictions are hardly realistic given their widely varying tax burdens.
- **Differences in the range and nature of revenues administered**: There are a number of differences that can arise here. In some jurisdictions, more than one major tax authority may operate at the national level, or taxes at the federal level may be predominantly of a direct tax nature, while indirect taxes may be administered largely by separate regional/state authorities. In other jurisdictions, one national authority will collect taxes for all levels of government, i.e. federal, regional and local governments. Similar issues arise in relation to the collection of social insurance contributions.
- **Differences in the range of functions undertaken**: The range of functions undertaken by tax administrations can vary from jurisdiction to jurisdiction. For example, in some jurisdictions the

tax administration is also responsible for carrying out activities not directly related to tax administration (for example, the administration of certain welfare benefits or national population registers), while in others some tax-related functions are not carried out by the tax administration (for example, the enforcement of debt collections). Further, differences in societal views may influence what an administration does, how it can operate and what services is has to offer. The latter may have a particularly significant impact on the cost/revenue relationship.

Finally, it should be pointed out that the "cost of collection" ratio ignores the revenue potential of a tax system, i.e. the difference between the amount of tax actually collected and the maximum potential revenue. This is particularly relevant in the context of international comparisons – administrations with similar cost/revenue ratios can be some distance apart in terms of their relative effectiveness.

Workforce

In 2022, the administrations included in this report employed approximately 1.7 million staff (see Table A.18) making the effective and efficient management of the workforce critical to good tax administration. Having a competent, professional, productive and adaptable workforce is at the heart of most administrations' human resource planning. With salary costs averaging more than 70% of operating expenditures, any significant budget change invariably impacts staff numbers. The "double pressure" created from budgetary constraints and technology change, mentioned in the 2017 edition (OECD, 2017[2]) (see also Figure 10.3.), continues to be a significant management issue for most administrations. The challenge is compounded for some administrations which, due to contract restrictions or government mandates, may find it difficult to strategically down-size their operations other than through the non-replacement of staff who leave of their own accord.

Figure 10.3. Double pressure on the workforce

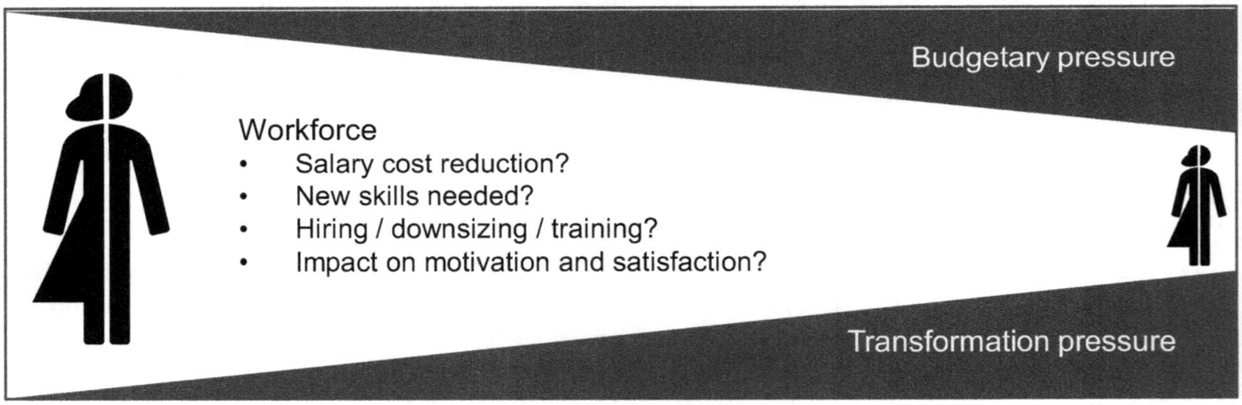

Staff usage by function

Figure 10.4. provides average allocation of staff resources (expressed in full-time equivalents) across seven functional groupings used to categorise tax administration operations. It should be noted that for the ISORA 2023 survey, the functional groupings were revised splitting the category "All other functions" into four: (i) Dispute management; (ii) Human resource management; (iii) Information and communication technology support; and (iv) All other functions. This allows obtaining a better picture of staff usage by tax administrations.

Figure 10.4. Staff usage by function, 2022

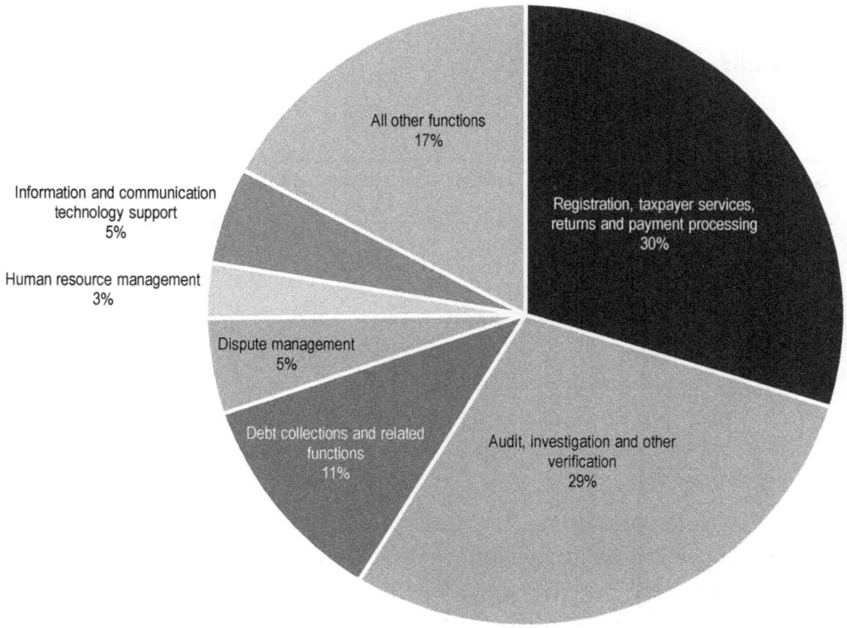

Note: Excluding administrations that were unable to provide the break-down for all functions.
Source: CIAT, IOTA, IMF, OECD, International Survey on Revenue Administration, Tables D.7 Staff allocation by location and function: Registration, services, processing, and audit and verification, D.8 Staff allocation by function: Debt collection, dispute management, and HR management, and D.9 Staff allocation by function: ICT support and all other functions, https://data.rafit.org/regular.aspx?key=74180899 (accessed on 10 September 2024).

StatLink https://stat.link/nz8wek

While the detailed data for each administration in Tables D.7. to D.9. shows a significant spread of values and a number of outliers for each function, on average the "Audit, investigation and other verification" function and the "Registration, services, returns and payment processing" function are equally resource intensive, each employing on average 30% of staff. Both ratios, as well as the ratio for "Debt collection and related functions" have remained stable over recent years.

With advancements in technology, an ever-increasing availability of data, and constantly changing taxpayer expectations as regards service offerings, tax administrations are enhancing their information and communication technology as well as analytics capabilities. They employ increasing numbers of people with specialist skills or, where those positions do not exist in-house, contract them from outside.

ISORA 2023 looked at three of those skills and asked administrations to indicate whether they employ or contract people with behavioural science skills, user interface design skills, and/ or data science skills. Table 10.4. summarises the results and shows that:

- Around half of the administrations use behavioural insights skills, either in-house, contracted as needed, or both in-house and contracted. How behavioural insights can help tax administrations is described in Chapter 6 and has also been explored in the 2021 OECD publication *Behavioural Insights for Better Tax Administration: A Brief Guide* (OECD, 2021[3])
- User interface design is another specialist skill that has become more and more important. User interface design is the process of designing the interface between software solutions and humans, with the goal of ensuring that the software is easy to use. Its importance can be seen by more than 70% of administrations employing and/ or contracting people with this skill.

- Data scientists are employed and/or contracted by close to 80% of administrations. With the increasing amounts of data available to and manged by tax administrations this is not surprising.

Table 10.4. Use of specialist skills, 2022

Percentage of administrations

Type of specialist skill	Specialist position exist **in-house only**	Specialist skills are **contracted only** as needed	Specialist positions **in-house and** skills **contracted** as needed
Behavioural science	25.9	3.4	19.0
User interface design	19.0	6.9	46.6
Data science	41.4	1.7	34.5

Source: CIAT, IOTA, IMF, OECD, International Survey on Revenue Administration, Table B.15 Specialist skills, https://data.rafit.org/regular.aspx?key=74180914 (accessed on 10 September 2024).

Staff metrics

The ISORA survey also gathers key data concerning the age profiles, length of service, gender distribution and educational qualifications of tax administration staff: see Tables D.10. to D.16. and A.22. to A.33. While interpreting this data it should be noted that combined tax and customs administrations were allowed to use their total workforce for answering the underlying survey questions as it may be difficult for them to separate the characteristics of the tax and customs workforce.

Age profiles

While there are significant variations between the age profiles of tax administration staff (see Tables D.12. and D.13.), it is interesting to see that there are also differences when viewed across different regional groupings. This may be the result of a complex mix of cultural, economic, and sociological factors (for example, economic maturity, recruitment, remuneration, and retirement policies).

Figure 10.5. illustrates that staff are generally younger in administrations in the regional groupings of "Asia-Pacific" and "Middle East and Africa" where, on average, around 30% of staff are below 35 years of age, whereas in the "Americas" and "Europe" this percentage drops to below 20%. At the same time, administrations in the "Americas" and "Europe" have a large percentage of staff older than 54 years.

Figure 10.5. Age profiles of tax administration staff, 2022

Percentage of staff by age bands for selected regional groupings

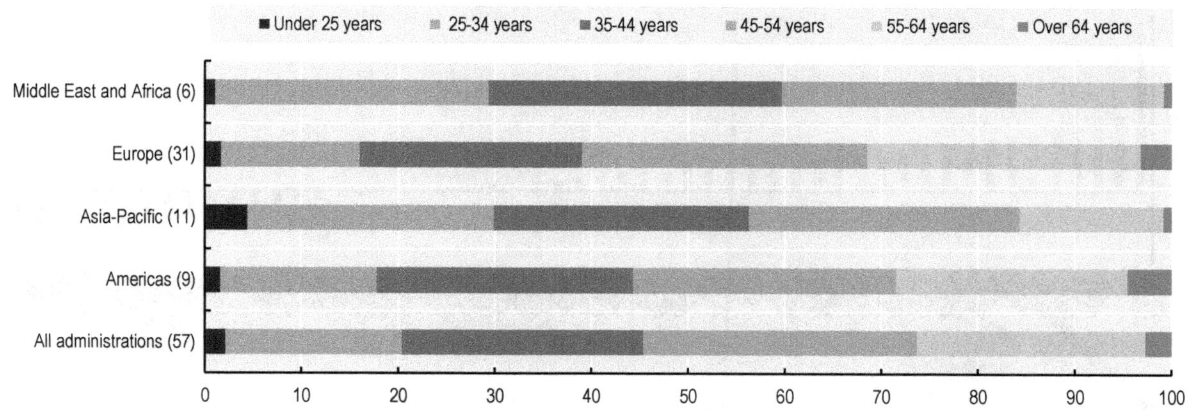

	All administrations (57)	Americas (9)	Asia-Pacific (11)	Europe (31)	Middle East and Africa (6)
■	2.1	1.6	4.5	1.7	1.1
■	18.2	16.2	25.5	14.3	28.3
■	25.0	26.5	26.4	23.1	30.3
■	28.3	27.3	28.0	29.5	24.3
■	23.6	23.9	14.9	28.2	15.2
■	2.7	4.5	0.8	3.2	0.8

Percent

Note: The following administrations are included in the regional groupings: Americas (9) – Argentina, Brazil, Canada, Chile, Colombia, Costa Rica, Mexico, Peru and the United States; Asia-Pacific (11) – Australia, China (People's Republic of), Hong Kong (China), India, Indonesia, Japan, Korea, Malaysia, New Zealand, Singapore and Thailand; Europe (31) – Austria, Belgium, Bulgaria, Croatia, Cyprus, Czechia, Denmark, Estonia, Finland, France, Georgia, Germany, Greece, Hungary, Iceland, Ireland, Italy, Latvia, Lithuania, Luxembourg, Malta, the Netherlands, Norway, Poland, Portugal, the Slovak Republic, Slovenia, Spain, Sweden, Switzerland and the United Kingdom; Middle East and Africa (6): Israel, Kenya, Morocco, Saudi Arabia, South Africa and Türkiye.

Source: CIAT, IOTA, IMF, OECD, International Survey on Revenue Administration, Tables D.12 Staff age distribution: Staff below 45 years and D.13 Staff age distribution: Staff 45 years and above, https://data.rafit.org/regular.aspx?key=74180899 (accessed on 10 September 2024).

StatLink https://stat.link/dk04f3

Looking at the jurisdiction specific data, the percentage of staff older than 54 years grew in two-thirds of administrations over the five-year period from 2018 to 2022 (see Figure 10.6).

Figure 10.6. Staff older than 54 years: Movement between 2018 and 2022

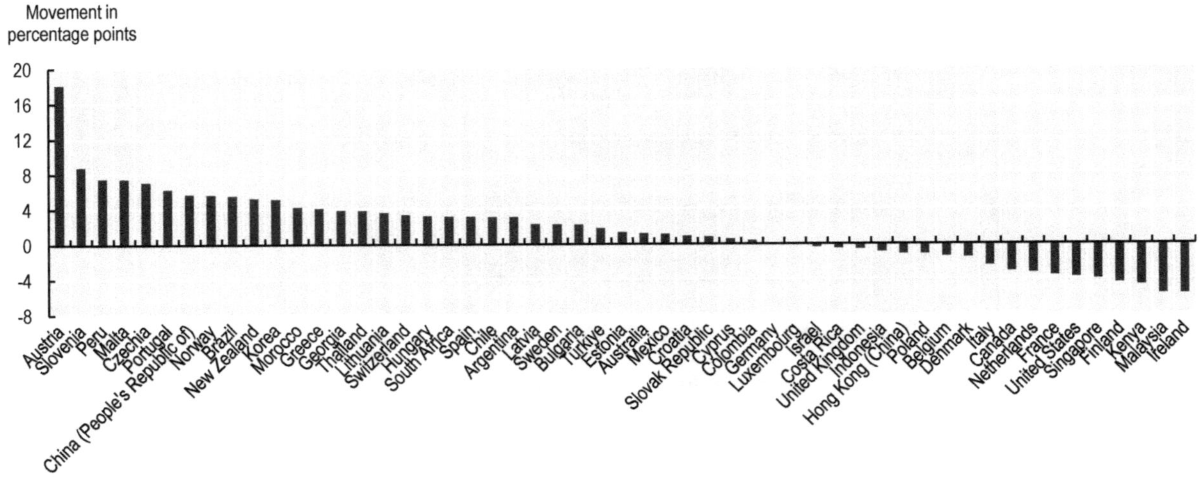

Note: Only includes jurisdictions for which data was available for both years. Data for Iceland and Saudi Arabia has been excluded due to the mergers of the tax administration with the customs administration.
Source: CIAT, IOTA, IMF, OECD, International Survey on Revenue Administration, Table D.13 Staff age distribution: Staff 45 years and above, https://data.rafit.org/regular.aspx?key=74180899 (accessed on 10 September 2024).

StatLink https://stat.link/p6d9s4

Figure 10.7. Average length of service vs. average age profile, 2022

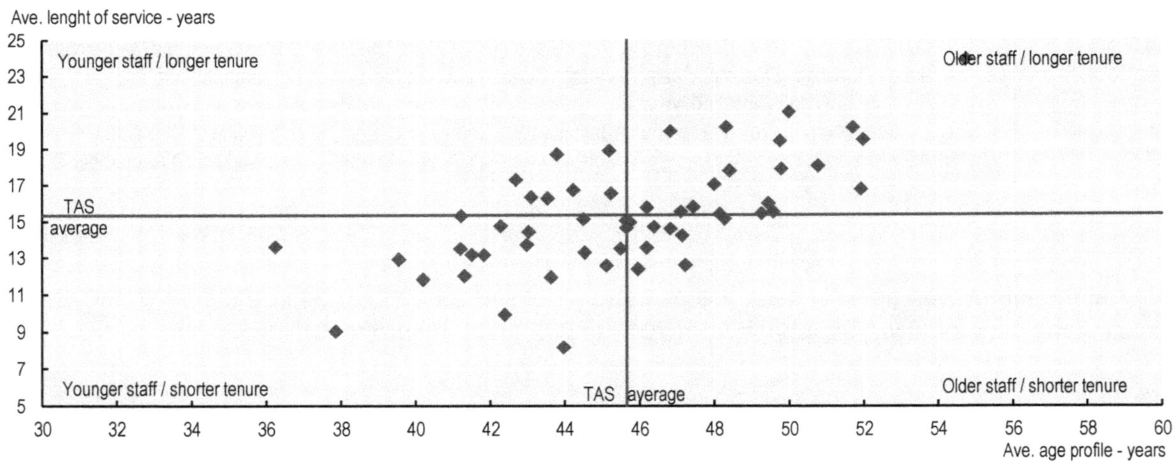

Source: OECD Secretariat calculations based on CIAT, IOTA, IMF, OECD, International Survey on Revenue Administration, Tables D.12 Staff age distribution: Staff below 45 years, D.13 Staff age distribution: Staff 45 years and above, D.14 Length of service: Less than 10 years, and D.15 Length of service: 10 years or more, https://data.rafit.org/regular.aspx?key=74180899 (accessed on 10 September 2024).

StatLink https://stat.link/lawmp6

Length of service

The difference in age profiles is also largely reflected in the length of service of tax administration staff. Figure 10.7. indicates that a significant number of administrations will not only face a large number of staff retiring over the next years, but that many of these staff will be very experienced, thus raising issues about retention of key knowledge and experience.

Gender distribution

In light of the strong public interest in gender equality, administrations were invited to report total staff and executive staff respectively by gender. As can be seen in Figure 10.8., while many administrations are close to the proportional line, typically female staff remains proportionally underrepresented in executive positions and significantly underrepresented in a number of administrations, something that has remained unchanged since the 2017 edition of this report (OECD, 2017[2]).

Figure 10.8. Percentage of female staff – total female staff vs. female executives, 2022

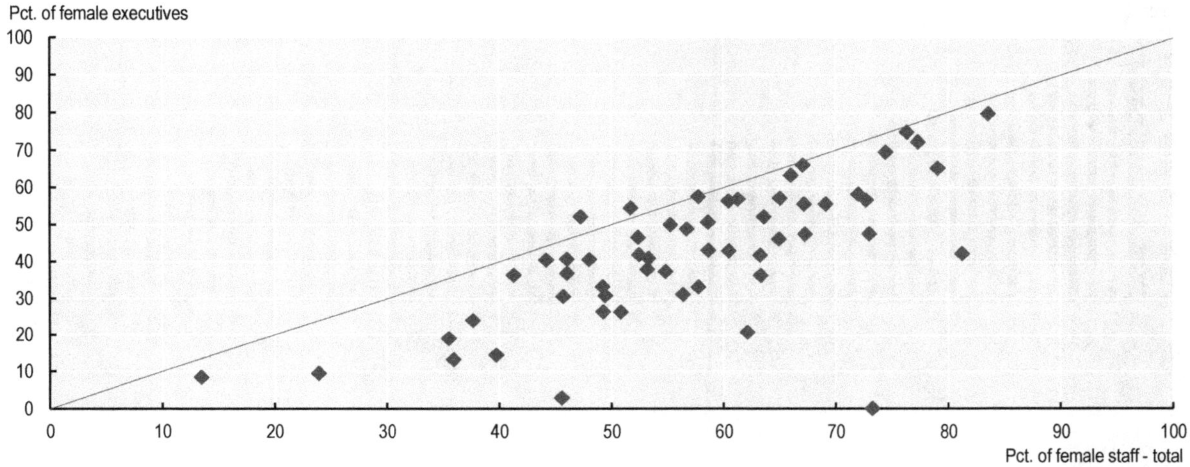

Source: CIAT, IOTA, IMF, OECD, International Survey on Revenue Administration, Table D.16 Gender distribution, https://data.rafit.org/regular.aspx?key=74180899 (accessed on 10 September 2024).

StatLink https://stat.link/uhxcrm

Looking at the overall averages, whilst there are variations between jurisdictions (see Table D.16.), on average the share of female employees of total staff and executive staff has remained largely unchanged over the five-year period from 2018 to 2022, with a small increase of around 7% of female executives (see Table 10.5.). The jurisdiction-level data shows that in about two-thirds of administrations the percentage of female executives has increased since 2018 (see Table D.16.).

Table 10.5. Average share of female staff and female executives (in percent), 2018-22

Staff category	2018	2019	2020	2021	2022	Change between 2018 and 2022 in percent
Female staff (55 jurisdictions)	56.8	57.4	57.3	57.4	57.6	+1.4
Female executives (54 jurisdictions)	39.9	41.6	41.2	42.4	42.9	+7.4

Note: The table shows the share of female employees of total staff and executive staff for the jurisdictions covered in this publication that were able to provide the information for the years 2018 to 2022. The number of jurisdictions for which data was available is shown in parentheses.
Source: CIAT, IOTA, IMF, OECD, International Survey on Revenue Administration, Table D.16 Gender distribution, https://data.rafit.org/regular.aspx?key=74180899 (accessed on 10 September 2024).

The ISORA survey also asked administrations to indicate whether staff has self-identified as neither female nor male (referred to as "other" gender for the purposes of the survey). Seven administrations report capturing information on "other" gender and two administrations, Australia and New Zealand, reported having staff who self-identified as "other," in the case of Australia also at executive level (see Tables A.24. and A.27.).

To understand how the gender distribution might develop in the future, the ISORA 2023 survey asked tax administrations for the first time to report the percentage of recruits who are female. As can be seen in Figure 10.9., in the vast majority of administrations covered in this publication, females make up more than half of all staff that joined the administration during the fiscal year.

Figure 10.9. Percentage of female recruits, 2022

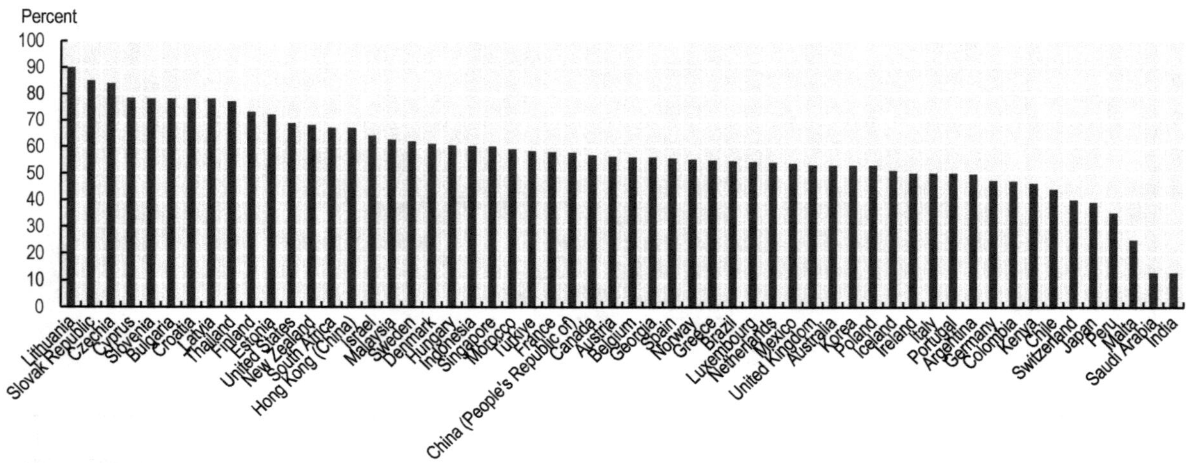

Source: CIAT, IOTA, IMF, OECD, International Survey on Revenue Administration, Table D.16 Gender distribution, https://data.rafit.org/regular.aspx?key=74180899 (accessed on 10 September 2024).

StatLink https://stat.link/okms17

Staff attrition

Staff attrition, also called staff turnover, refers to the rate at which employees leave an organisation during a defined period (normally a year). High attrition rates may result from a variety of factors, such as downsizing policies, demographics or changing staff preferences. The attrition rate should be considered together with other measures, such as the hire rate, which looks at the number of staff recruited during a defined period, when evaluating the human resource trends of an administration.

While a high attrition rate combined with a low hire rate is usually associated with a general downsizing policy, administrations should perhaps be concerned where both rates are high. Recruitment is costly, not only the recruitment process itself but also the cost and time for training and supporting new staff members.

Having attrition rates that are too low may also not be ideal. While an organisation is growing, a low attrition rate may be desirable. However, in situations where both the attrition rate and the hire rate are low, an organisation may not have the ability to recruit new skills as all positions are filled. This could be an issue particularly for administrations that are undergoing transformation and are therefore in need of staff with skills that are different from what is currently available within the administration.

While what is considered a "healthy" attrition rate differs between industry sectors or jurisdictions, the average attrition and hire rates for administrations participating in this publication of around 7% in 2022 would seem to present a reasonable range for tax administrations of between 5% and 10%. It is worth noting that the average attrition and hire rates for 2022 are now back to pre-pandemic levels, even slightly above. (See Table 10.6.)

Table 10.6. Average attrition and hire rates (in percent), 2018-22

Rates	2018	2019	2020	2021	2022	Change between 2018 and 2022 in percent
Attrition rate (49 jurisdictions)	6.6	7.1	6.0	6.8	7.4	+12.8
Hire rate (49 jurisdictions)	6.8	7.1	5.9	6.0	7.4	+8.4

Note: The table shows the average attrition and hire rates for the jurisdictions covered in this publication that were able to provide the information for the years 2018 to 2022. The number of jurisdictions for which data was available is shown in parenthesis. Data for China (People's Republic of), Iceland, Norway and Saudi Arabia was excluded from the calculation as the result of extraordinary staff transfers over the period 2018 to 2021 which were recorded as recruitments, thus distorting their averages for those years (see notes in Table A.23).
Source: CIAT, IOTA, IMF, OECD, International Survey on Revenue Administration, Table D.10 Staff dynamics, https://data.rafit.org/regular.aspx?key=74180899 (accessed on 10 September 2024).

However, when looking at specific administration data, it becomes apparent that "attrition and hire" rates cover a very broad range. Figure 10.10. shows the relationship between tax administration attrition and hire rates. It illustrates that there are a number of administrations with attrition and hire rates well above 10% (upper-right box), while others show very low attrition and hire rates (lower-left box).

Figure 10.10. Attrition and hire rates, 2022

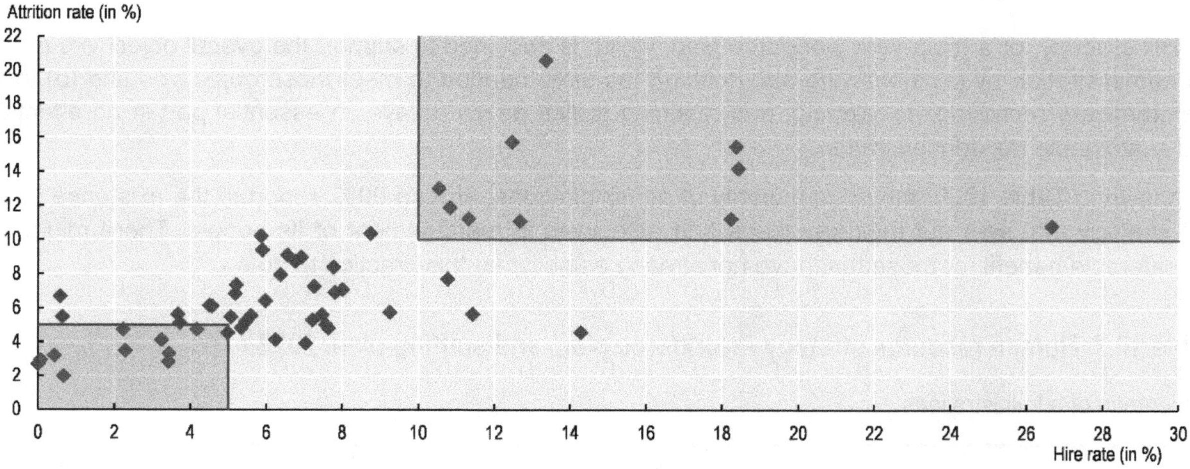

Note: Attrition rate = number of staff departures/average staffing level. Hire rate = number of staff recruitments/ average staffing level. The average staffing level equals opening staff numbers + end-of-year staff numbers/2.
Source: CIAT, IOTA, IMF, OECD, International Survey on Revenue Administration, Table D.10 Staff dynamics, https://data.rafit.org/regular.aspx?key=74180899 (accessed on 10 September 2024).

StatLink https://stat.link/ex1hoq

People management

Effective people management in tax administration involves comprehensive recruitment, training, and retention strategies. By investing in continuous professional development, tax administrations can keep their staff informed of the latest laws, technologies, and working practices and methods. Moreover, a focus on employee well-being and engagement can lead to higher job satisfaction, lower attrition rates, and a more dedicated workforce. This can help in cultivating a positive organisational culture that values integrity, accountability, and excellence, which are crucial for a well-functioning tax system. Administrations invest in this and around 3% of staff are engaged with human resource (HR) management (see Figure 10.4.).

To better understand tax administrations approaches towards people management, the ISORA 2023 survey gathered a significant amount of data points which are summarised below in four categories: (i) talent recruitment and retention, (ii) learning and development, (iii) staff motivation and performance, and (iv) diversity management.

Talent recruitment and retention

Recruiting and keeping talent are important factors for the long-term success of a tax administration. This includes identifying the needs for future talent and having a strategic approach towards managing the workforce. This section is looking at four areas that contribute to having a successful talent recruitment and retention approach:

- The availability of an HR strategy or multi-year workforce plan,
- The existence of a staffing plan,
- The assessment of capability needs within the administration, and
- The administration's autonomy in human resource management.

Human resource strategy / workforce plan

An HR strategy, or a multi-year workforce plan, which is designed to support the overall objectives of the tax administration by (a) identifying and defining the skills needed to meet those objectives and (b) then systematically recruiting, developing, and retaining skilled people, plays an essential part in an effective and sustainable tax administration.

As shown in Table 10.7., the large majority of administrations, around 90%, reported the existence of an HR strategy that sets out their key plans and objectives in management of its people. There might be considerable benefit for those that have not already established this practice to do so.

Table 10.7. Human resource strategy / workforce plan, and staffing plan, 2022

Percentage of administrations

Strategy / multi-year workforce plan included in the HR management approach	If yes,				Staffing plan included in the HR management approach	If yes,
	Strategy / multi-year workforce plan is competency based	Job competency dictionary is in place	Job catalogue is in place	Job descriptions exist		Recruitment plan exists
87.9	78.4	74.5	84.3	90.2	82.8	93.8

Source: CIAT, IOTA, IMF, OECD, International Survey on Revenue Administration, Tables B.10 HR management approach: Strategy / multi-year work force plan and training strategy, and B.11 HR management approach: Support for new staff and staffing plan, https://data.rafit.org/regular.aspx?key=74180914 (accessed on 10 September 2024).

For those that have an HR strategy, around 80% indicated that they take a competency-based approached, where the competencies and performance criteria are described for each position, and around three-quarters of administrations reported that they have a job competency dictionary. In addition, close to 85% reported having a job catalogue in place, while 90% of administrations indicated that there are job descriptions for the various positions. (See Table 10.7.)

Staffing plan

A workforce plan or strategy is essential to define the longer-term approach for recruiting, developing and retaining people and to ensure that the right skills are available at the right time. Contrary to this, a staffing plan will focus on the short-term needs of the administration and will help understand the immediate personnel requirements, including the number and types of staff required.

As can be seen in Table 10.7., around 80% of administrations reported having a staffing plan, and almost all of those have also put in place a recruitment plan.

Assessment of capability needs

The changes tax administrations are managing at present, whether technological, international, policy or budget driven, are significant. Tax administrations will have to adapt to the culture and services expected by taxpayers, particularly the next generation of taxpayers. To assist in the HR short-term and long-term planning process, around three-quarters of tax administrations covered in this publication reported assessing the current and future capability needs (see Table 10.8.).

Utilizing the power of data, close to 90% of administrations that assess capability needs reported the use of data analysis as part of the evaluation process and all of them review the evaluation on a regular basis. Illustrating the strong linkages between the capability needs assessment and workforce planning, 86% reported that the evaluation outcomes are reflected in the HR strategy. Moreover, around 80% indicted having a formal plan to address gaps in staff capability (see Table 10.8.).

Table 10.8. Human resource strategy / workforce plan, and staffing plan, 2022

Percentage of administrations

Current and future capability needs are assessed	If yes,			
	Evaluation process uses data analysis	Evaluation is reviewed on a regular basis	HR strategy reflects evaluation outcomes	Formal plan to address gaps in staff capability exists
72.4	88.1	100.0	85.7	83.3

Source: CIAT, IOTA, IMF, OECD, International Survey on Revenue Administration, Table B.14 Capability needs assessment, https://data.rafit.org/regular.aspx?key=74180914 (accessed on 10 September 2024).

Box 10.3. Examples – Recruitment processes

China (People's Republic of) – Intelligent management of employee information

To aid in the selection and recruitment of employees across different departments and roles, the State Tax Administration (STA) has conducted in depth comparative analysis of employee data to build an accurate profile of each employee:

- Integrated analysis through collecting employee data from numerous sources: By collecting tax officials' data recorded in government affairs, business systems and other relevant systems a "live profile" is built for each tax official which can be analysed and compared with the profiles of other officials.

- Real-time employment updates: The recruitment of new employees and change in role or promotion of current employees is updated on the online management system, allowing for the real-time monitoring and analysis of personnel. This allows for planning and helps to ensure all areas are adequately resourced.
- Intelligent Management Network: Through building an "intelligent management network" that connects the five levels of the national tax system, the structure of all the different teams of officials is presented in a panoramic manner. This allows for the comparison and analysis of human resource allocation and personnel performance across the whole tax administration, aiding in any decision-making on resource management.

France – Recruitment Campaign

The Directorate General of Public Finances (DGFiP) has launched a major digital communications campaign aimed at making its jobs more attractive to prospective employees. The campaign includes the creation of a new website dedicated to recruitment highlighting the wealth of jobs and career paths within DGFiP, and the roll-out of a new advertising campaign.

By clearly communicating its values and culture through online channels (social networks and its website), DGFiP is attracting the interest of a wider range of potential candidates. To do this, it shares inspiring stories of its managers, social and environmental initiatives, and significant events, in order to show the human side of DGFiP. The campaign uses video testimonials to capture attention and showcase to candidates the diversity of jobs available, career opportunities and the various benefits.

Employees and managers of DGFiP are actively involved in the strategy by promoting DGFiP and their day-to-day work in various ways. For example, the local directorates consolidate the image of public finances by taking part in major local student fairs and relaying campaigns to partner administrations.

Sources: China (People's Republic of) (2024) and France (2024).

Autonomy in human resource management

As set-out in Chapter 9 on governance arrangements, tax administrations can benefit from a high degree of autonomy in relation to recruitment, development and remuneration to ensure the effective and efficient operation of the tax system. As can be seen in Table 10.9., the vast majority of administrations report having autonomy in HR related matters. However, a look at the data by jurisdiction does show that a small number of administrations only have autonomy in some areas. Moreover, even where tax administrations have autonomy, there are often regulatory or budgetary constraints that may inhibit the effective use of these powers.

While the degree of autonomy remains largely consistent across the different areas, there is one notable exception, namely the "Placement of staff within a salary range" which, with 64%, is significantly below the ratings of other HR powers administrations typically have. This may be a particular concern in the areas of information and communication technologies, data science, cyber security, and other positions where tax administrations compete with private sector entities for skilled people.

Table 10.9. Autonomy in human resource management, 2022

Percentage of administrations

Administration has the authority to ...							
Determine work requirements	Make appointments of new staff	Decide on promotion of existing staff	Decide skills and qualifications required for appointment or promotion	Determine whether work is carried out by permanent staff or contractually	Place staff within a salary range	Terminate employment	Apply disciplinary sanctions
98.3	91.4	89.7	93.1	87.9	63.8	86.2	96.6

Source: CIAT, IOTA, IMF, OECD, International Survey on Revenue Administration, Table B.7 Human resource authority, https://data.rafit.org/regular.aspx?key=74180914 (accessed on 10 September 2024).

Learning and development

The changes that digitalisation and the digital transformation of tax administrations bring to the operating models of tax administrations means that not only will new staff need to be hired, but the skills of existing staff may need to be developed. A key issue in this respect is how to transition and support staff through this change. At the same time, administrations need to remain conscious of the large number of staff retiring over the next few years (see in the sub-section on "Staff metrics") and how to transfer their knowledge and experience to new employees.

Training strategy

As shown in Table 10.10., tax administrations have recognised the importance of preparing existing staff for this transition and more than 90% have developed training strategies that allow existing staff to upgrade their skills. The need to increase capability internally is particularly important where employment conditions, contractual requirements, and remuneration levels, make it difficult to hire skilled staff, particularly, when competing with the private sector for skills.

Of those administrations that have training strategies, almost 90% have put in place a formal training cycle process, and more than 95% have a specific training plan which is important when investing in new capabilities to support the ability to implement change more rapidly and to support the development and adoption of new services and products, particularly involving digital technology.

Box 10.4. Türkiye – Workshop on the application of behavioural approaches in voluntary tax compliance

Türkiye has provided training to colleagues working in behavioural approach teams through in-person workshops. Behavioural approaches are getting increased attention by tax administrations as an area of interest to improve compliance levels. This training aims to provide a forum where views can be exchanged on the best way to deliver a consistent high quality customer service.

The first workshop was held in December 2023 in Ankara and brought together 141 people from the central and provincial behavioural approach units, to develop evidence based and taxpayer focused policies. Taxpayer decisions and the factors affecting these decisions were examined, to work out how to achieve higher levels of voluntary tax compliance. Staff were also briefed on other behavioural public policy units established in different jurisdictions. This was concluded with communication and diction training, to aid officials in communicating effectively with taxpayers.

Source: Türkiye (2024).

Table 10.10. Training strategy, 2022

Percentage of administrations

Training strategy included in HR management approach	If yes,	
	Formal training cycle process exists	Specific training plan exists
91.4	88.7	96.2

Source: CIAT, IOTA, IMF, OECD, International Survey on Revenue Administration, Table B.10 HR management approach: Strategy / multi-year work force plan and training strategy, https://data.rafit.org/regular.aspx?key=74180914 (accessed on 10 September 2024).

Supporting new staff

Supporting new staff when they join the administration is important for ensuring a smooth integration, so that they are quickly operational and can perform at the highest level. Induction programmes and mentoring initiatives provide newcomers with the essential knowledge, skills, and cultural understanding needed to navigate their new environment effectively. It can also have a positive impact on the long-term motivation of new staff.

As illustrated in Table 10.11., more than 90% of tax administrations covered in this publication have programmes in place to support new staff, with almost all of those running formal induction programmes. At the same time, only around two-thirds of the administrations have introduced formal mentoring programmes for new staff. This could be a missed opportunity, particularly in a remote working environment where new staff might not directly feel part of the wider organisation. Here, remote mentoring programmes might contribute to lower attrition rates, quicker skill development, and an increased engagement.

Leadership development and succession planning

Leadership development and succession planning are important for continuity and stability within tax administration. It ensures there are always viable candidates within the administration who can quickly take over when required, increasing the resilience of the tax administration. It also aids in the vital transfer of knowledge between successors, and provides leadership certainty to staff.

Around three-quarters of administrations have leadership and talent management programmes. As regards knowledge transfer, around 75% have a personalised knowledge transfer approach, i.e. where knowledge is transferred from one tax official to another on a one-to-one basis, and around 90% operate a system where knowledge transfer is documented, i.e. the knowledge is converted into products, such as documents or videos, that can be consumed by many. (See Table 10.11.)

Table 10.11. Supporting new staff, and leadership development and succession planning, 2022

Percentage of administrations

Program to support new staff included in HR management approach	If yes,		Leadership development and succession planning		
	Formal induction program for new staff exists	Formal mentoring program for new staff exists	Leadership and talent management program exists	Knowledge transfer is personalised (one-to-one transfer)	Knowledge transfer is documented
91.4	98.1	64.2	72.4	73.8	90.5

Source: CIAT, IOTA, IMF, OECD, International Survey on Revenue Administration, Tables B.10 HR management approach: Strategy / multi-year work force plan and training strategy, and B.11 HR management approach: Support for new staff and staffing plan, https://data.rafit.org/regular.aspx?key=74180914 (accessed on 10 September 2024).

Virtual training

During the COVID-19 pandemic, many tax administrations reported transitioning their training programmes from face-to-face contact to a virtual environment. Tax administrations report that these practices brought significant benefits to the administration and participants, and as a result they continue being adapted for the longer term. Previous editions of this report showcased examples of this, such as the use of live online training sessions or pre-recorded videos/webinars (OECD, 2021[4]) or interactive applications that can also be used as part of recruitment efforts (OECD, 2023[1]).

While moving to a virtual training environment may have some up-front costs, it may save costs in the longer term as once produced, pre-recorded training material can be viewed at any time, from anywhere. Remote training can reduce travel expenses and can allow staff to learn at their own pace and convenience as well as increasing the number of staff members that can follow a course. New technologies are also helping facilitate the collaborative learning aspects, increasing the quality of the training experience.

In addition to the virtual training programmes produced by tax administrations themselves, international organisations are also producing e-learning courses specifically designed for tax administrations. One of these programmes is the Virtual Training to Advance Revenue Administration (VITARA) initiative, a joint project of four organisations, which is described in more detail in Box 10.5.

Box 10.5. The VITARA initiative

VITARA is an online course specifically designed for tax administrations. The course consists of several short, structured online modules. It is a joint project of four organisations, the Inter-American Center of Tax Administrations (CIAT), the International Monetary Fund (IMF), the Intra-European Organisation of Tax Administrations (IOTA) and the OECD.

The VITARA course content is tailored to senior managers and executives of tax administrations of developing countries. Yet other tax officials, including from advanced economies, could also benefit from following the different course modules. All modules are free of charge and there are no prerequisites or qualification requirements.

The VITARA curriculum represents a comprehensive training package for tax administration management. It consists of two parts and includes the following topics:

- Part A. Institutional governance, management, and support
  - Institutional governance
  - Compliance risk management
  - Organization
  - Strategic management
  - Information technology and data management
  - Reform management (Fundamentals and Specific Topics)
  - Human resource management
  - Performance management
  - Enterprise risk management
- Part B. Core functions of tax administration
  - Introduction to tax administration
  - Taxpayer registration
  - Taxpayer services

- Filing of declarations
- Payment and debt collection
- Audit program
- Dispute resolution
- Revenue management

By September 2024, ten VITARA modules have been developed in English, and some are also available in Spanish, French and Arabic. New English modules as well as further translations will follow. The available modules (underlined above) can be accessed here: https://www.imf.org/en/Capacity-Development/Training/ICDTC/Search?sortby=Relevancy&sortdir=Descending&keywords=VITARA (accessed on 10 September 2024).

To support learners, and to provide easy and free access to the content of the VITARA online modules (particularly to those that have no stable internet access), the VITARA partners have started reproducing the module content in so called "Reference guides". By September 2024, five Reference guides have been published:

- Human Resource Management (CIAT, IMF, IOTA, OECD, 2024[5])
- Organisation (CIAT, IMF, IOTA, OECD, 2024[6])
- Strategic management (CIAT, IMF, IOTA, OECD, 2023[7])
- Reform Management Fundamentals: Setting Up a Reform Program (CIAT, IMF, IOTA, OECD, 2024[8])
- Reform Management Specific Topics: Managing a Reform Program (CIAT, IMF, IOTA, OECD, 2024[9])

Staff motivation and performance

Maintaining the motivation of employees is crucial to running a successful organisation, driving productivity and engagement which in turn helps the administration to achieve its objectives. Having a performance management system in place can complement this, through establishing clear goals, expectations, and providing a mechanism for regular feedback and development opportunities.

Staff surveys

Conducting regular surveys to gather employee perceptions of the workplace and HR management to better inform decision making in these areas can be of particular importance in times of change. Measuring staff engagement, satisfaction and motivation, sharing the results of surveys of these areas with staff, and involving them in the selection, design and implementation of changes has proven a successful formula to increase productivity in a number of tax administrations.

Around 70% of administrations survey their staff periodically on attitudes, perceptions and workplace satisfaction, although the frequency of surveys may vary. More than 90% of those administrations assess staff engagement, share the results with staff, and involve their staff when considering responses to survey findings. (See Table 10.12.)

Table 10.12. Staff surveys, 2022

Percentage of administrations

Periodic staff surveys on attitudes, perceptions and workplace satisfaction are conducted	If yes,		
	Assessment of staff engagement	Results shared with staff	Staff engaged when responding to assessment
70.7	97.6	95.1	90.2

Source: CIAT, IOTA, IMF, OECD, International Survey on Revenue Administration, Table B.9 HR management approach: Staff surveys, https://data.rafit.org/regular.aspx?key=74180914 (accessed on 10 September 2024).

Performance management systems

Almost all tax administrations report that they have performance management systems in place. Most of these conduct the evaluation on an annual basis (or even more often) and include specific objectives for each staff member in this process. The importance of individual development plans has also been recognised and only 15% of the administrations do not include them in their performance management system. (See Table 10.13.)

Table 10.13. Performance management systems, 2022

Percentage of administrations

Performance management system in place	If yes,		
	Includes individual development plans	Includes specific objectives	Formal evaluation at least annually
93.1	85.2	90.7	92.6

Source: CIAT, IOTA, IMF, OECD, International Survey on Revenue Administration, Table B.8 Remuneration and performance management, https://data.rafit.org/regular.aspx?key=74180914 (accessed on 10 September 2024).

Remuneration and staff performance

Linking performance to pay or some other types of rewards may be a powerful motivator and increase staff engagement. The nature of the reward mechanisms varies greatly and can include individual or collective salary increases, flexibility to adjust salary scales, promotions, individual or collective bonuses, and non-monetary rewards. At the same time, it may have adverse effects on the workplace and culture by creating a competitive environment.

A significant number of administrations, three-quarters, can link performance to pay and reward. While good performance can typically result in increased remuneration (93%), there are a number of administrations where poor performance can result in reduced salary (36%) or the denial of annual increments (50%).

Table 10.14. Remuneration and staff performance, 2022

Percentage of administrations

Performance linked to pay and reward	If yes, Good performance can result in increased remuneration	Poor performance can result in reduced salary	Poor performance can result in denial of annual increment
75.9	93.2	36.4	52.3

Source: CIAT, IOTA, IMF, OECD, International Survey on Revenue Administration, Table B.8 Remuneration and performance management, https://data.rafit.org/regular.aspx?key=74180914 (accessed on 10 September 2024).

Supporting staff

The changes tax administrations are managing, whether technology, policy or budget driven, are constant. In addition, the wider digital transformation of the economy is changing the service expectations of taxpayers. To maintain staff motivation and performance, tax administrations are considering the best way to support staff through these changes, as well as ensuring they have the right tools for the tasks.

Technology is playing a key role in this. This includes the use of artificial intelligence, machine learning and robotic process automation (RPA) to automate some of the core tasks within a tax administration. Table 6.10. in Chapter 6 highlights the rapid growth in the use of such services with, for example, almost two-thirds of administrations reporting that they now using or planning to use RPA. This is helping tax administrations respond to budgetary and workforce pressures as it is freeing up resource for staff to be focussed on more complex tasks.

Box 10.6. illustrates the wide range of uses that automation is being put to. Further examples are included in Box 9.5. of the 2023 edition of this series (OECD, 2023[1]).

Box 10.6. Examples – Supporting staff through automation

France – Using generative artificial intelligence to assist with processing parliamentary amendments to the budget bill

The LLaMandement Project, developed by DGFiP, represents a significant leap forward in the legislative process, particularly in the handling of the Finance Bill which is the cornerstone of France's annual budget.

The Project uses Artificial Intelligence (AI) to streamline the processing of parliamentary amendments by DGFiP, automating the summary and allocation of these amendments to the correct teams. This innovation is instrumental in shaping the nation's budget by ensuring that financial legislation is handled with the utmost efficiency and accuracy.

This initiative directly impacts the legislative process by enhancing the capacity of parliamentary and administrative staff to manage and scrutinise the vast number of amendments presented during the Finance Bill discussions. With LLaMandement, the process of reviewing over 10 000 amendments becomes significantly more manageable, allowing for a more focused and informed debate on the nuances of financial legislation. This in turn facilitates a more thorough consideration of the budgetary implications of each amendment, ensuring that the final Finance Bill is both comprehensive and reflective of the legislative intent.

DGFiP has released the tool's source code, training data, and usage documentation to the public domain. This open-source philosophy enhances the project's transparency, inviting collaboration, external evaluation, and further development from a wider community. It fosters an environment that enables citizens, academic institutions, and industrial partners to contribute to and benefit from the state's advancements in generative AI.

For more information, please see here: https://arxiv.org/pdf/2401.16182.pdf (accessed on 10 September 2024).

Lithuania – Robotic Process Automation

In striving to achieve operational excellence, Lithuania's State Tax Inspectorate (STI) recently completed the automation of its processes by investing in Robotic Process Automation (RPA) software and the requisite licenses.

Two pivotal areas targeted for automation were the revision of unpaid taxes and the compilation of administrative protocols. By automating the process of compiling the protocols of administrative misconduct, the STI can now swiftly implement fines for non-submitted tax returns to a larger number of taxpayers. This measure not only encourages timely tax return submissions, but also contributes additional funds to the state budget. Furthermore, automating the process of reviewing unpaid taxes and fines for administrative misconduct streamlines the administration of fines. It enables the STI to respond promptly to changes in a person's assets, and collection imposed fines in instalments.

By the end of 2023, 22 200 decisions were automated. This translated to a saving of 581 working days, underscoring the efficiency gains brought about by automation. Similarly, the automation of administrative offense protocols proved fruitful for STI. Originally targeting 18 000 protocols in 2023, the organization surpassed expectations by drafting 31 285 protocols by year-end which translated to a saving of 9 995 working days.

Looking ahead, STI is dedicated to enhancing its operations by empowering its specialists to automate new processes.

Saudi Arabia – Using Robotic Process Automation for operational tasks

ZATCA in Saudi Arabia has implemented RPA to significantly improve its operational efficiency and accuracy. By automating repetitive and rule-based tasks, RPA has relieved the burden on ZATCA's workforce and accelerated tax and customs processes. This automation has resulted in faster response times and reduced errors associated with manual data entry, leading to greater overall accuracy in financial transactions, reporting, and customs operations.

The integration of RPA has brought several key benefits to ZATCA across various areas. Duties such as data entry, document verification, and compliance inspections have been automated, improving efficiency and minimizing potential human errors. Similarly, RPA has streamlined HR operations, optimizing employee management and administrative tasks. Customer service has also been enhanced through the automation of routine ticketing processes, resulting in quicker resolutions and improved customer satisfaction.

ZATCA has further leveraged RPA in infrastructure system monitoring, enabling continuous and automated monitoring for proactive issue detection and ensuring system reliability. Additionally, data gathering and report generation have been automated, ensuring high accuracy in reporting and facilitating faster decision-making processes.

Overall, ZATCA's adoption of RPA demonstrates its commitment to innovative solutions in managing tax and customs procedures. By automating key areas such as Customs, HR operations, Ticket Handling, Infrastructure System Monitoring, and Reporting, ZATCA has not only streamlined processes but also improved customer service and decision-making capabilities. This strategic implementation of RPA has propelled ZATCA towards greater operational efficiency and accuracy.

Sources: France (2024), Lithuania (2024) and Saudi Arabia (2024).

Diversity management

Having a diverse workforce that represents the population helps the administration to better serve its customers and encourages an inclusive working environment. Introducing a comprehensive diversity policy can be a good way to promote this, by integrating diversity and inclusion into formal processes within the administration and promoting a culture where different perspectives are valued and encouraged, improving staff morale. As can be seen in Table 10.15., tax administrations have embraced this approach with 85% having a formal diversity policy.

Having a workforce with a wide range of viewpoints and experiences can also improve decision making and aid the tax administration in its service delivery, through enhancing trust with taxpayers. Conducting periodic staff surveys on diversity and inclusion can be a helpful tool in both assessing the effectiveness of current diversity policies and identifying possible areas for improvement and new focus areas. They can guide leadership teams in developing new initiatives to target any inequalities or challenges identified by the survey. To understand how staff perceive the administration's approach towards diversity, around half of the administrations reporting conducting staff surveys on diversity and inclusion on a periodic basis (see Table 10.15.) Additionally, there may be other tools that administrations identify to maintain an inclusive and diverse workforce, such as staff networks and education campaigns.

Table 10.15. Diversity management approaches, 2022

Percentage of administrations

Formal diversity policy exists	Periodic staff surveys on diversity and inclusion are conducted	Policies for flexible working arrangements included in HR management approach	If yes,			
			Staff can work flexible working hours	Staff can work from home or elsewhere on an occasional basis	Staff can work from home or elsewhere on a regular basis	Executives can work part-time
84.5	46.6	89.7	96.2	88.5	78.8	40.4

Source: CIAT, IOTA, IMF, OECD, International Survey on Revenue Administration, Tables B.9 HR management approach: Staff surveys, B.12 HR management approach: staffing plan and flexible working arrangements, B.13 HR management approach: Leadership development, time reporting, diversity policy, https://data.rafit.org/regular.aspx?key=74180914 (accessed on 10 September 2024).

Box 10.7. Finland – Promoting equality and non-discrimination

The Finnish Tax Administration promotes equality and non-discrimination in all its operations, both as an employer and providing taxpayer services.

Several measures are in place to ensure fair treatment and opportunities for all employees. A code of conduct has been established for both personnel and supervisors, emphasising the prevention of harassment, discrimination, and other inappropriate behaviours. Diversity initiatives are integrated into the employee experience and early care models. Anonymous job searches have been piloted, ensuring recruiters initially have no access to personal data to avoid bias. Remote work options have expanded, enabling hiring from various locations across Finland. Job titles have been changed into gender-neutral forms, and access to information in the second official language, Swedish, has been improved. There is also a dedicated working group on equality focused on promoting diversity and inclusion in everyday work.

In terms of equality towards taxpayers, the focus is on being inclusive and accessible. Diverse service channels are provided to accommodate different needs, with services designed to be accessible and user-friendly. Timely and accessible customer communication is prioritised and staff are trained in equality principles and practices. Monitoring and collecting customer feedback ensures the quality and accuracy of services.

Furthermore, there is ongoing dialogue with taxpayers and stakeholders, including minority organisations, to help identify development needs and set priorities. For the years 2023-2025, the main priorities are cognitive and linguistic accessibility, staff skills and culture.

Source: Finland (2024).

Flexible working arrangements

One way to support diversity in tax administrations is to facilitate flexible working arrangements, such as flexible working hours or remote working opportunities. These arrangements are increasingly important in today's work environment as they enable employees to balance their professional and personal lives more effectively, leading to a higher job satisfaction and productivity. By accommodating diverse work preferences and needs, administrations can attract and retain top talent, reduce absenteeism, and foster a more engaged and motivated workforce.

Policies for flexible working arrangements exist in around 90% of the administrations covered by this publication. In almost all of those administrations staff can work flexible working hours and the vast majority offer staff the possibility to work from home or elsewhere on an occasional and regular basis. (See Table 10.15.)

Figure 10.11. illustrates the percentage of:

- Staff that is able to work remotely, i.e. staff have the IT infrastructure to enable them to perform remotely all the tasks they would perform in the office, and
- Staff that works remotely at least 20% of the year, i.e. one or more days per week, on average.

Figure 10.11. Remote working, 2022

Percentage of staff able to work remotely and those working remotely at least 20 percent of the year

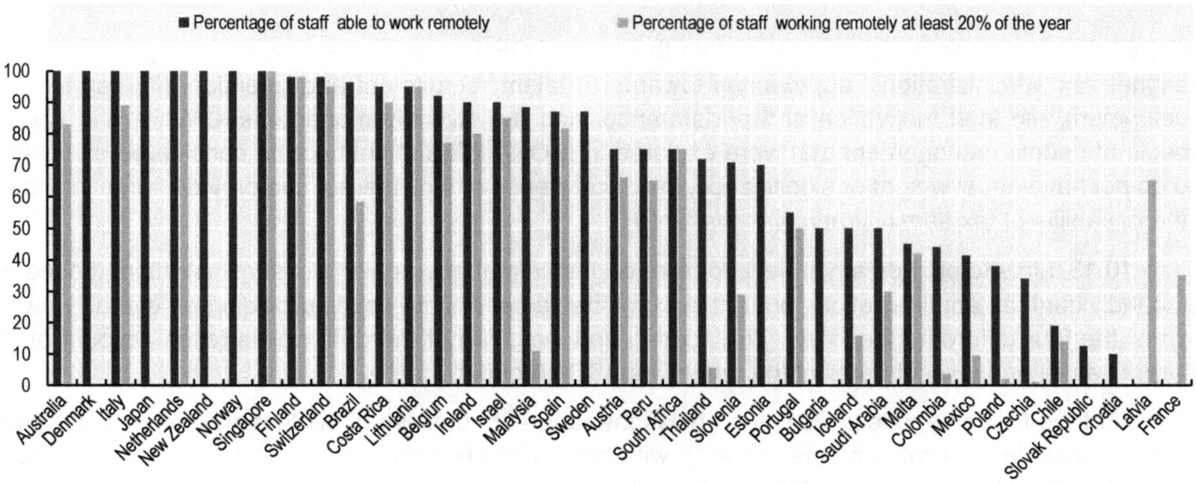

Source: CIAT, IOTA, IMF, OECD, International Survey on Revenue Administration, Table B.12 HR management approach: staffing plan and flexible working arrangements, https://data.rafit.org/regular.aspx?key=74180914 (accessed on 10 September 2024)

StatLink https://stat.link/s6tah1

Further, Table 10.15. shows that around 40% of administrations have also introduced the possibility for executives to work part-time, and as can be seen in Figure 10.12. executives make use of those arrangements.

Figure 10.12. Percentage of executives working part-time, 2022

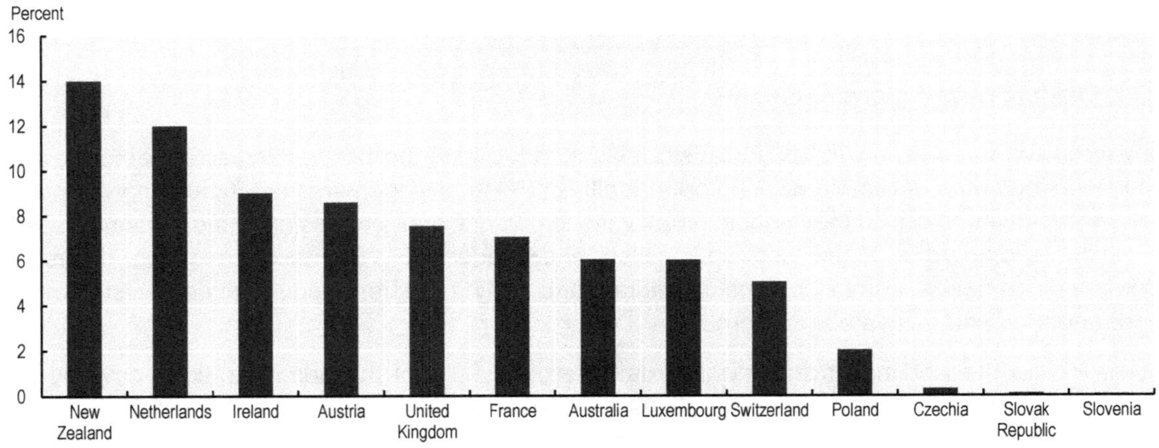

Source: CIAT, IOTA, IMF, OECD, International Survey on Revenue Administration, Table B.12 HR management approach: staffing plan and flexible working arrangements, https://data.rafit.org/regular.aspx?key=74180914 (accessed on 10 September 2024)

StatLink https://stat.link/01swgf

As tax administrations reflect on the working practices established as part of the pandemic response, the impact of longer-term hybrid or remote working is also being considered. This was explored in more detail in the OECD report *Tax Administration: Towards sustainable remote working in a post COVID-19 environment* (OECD, 2021[10]).

People management: A high-level picture

Using different aspects and data points from the 2023 ISORA survey, the people management section examines tax administrations' approaches towards (i) talent recruitment and retention, (ii) learning and development, (iii) staff motivation and performance, and (iv) diversity management. Whilst the various aspects of people management that were explored in ISORA 2023 should not be considered exhaustive and do not have equal weight or significance, their occurrence or lack thereof can provide some indication of the capability of tax administrations in that area.

Figure 10.13. aims to provide a high-level picture of people management in tax administration. It does not name individual tax administrations but rather combines a set of data points providing an overall view for each of the four different categories. The scoring and weighing of the data points takes account of the different nature and level of detail of the underlying ISORA questions.

For each of the four categories, the figure shows the range of administrations that are between the lower and upper quartile (illustrated by the "boxes"), with the median represented by the horizontal lines drawn through the boxes. The lines extending the boxes vertically (the "whiskers") indicate the range of administrations that are in the upper and lower quartiles.

The figure indicates that tax administrations have relatively advanced approaches regarding talent recruitment and retention, learning and development, and staff motivation and performance. The median score for tax administrations as regards those categories is at 80% or above, which indicates that based on ISORA data the majority of administrations have built their capabilities in those areas.

The picture is slightly different as regards diversity management where the median score for tax administrations is below 70%. While still positive, in contrast to the other categories this an area with scope for additional gains.

Figure 10.13. People management: A high-level picture, 2022

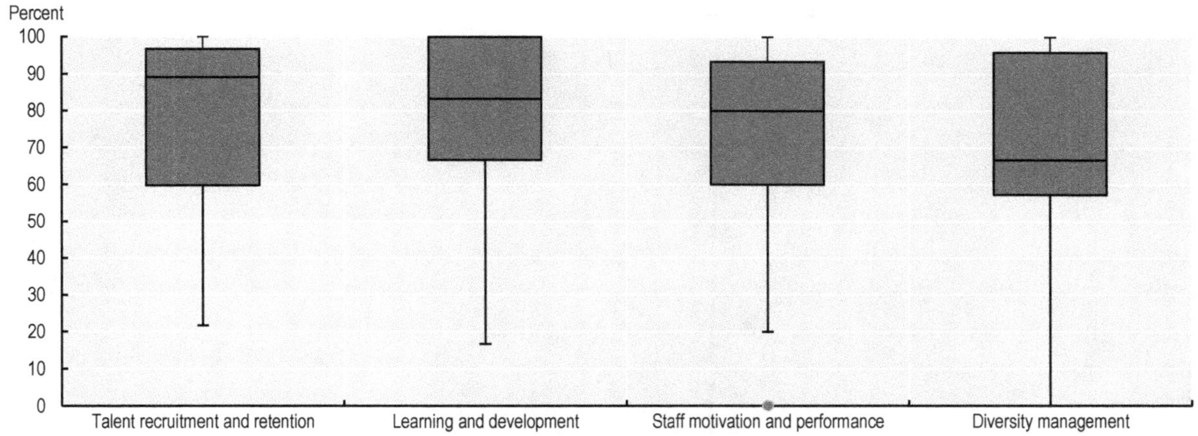

Source: OECD Secretariat calculations based on CIAT, IOTA, IMF, OECD, International Survey on Revenue Administration, https://data.rafit.org/regular.aspx?key=74180914 (accessed on 10 September 2024)

StatLink https://stat.link/k28x7o

References

CIAT, IMF, IOTA, OECD (2024), *Reform Management Fundamentals: Setting Up a Reform Program*, OECD Publishing, Paris, https://doi.org/10.1787/4d33b619-en. [8]

CIAT, IMF, IOTA, OECD (2024), *Reform Management Specific Topics: Managing a Reform Program*, OECD Publishing, Paris, https://doi.org/10.1787/1fc51bcf-en. [9]

CIAT, IMF, IOTA, OECD (2024), *VITARA Reference Guide: Human Resource Management*, OECD Publishing, Paris, https://doi.org/10.1787/6ef70142-en. [5]

CIAT, IMF, IOTA, OECD (2024), *VITARA Reference Guide: Organization*, OECD Publishing, Paris, https://doi.org/10.1787/ab075e83-en. [6]

CIAT, IMF, IOTA, OECD (2023), *VITARA Reference Guide: Strategic Management*, International Monetary Fund, Washington, DC, https://doi.org/10.5089/9798400223488.069. [7]

OECD (2023), *Tax Administration 2023: Comparative Information on OECD and other Advanced and Emerging Economies*, OECD Publishing, Paris, https://doi.org/10.1787/900b6382-en. [1]

OECD (2021), *Behavioural Insights for Better Tax Administration: A Brief Guide*, OECD Publishing, Paris, https://doi.org/10.1787/582c283e-en. [3]

OECD (2021), *Tax Administration 2021: Comparative Information on OECD and other Advanced and Emerging Economies*, OECD Publishing, Paris, https://doi.org/10.1787/cef472b9-en. [4]

OECD (2021), "Tax administration: Towards sustainable remote working in a post COVID-19 environment", *OECD Policy Responses to Coronavirus (COVID-19)*, OECD Publishing, Paris, https://doi.org/10.1787/fdc0844d-en. [10]

OECD (2017), *Tax Administration 2017: Comparative Information on OECD and Other Advanced and Emerging Economies*, OECD Publishing, Paris, https://doi.org/10.1787/tax_admin-2017-en. [2]

11 Tax gap estimation

Improving tax compliance and reducing the tax gap is typically one of the main objectives of a tax administration. Therefore, many jurisdictions are estimating the size of their tax gap. Although a tax gap may have a relatively simple definition, its estimation is complex and includes many nuances. This chapter provides an overview of key tax gap concepts and examples of international experiences in tax gap research.

An increasing number of jurisdictions are estimating tax gaps as these estimates can provide insights on size and nature of non-compliance, emerging trends, and the general health of the tax system. To estimate the tax gap, a jurisdiction needs to take into account many aspects such as legislative frameworks the overall administrative design of their tax systems, internal operations, availability of data, and economic events. Moreover, jurisdictions need to capture unobserved events or deliberately hidden activities that add challenges to tax gap estimation.

This chapter provides an overview of:

- Tax gap definition and its types;
- Tax gap methodologies;
- Tax gap components;
- How tax gaps are used by tax administrations; and
- The impact of the COVID-19 pandemic on the tax gap.

It also highlights international experience with tax gap research.[1]

Tax gap definition

Tax gap is generally defined as a difference between the potential tax revenue and actual tax revenue (Hutton, 2017[1]). It can be separated into two types: compliance gap and policy gap.

- ***Compliance gap*** is a potential tax revenue loss due to non-compliance under current tax laws. One of the main functions of most tax administrations is reducing tax non-compliance, therefore, they mostly focus on a compliance gap rather than a policy gap (Hutton, 2017[1]). Moreover, most jurisdictions do not take into account illegal activities in their tax gap estimation due to uncertainties in taxes that could be applied.
- ***Policy gap*** measures other tax revenue loss due to various tax policies. This gap can include intentional tax expenditure such as tax credits to achieve certain policy outcomes or unintentional tax expenditure such as tax avoidance due to loopholes in tax law (Hutton, 2017[1]). Since tax policies are often managed by a ministry of finance or a department of treasury, it is often out of the control of tax administrations.

Since a compliance gap is more common for tax administrations than a policy gap, the remainder of this chapter mostly focuses on methodologies and nuances for the compliance gap.

Box 11.1. Examples – Policy gap

Belgium

The Belgian tax administration defines a policy gap as the difference between potential collections under the existing policy framework and potential collections under a normative or referential policy framework. Although often overlooked, policy gap estimations allow for a comparison of the sizes of the compliance gap and policy gap and their respective contribution to the total gap. Defining the gap in such a way allows decision makers to also focus on how policy choices have an effect on the total gap and if policy changes have an effect on the compliance gap.

Furthermore, the policy gap can be broken down into a "non-taxable" or a non-actionable gap, such as items that are included in the national accounts consumption statistics, but are not subject to VAT. These results can also be used in the modelling of certain tax expenditures. For example, it can give an overview of not only the size of the zero-rated goods and services, exemptions, but also of the size of public goods, non-market services.

In other words, a policy gap estimation offers an opportunity to increase budget transparency, to establish a closer link between tax expenditures and direct expenditures and potential avenues of actions for improving revenue performance by addressing either component of the gap.

European Commission

The European Commission's annual study on the *VAT gap in the EU* (European Commission, 2023[2]) estimates the VAT policy gap in addition to the VAT compliance gap. The VAT policy gap is a proxy of the additional VAT revenue that could be generated if a uniform VAT rate – without any exemptions or reduced rates – were applied to all final domestic consumption of goods and services by households, government, and non-profit institutions serving households (NPISH), assuming full taxpayer compliance. In policy terms, this is a more "actionable" estimate than the estimate of the VAT compliance gap, because EU Member States have, in general, direct control over reduced rates and, to some extent, on exemptions.

The VAT policy gap consists of two main components: the VAT exemption gap, which accounts for revenues lost due to exemptions and exclusions from the tax base, and the VAT rate gap, which accounts for revenues foregone due to preferential treatment such as reduced rates and zero-rates. Changes in the size of the VAT policy gap can be attributed to changes in legal rules, such as national adjustments to reduced rates or exemptions, as well as shifts in demand composition.

Estimating the VAT policy gap provides transparency on the cost of policy choices that depart from uniform VAT rates and helps identify areas where tax policy changes could increase revenue and improve tax efficiency. The European Commission publishes annual estimates of the VAT policy gap and its components as part of its *VAT gap in the EU* study, which provides a standardised framework for EU Member States to assess their VAT systems. Over time, these estimates have been continuously improved in accuracy and detail, enabling policymakers to track progress and target reforms.

The latest report finds that the average VAT policy gap in the EU-27 stood at approximately 45 percent of the notional ideal revenue in 2022. The VAT rate gap has increased since 2020. In the same time frame, the VAT exemption gap, which constitutes the largest portion of the policy gap, has decreased. This decline in the VAT exemption gap is attributed to changes in demand composition, as there have been no significant changes to the VAT Directive regarding exemptions.

Note: While individual EU Member States are allowed to abolish reduced rates, most exemptions are mandated by EU law, specifically the VAT Directive (Council Directive 2006/112/EC). As a result, abolishing these exemptions would necessitate an amendment to the Directive at the European level, which demands unanimous agreement among EU Member States.
Sources: Belgium (2024) and the European Commission (2024).

Even though there is a common definition of a tax gap, it may not be exactly the same for various jurisdictions. For example, some jurisdictions include late payments as part of their tax gap while others do not. Others might not include a payment gap in their overall tax gap at all. In addition, tax gap estimates could be linked to a year of economic activity (e.g. tax year) or imply all incoming revenue during certain time frame (e.g. fiscal year). Therefore, a direct comparison of various jurisdictions should be interpreted with caution and account for differences in tax systems, definitions and methodologies.

Tax gap types

A tax gap can be divided based on non-compliance sources such as registration, filing, reporting or payment (see Figure 11.1. and Figure 11.2.). Some jurisdictions use a term “lodgement” instead of “filing” indicating a process of filing or lodging a tax form. Jurisdictions may also use different names for their tax gaps based on the sources of non-compliance. For example, a tax gap related to payment non-compliance could be called a payment gap, underpayment gap, non-payment gap or collection gap. The most popular terms for a tax gap related to reporting non-compliance are a reporting gap, underreporting gap and assessment gap.

Most of the jurisdictions are focusing on estimating reporting (75%) and payment (64%) non-compliance as they are major sources contributing to the tax gap. (See Annex Table 11.A.2.) Moreover, registration and filing non-compliance can be more challenging to estimate as they cover a population that may be unknown to the tax administration.

Figure 11.1. Non-compliance sources that contribute to the tax gap

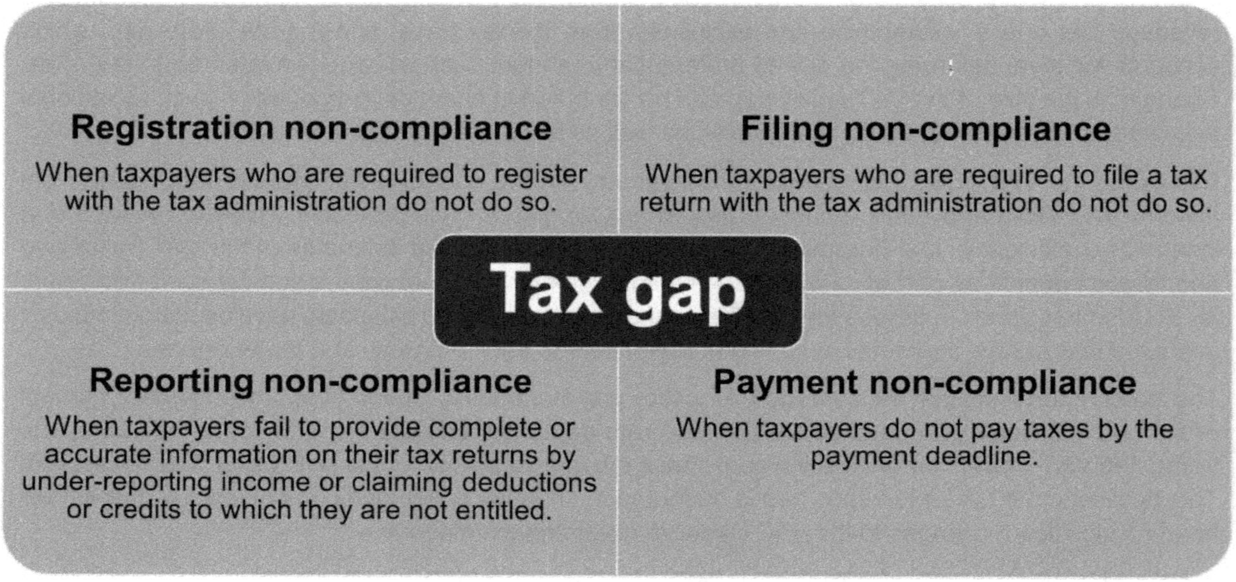

Figure 11.2. Tax gap estimation and non-compliance sources

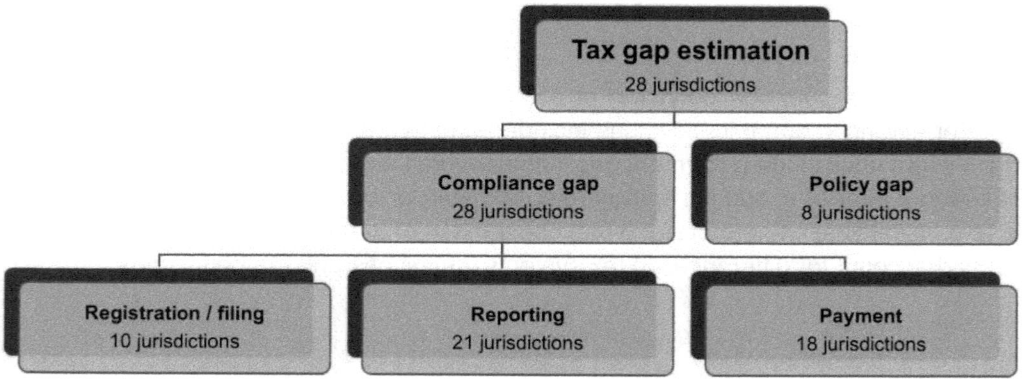

Source: Annex Table 11.A.1 and Annex Table 11.A.2.

To provide a clearer view on what exactly is included in the tax gap, jurisdictions define gross tax gap versus net tax gap (see Figure 11.3.). Most jurisdictions estimate the gross tax gap (82%) and half measure the net tax gap. Close to 40% measure both gross and net tax gaps. Net tax gap usually includes some challenges as there could be a lag time in completing compliance and collections activities. (See Annex Table 11.A.2.)

Some jurisdictions (36%) use projections at least for one tax gap component to balance timeliness with other considerations such as the quality of tax gap estimates. (See Annex Table 11.A.3.)

Figure 11.3. Gross tax gap vs net tax gap

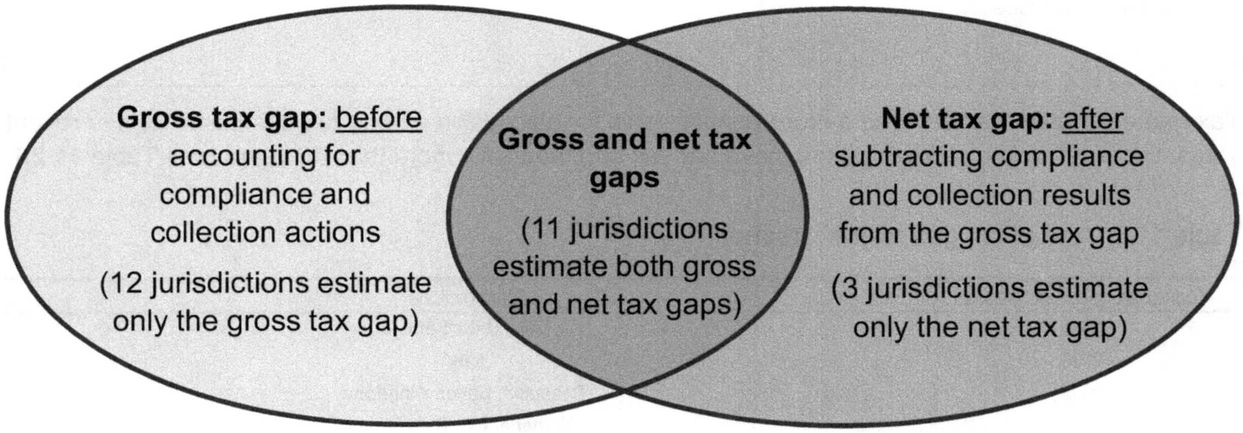

Source: Annex Table 11.A.2.

A small number of jurisdictions publish their overall tax gap estimates in the public domain (29%) and some of them have a legal requirement to do so. Several jurisdictions do not publish their overall tax gap, but they make one tax gap component (usually, Value Added Tax) publicly available. The frequency of the publications varies from annual to every four years or it is on an irregular schedule. Almost 40% of the jurisdictions that publish their tax gap estimate, do so annually. (See Annex Table 11.A.1.)

Box 11.2. United States – Tax gap by source of non-compliance

In the United States, the Internal Revenue Service (IRS) estimates the gross tax gap that comprises of three components:

- Non-filing: tax not paid on time by those who do not file on time,
- Underreporting: tax understated on timely filed returns, and
- Underpayment: tax that was reported on time, but not paid on time.

The majority of the tax gap comes from underreporting gap (around 80%), and non-filing and underpayment are smaller sources (on average, 9% and 11% respectively) that contribute to the gross tax gap.

Tax gap analysis has consistently shown that compliance is higher when income is subject to information reporting and even higher when also subject to withholding.

Table 11.1. Tax gap estimates by compliance source for tax years 2014-16 and projections for tax years 2017-19, 2020 and 2021 in the United States

Tax gap component	Tax Years (TY) 2014-16	Projections			
		TY 2017-19	TY 2017-19	TY 2020	TY 2021
Non-filing Tax Gap	8%	8%	7%	9%	11%
Underreporting gap	80%	80%	81%	80%	79%
Underpayment gap	12%	12%	12%	11%	10%
Gross tax gap	100%	100%	100%	100%	100%

Source: The United States (2024).

Tax gap estimation has become a more popular topic for discussion among tax administrations in recent years. However, some administrations have had tax gap teams for more than 40 years (see Table 11.2.).

Table 11.2. Year of tax gap teams' creation

Year of tax gap team creation	Jurisdictions
1980	Chile, **United States***
2000	**Italy***
2005	Denmark*, **United Kingdom***
2006	**Netherlands***, Switzerland
2007	Portugal
2012	Iceland*, European Commission
2013	Israel
2014	**Australia***, Latvia, Lithuania
2015	Romania
2016	**Canada***
2017	**Sweden**
2018	Greece, Slovakia
2019	Indonesia*
2020	**Brazil***, Hungary
2021	Spain
2022	Finland
2023	Colombia*
2024	France

Note: Jurisdictions that estimate the overall tax gap have an asterisk (*) and jurisdictions that publish their overall tax gap estimates are **bolded**.
Source: FTA 2023 survey on tax gap estimations.

According to a presentation by the IMF during the 2024 meeting of the FTA Community of Interest (COI) on Tax Gap, the main factors to succeed in tax gap research are data, a methodology, human resources, management support, and institution orientation (see Table 11.3.).

Table 11.3. Key factors of a successful tax gap program

Data	Methodology	Human resources	Management support	Institution orientation
Investing in data management and data cleaning. Ensuring data covers a target population. Accumulation of longitudinal data/analysis. Periodical revision to improve estimates' reliability.	Selecting the most appropriate methodology tailored to the data available. Establishing clear objectives. Using both bottom-up and top-down techniques. Consistent estimation techniques over time.	Building a multidisciplinary team with diverse expertise (i.e. in data analytics, statistics, econometrics, audit, tax policy). Avoiding frequent turnovers and keep the team stable.	Senior management endorsement. Patience in team development.	Public mandate to estimate tax gap. Regular publication. Adopting transparency.

Source: IMF presentation at the 2024 meeting of the OECD's Forum on Tax Administration Community of Interest on Tax Gap.

Tax gap methodologies

Tax gap estimation is complex and requires nuanced analysis. In general, there are two main approaches to estimating the tax gap (see Figure 11.4.):

- ***Top-down methodologies***: Generally using aggregated macro-economic data (e.g. national accounts data) to estimate the size of the tax base and the theoretical tax liability. The difference between the theoretical tax liability and the actual amount of tax paid or reported is the estimated tax gap.
- ***Bottom-up methodologies***: Generally using micro-economic data (for example, audit data) to extrapolate potential non-compliance and estimate the tax gap. The most common data sources for these methodologies are either data from random audits or risk-based audits.

Most jurisdictions (89%) prefer using top-down approaches, and slightly more than half (57%) use bottom-up approaches. A top-down approach is usually a good starting point for jurisdictions new to tax gap estimation. In addition, jurisdictions tend to start with the VAT gap which has a fairly established top-down methodology. Some administrations (54%) use third-party support for the tax gap estimation such as from IMF, academics, a ministry of finance, independent consultants or other organisations. (See Annex Table 11.A.1. and Annex Table 11.A.3.)

Figure 11.4. Two main approaches to estimate a tax gap

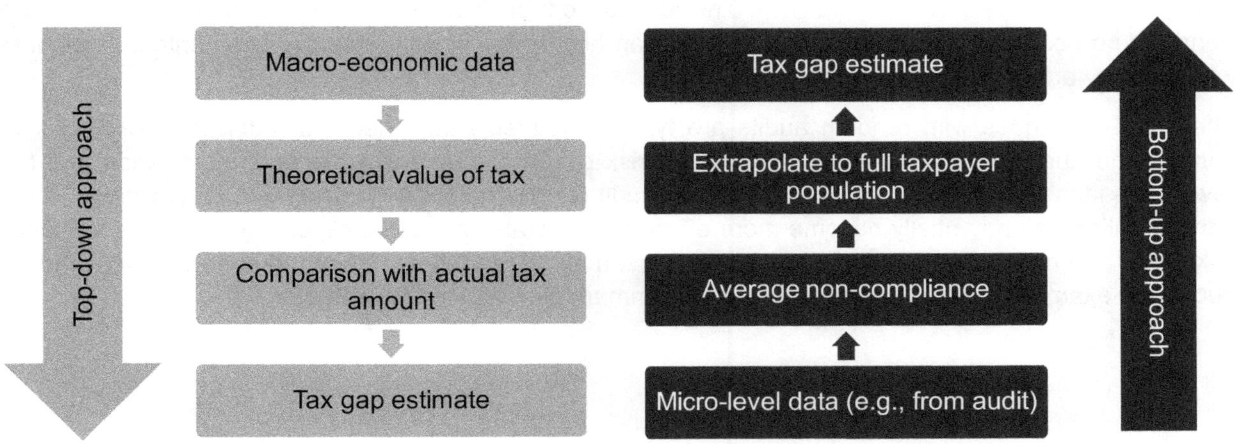

Top-down methodology

Ideally, a jurisdiction estimates the tax gap using both approaches as they provide different insights. A top-down methodology can provide additional information about the whole population that might be unknown from the operational data and give an overview of non-compliance and risk sectors in the economy. However, it is limited and cannot provide more detailed findings. The insights from top-down methodologies can be used to inform compliance strategies at a high level.

A top-down methodology could be used as an alternative to bottom-up approaches when random audits are unavailable and risk-based audit results cannot be extrapolated to the taxpayer population. At the same time, it could be used as a complement to view a tax gap from another prospective.

Bottom-up methodology

A bottom-up methodology usually provides more insights on non-compliance at the micro level. Therefore, it can be disaggregated and could be used to improve risk-assessment processes. However, estimates from this methodology could be limited to specific populations or taxes. Bottom-up methodologies require statistical or econometrical expertise and tax administration operational knowledge with good data understanding (OECD, 2017[3]).

One of the main data sources for bottom-up approaches is random audit, but it may not always be available in all jurisdictions. Therefore, some tax administrations use operational audits (for example, data from risk-based audits) or other available micro-level data. For example, some bottom-up methodologies make use of Census data, third-party information reporting data and administrative filing and payment data instead of audit data.

Random audits

Random audits are usually conducted based on a random sample drawn from the population of taxpayers. There are different types of random sampling such as simple random sampling, systematic sampling, stratified sampling and clustering sampling, where simple random sampling and stratified sampling are the most common among tax administrations. Some of these sampling techniques are explained in two Technical Guidance Notes published by the IMF in 2021 (Thackray, Jennings and Knudsen, 2021[4]) and 2023 (Barra, Hutton and Prokof'yeva, 2023[5]).

Random audit programmes are considered a high-quality method to estimate tax gaps in large populations of registered taxpayers (OECD, 2017[3]). The results from such audits can also help identify emerging trends in non-compliance for all taxpayers, and can help verify existing risk selection criteria, including whether they are still relevant and optimal.

The main challenges with random audits are typically related to the need for additional resources to conduct the audits and, as those audits are not risk-based but random, often not much additional tax revenue is identified. However, by using random audit results in improving risk-assessing systems, a tax administration can potentially become more efficient at operational audits, allocating resources to higher risk areas and recovering more taxes. Also, some sampling designs can help to reduce costs of random audits (for example, stratifications by risks, see Denmark's example in Box 11.3.).

Box 11.3. Examples – Random audit programmes

Denmark – Stratification by risks for a random audit programme for private individuals

The Danish Tax Administration stratifies or groups its private individual taxpayer population by risks and then draws a random sample of each risk group. To balance between recovering higher tax revenue and receiving insights on the overall taxpayer population, larger samples are drawn from higher risk groups than from low-risk ones. In that case, the results can still be extrapolated to the overall population, but at the same time, there is more efficient audit resource allocation than in a regular random audit program. This can also lead to higher returns on investments.

Denmark uses the results of random audits as an input to new legislation and to risk-assessment for improving tax compliance.

Netherlands – Know your taxpayer, understand their behaviour

The Dutch Tax Administration focuses on random audits as it can be an instrument for improving compliance risk management. Random audits not only give insight in compliance levels among populations, but also in what area of behaviour the compliance level could be improved. This creates the opportunity to develop specific interventions to target behaviour.

Compliance risk management in the Netherlands consists of five steps, namely identification of uncertainties (possible mistakes), analysing underlying causes, prioritisation, treatment (intervention) and evaluation. The Netherlands' random audits programme contributes to step 1, identification of uncertainties (and therefore compliance risks) and step 2, analysis of what causes the mistakes made to enable designing interventions that change non-compliant behaviour into compliant behaviour or to strengthen existing compliant behaviour.

Improving compliance behaviour depends on behavioural change. The administration uses the COM-B system as a model of behaviour that provides a basis for designing interventions aimed at behavioural change. In this behaviour system capability, opportunity and motivation interact to generate behaviour that in turn influences these components. Applying this to intervention design, the task is to consider what the behavioural target would be, and what components of the behavioural system would need to be changed to achieve that.

Firms, for instance, that are selected into the random audits programme are checked completely, that is on all types of taxes such as Value Added Tax and Corporate Income Tax. Therefore, random audits give a complete overview of tax behaviour of firms. But they do not give insight into why firms behave in this manner. To understand the behaviour of firms, information is collected using a survey among tax officers. Questions with respect to characteristics of firms, use of tax practitioners and judgements on what underlying causes might lead to mistakes made (for example, causes based on capability, opportunity and motivation such as lack of knowledge and financial constraint) are answered after every audit. These survey results help to understand the audit data and, hence, behaviour of firms.

The combination of insight in compliance levels due to audits and in underlying causes help to shape specific interventions to change the compliance behaviour of taxpayers.

Sources: Denmark (2024) and the Netherlands (2024).

Risk-based audits

Some jurisdictions that do not have random audit programmes rely on either top-down approaches or a use of risk-based audit results. Even though random audit methods are usually considered a high-quality method for tax gap estimation (OECD, 2017[3]), risk-based audits could provide additional insights on non-compliance due to deeper audit procedures.

However, risk-based audits tend to capture information on taxpayers with higher risks and, thus, these results are not representative of the overall population. The audited population is usually selected by specific criteria and not chosen randomly, leading to results with selection bias. This bias could be addressed by applying statistical or econometrical methods. The common methods include a Heckman method or Heckman Correction approach, extreme value method, cluster analysis, post stratification, and propensity score matching (Fiscalis TGPG, 2018[6]; Barra, Hutton and Prokof'yeva, 2023[5]).

On average, there are more bottom-up methodologies from random audits than from risk-based audits (see Figure 11.5.).

Figure 11.5. Number of bottom-up methodologies by data sources

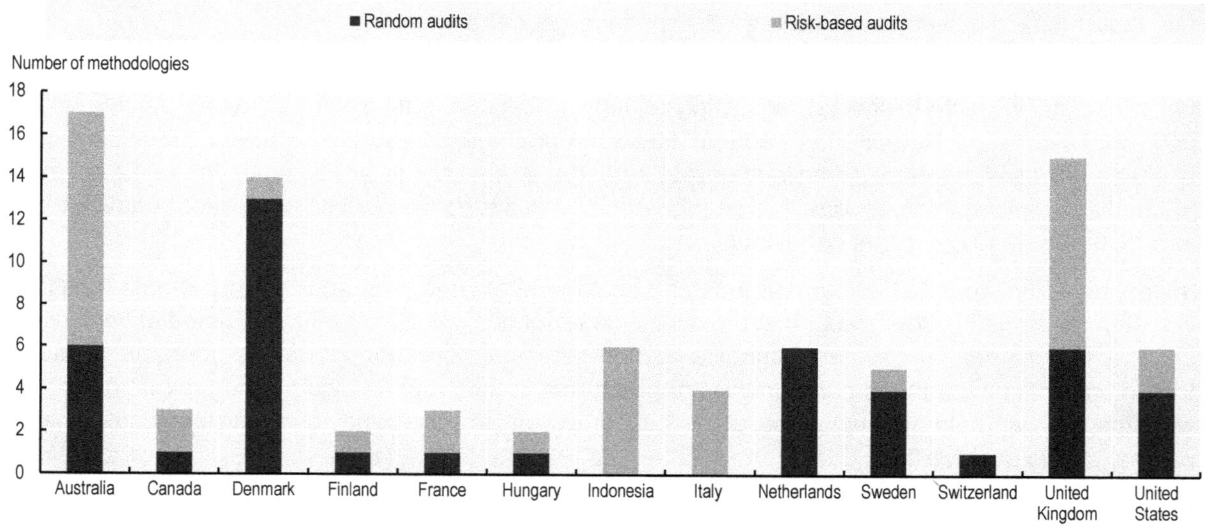

Source: Annex Table 11.A.4.

StatLink https://stat.link/w4mgz7

Non-detection multiplier

Some jurisdictions (21%) are applying a non-detection multiplier to their tax gap estimates (see Annex Table 11.A.3.). Non-detection multiplier or uplift factor is a multiplier that is applied to a tax gap estimate to account for undetected non-compliance not captured through tax gap estimates. For example, auditors may not always identify all sources of non-compliance when conducting audits due to various reasons. Therefore, any tax gap estimates from these audit data may be missing undetected non-compliance. Non-detection multipliers could be applied to some tax gap components or some methodologies and not necessarily to the overall tax gap.

There are several methods to develop a non-detection multiplier as can be seen in Table 11.4. One of the methods used is called the "Delphi technique" and tax administrations from both Sweden and the United Kingdom have published papers on the use of this method (HMRC, 2020[7]; Swedish Tax Agency, 2023[8]).

Table 11.4. Methods to estimate non-detection multiplier

Detection controlled estimation (DCE)	Secondary review by expert auditors	Third-party data matching	Expert judgement (Delphi technique)	Adopting others' multipliers
Econometric approach based on a separate study: brings all audit cases to the same level as they were examined by the "best" examiner. Developed by researchers in late 80s for the United States. First used by the United States for the Tax Year 2001 tax gap estimates.	Audits are passed to a separate group of experts to review and estimate a non-detected tax value. Requires additional resources and is limited to the ability of experts to find non-detected taxes.	Audits are conducted without third-party information and the results are then compared to available third-party data. Is not applicable for income sources without third-party information. Does not work if third-party information is already used in audits.	Panel of experts estimate how much tax generally does undetected in different types of audits at an aggregated level. Requires less resources but is limited to experts' ability to estimate non-detection amount in groups of taxpayers. Is used by the United Kingdom.	Adopting multipliers calculated by other tax administrations or other experts or using international ranges. May not represent a country-specific tax system and audit process. May be a good alternative in an absence of other methodologies.

Sources: FTA 2023 survey on tax gap estimations and Thackray, M., S. Jennings and M. Knudsen (2021), *The Revenue Administration Gap Analysis Program: An Analytical Framework for Personal Income Tax Gap Estimation*, https://doi.org/10.5089/9781513577173.005.

Box 11.4. Examples – Non-detection multiplier or uplift factor

United Kingdom – Non-detection multiplier using Delphi technique

Historically, the United Kingdom's (UK's) HM Revenue and Customs (HMRC) used multipliers derived from analysis by the IRS in the United States and adopted them to their random audit results. In recent years, HMRC have developed new non-detection multipliers using the Delphi technique to better apply to the types of risks seen in the UK tax system. These multipliers help adjust tax gaps for missing non-compliance in cases that were audited.

Non-detection arises for several different reasons, including the detection capability of the auditor, tax complexity, taxpayer co-operation, availability of data, available time to conduct the audit, and the level of concealed non-compliance.

The Delphi technique is a consultative method to gather expert opinion in a systematic way and establish consensus. The technique includes three rounds of questionnaires to acquire a consensus from a panel of experts in each tax regime. Response summaries are given at the beginning of last two rounds, where the panel could amend or agree their responses. In most recent years, a Delphi technique has been applied to estimate a non-detection multiplier for Pay-as-You-Earn (PAYE) employer compliance for small businesses and corporation tax for small businesses.

It is important to review a non-detection multiplier to adjust based on more recent information as detection may change over time, for example, due to improved compliance strategies. Non-detection multipliers can also differ for results from randomly selected audits and for risk-based audits. Further information is included in the HMRC Working Paper *Non-detection multipliers for measuring tax gaps* (HMRC, 2020[7]).

United States – Non-detection multiplier

The IRS tax gap estimates for the Tax Year (TY) 2001 incorporated Detection Controlled Estimation (DCE) for the first time. The first iteration of DCE using TY 2001 random audit data involved estimation for two categories of income (based on the extent of third-party information reporting) and for two categories of taxpayers (based on nature and size of income). The results were then synthesised down to four "multipliers".

Further research determined that there was an opportunity to expand DCE to allow for greater variability in the average detection rates across line items. Beginning with TY 2006, the IRS moved away from explicit multipliers and implemented a microsimulation approach to allocating DCE estimates of undetected income. The IRS has continued research on refining the microsimulation approach, focusing on improving estimates of the distribution of the tax gap.

Sources: The United Kingdom (2024) and the United States (2024).

Challenges related to tax gap estimation

Main challenges for tax gap estimation are usually related to data, methodology, resources and legislation (see Table 11.5.). Jurisdictions try to learn from international best practices and apply various techniques to overcome these challenges, but some constraints may limit capacity for tax gap estimation.

Table 11.5. Key challenges for tax gap estimation

Data	Methodology	Resources	Legislation
No random audits Small or not representative samples Data availability Lags in data Matching various data sources Non-detection Heterogeneous population Need of multiple data sources	Extrapolating from risk-based audits Difficulties in modelling complex non-compliance schema Finding appropriate methods for given data Accounting for emerging trends Limitations of top-down methods Need of multiple approaches	Limits in audit capacity Lack of tax gap experts Lack of budget Time-consuming audits Lack of internal support	Frequent changes in tax laws Complex tax systems

Source: FTA 2023 survey on tax gap estimations

Tax gap components

Tax systems vary, and therefore, tax gap components may differ between jurisdictions. In general, they can be divided into five main groups:

- Personal income tax (PIT),
- Corporate income tax (CIT),
- Value-added tax (VAT), equivalent to Goods and Services Tax (GST) for some jurisdictions,
- Excise taxes and duties, and
- Other tax types.

All jurisdictions that completed the underlying survey estimate the VAT gap (except the IRS as the United States that does not have this type of tax in their federal tax system), but only 39% of them estimate the overall tax gap that includes a combination of major tax types (see Figure 11.6.). Some jurisdictions are at early stages of the development of their tax gap programme and focus more on the VAT gap with a well-established top-down methodology. In certain cases, the IMF helps estimate the VAT gap for jurisdictions new to the tax gap research.

The second and third most popular tax gap components are PIT and CIT gaps, where more than 50% of jurisdictions are estimating either one of them or both. Excise gap is the rarest estimate (estimated by 29% of jurisdictions), and it typically includes excise taxes and duties on multiple excise products. Other tax gaps are also not very common (estimated by 36% of jurisdictions) and sometimes may get deprioritised due to the relatively small scale of their contribution to the overall tax gap.

Some jurisdictions may not segregate the tax gap by tax types in the same way. For example, the Netherlands Tax Administration does not use their bottom-up approach to estimate a tax gap for a specific tax revenue such as VAT but rather estimates the total gap for each entity.[2]

Figure 11.6. Number of jurisdictions that measure the relevant tax gap components

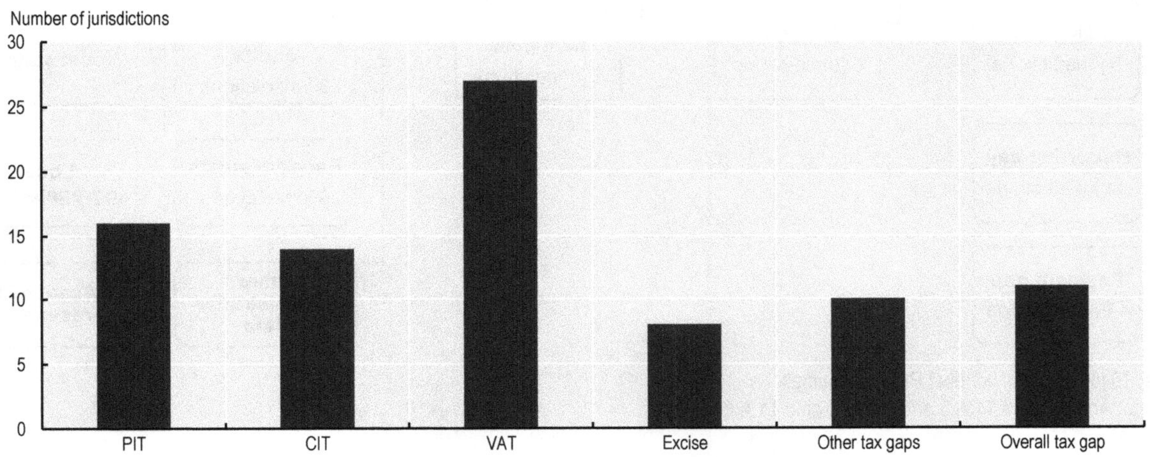

Source: Annex Tables 11.A.1. to 11.A.13.

StatLink https://stat.link/8hv9od

Personal income tax gap

The PIT gap usually includes tax non-compliance from private individuals (for example, from shadow economy activities, offshore investments, capital gains), self-employed individuals, and non-residents. A tax gap for self-employed individuals or small businesses could be included in the PIT gap or CIT gap, depending on the tax system and internal processes of a tax administration.

Almost 60% of jurisdictions estimate the PIT gap. Of those:

- 88% estimate the reporting gap and 69% estimate the payment gap; and
- 81% estimate the gross tax gap and half of them estimate the net tax gap.

Top-down and bottom-up approaches are equally popular, and random audits are prevalent in bottom-up methodologies. Top-down methodologies usually include global statistics, local aggregated data and academic research. See Figure 11.7. for details.

The IMF published a Technical Guidance Note containing various methodologies for PIT gap in *The Revenue Administration Gap Analysis Program: An Analytical Framework for Personal Income Tax Gap Estimation* (Thackray, Jennings and Knudsen, 2021[4]).

Figure 11.7. Overview of the PIT gap estimation

Number of jurisdictions that conduct the relevant analysis or apply the relevant methods

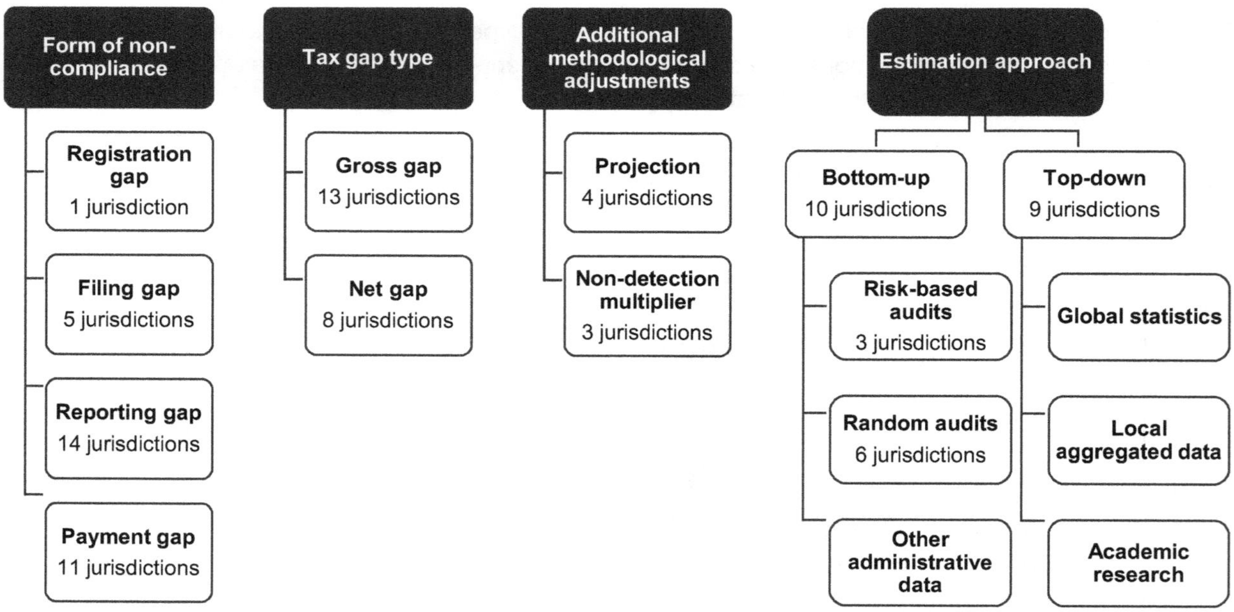

Note: 16 jurisdictions conduct PIT gap estimations.
Source: Annex Table 11.A.5 and Annex Table 11.A.6.

Box 11.5. Denmark – PIT gap from undeclared Danish labour

The Danish Tax Administration estimates the PIT gap for private and self-employed individuals using random audits. In addition to the random audit programmes, the part of the PIT gap attributed to undeclared work is estimated separately using the labour input method.

The application of the labour input method relies on data from the Danish Labour Force Survey, which is compared to Danish tax data. In short, undeclared work is assumed to be represented by the number of self-reported working hours in the Labour Force Survey that is in excess of the working hours officially recorded in the tax data. By calculating the discrepancy between the two, the prevalence and value of undeclared work in Denmark, together with the associated PIT gap, can be estimated.

Source: Denmark (2024).

Corporate income tax gap

The CIT gap usually includes tax non-compliance from large corporations, small and medium enterprises, public enterprises and institutions. Half of the jurisdictions estimate the CIT gap. Of those:

- All jurisdictions focus on the reporting gap and 86% on the payment gap; and

- 93% estimate the gross tax gap and 64% estimate the net tax gap.

While jurisdictions use either bottom-up or top-down approaches, there are two jurisdictions that estimate the CIT gap using both approaches at the time. On average, there are more bottom-up approaches used by jurisdictions. Bottom-up approaches are usually based on random or risk-based audit data. Local aggregated data is usually the main source for top-down approaches (see Figure 11.8.).

In addition, specific methodologies for CIT gaps can be found in the IMF Technical Guidance Note *Corporate Income Tax Gap Estimation by using Bottom-Up Techniques in Selected Countries: Revenue Administration Gap Analysis Program* (Barra, Hutton and Prokof'yeva, 2023[5]).

Figure 11.8. Overview of CIT gap estimation

Number of jurisdictions that conduct the relevant analysis or apply the relevant methods

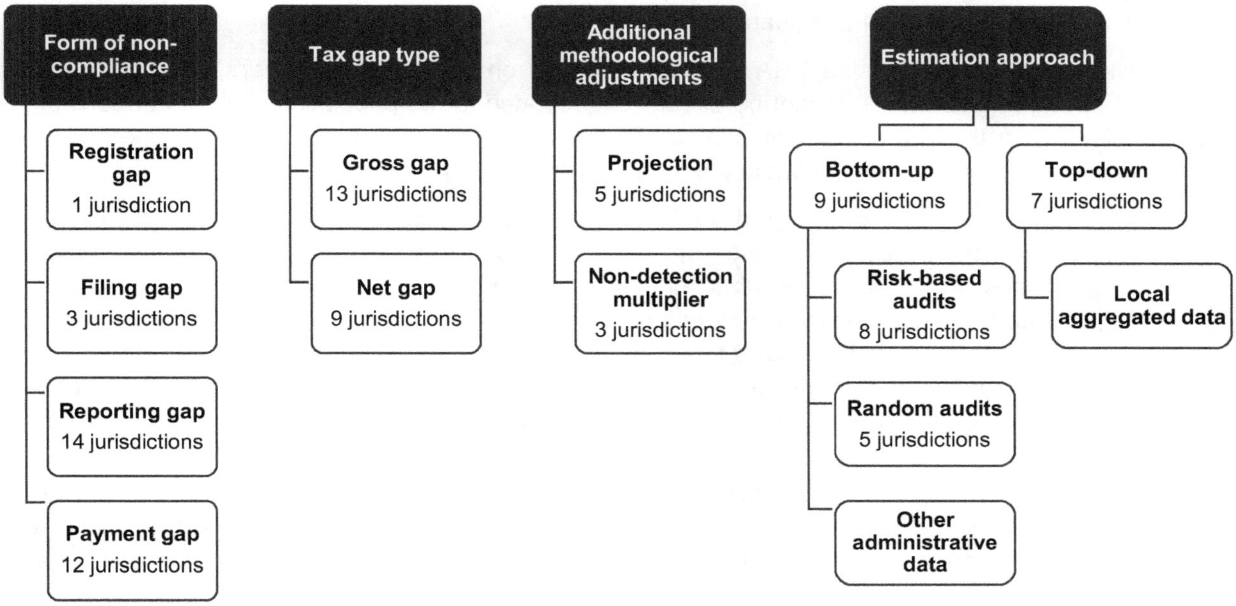

Note: 14 jurisdictions conduct CIT gap estimations.
Source: Annex Table 11.A.7 and Annex Table 11.A.8.

Box 11.6. Examples – CIT gap estimation

Brazil – Stochastic Production Frontier for CIT

The Brazilian Tax Administration had some difficulties to estimate CIT tax gap of small companies (Simples Nacional) using traditional methods, due to the lack of reliable and detailed data originated from the simplified tax forms. However, there was some third-party information available to be used in the estimation for small companies. This scenario contributed to choosing an alternative method as a CIT tax gap estimation tool, known as Stochastic Production Frontier (SPF).

The SPF method was originally developed to estimate the production possibilities of a set of companies based on a set of inputs such as capital and labour, through production functions. Thus, a classical production frontier model establishes the theoretical limits of the production capacity of firms using such inputs. The customisation of the SPF model to a tax approach in Simples Nacional was based on the use of tax information such as: purchases obtained from electronic invoices, bank flows and remuneration paid as inputs of a production function whose product was the revenue from the company. Thus, the econometric model was adapted to estimate a frontier for revenue generation (close to which the most compliant firms would be situated) and, consequently, to estimate the degree of noncompliance for firms, as a function of the gap between their declared revenue and the corresponding boundary. The use of discriminant variables with the model also allowed to obtain a good level of details in terms of geographic and sectorial cutouts.

After the Brazilian VAT tax reform, the model is planned to be updated to allow estimation of the VAT tax gap, through the prediction of the value added by companies (revenues minus inputs).

Canada – CIT gap estimation for large corporations using risk-based audits

The Canada Revenue Agency (CRA) continually monitors large corporations and risk assesses 100% of the corporations that are determined to be at a higher risk of non-compliance. These corporations are subject to rigorous compliance audits where the CRA examines relevant books and records to ensure that all tax obligations have been met.

While risk-based audits allow the CRA to focus its efforts on higher-risk taxpayers, non-compliance identified through these audits cannot be directly extrapolated to the population given that audits are selected based on the risk of non-compliance. Therefore, the CRA uses two statistical methods to minimise this selection bias and estimate the federal CIT reporting gap for large corporations:

- ***Extreme value methodology***, a statistical approach that assumes the majority of tax non-compliance in the large corporate population is concentrated in a relatively small number of corporations. It also assumes that the magnitude of non-compliance will tend to drop off exponentially when ranking corporations according to their level of non-compliance. A regression analysis is then used to extrapolate tax non-compliance to the rest of the large corporate population in order to obtain an estimate of the tax gap. One key limitation of this method is that it can underestimate the tax gap. Therefore, the CIT reporting gap from the extreme value methodology is used as a lower-bound estimate.
- ***Cluster analysis***, an unsupervised machine learning technique in the field of artificial intelligence that helps identity subgroups or "clusters" in a population, where objects in the same cluster are more similar to each other than to those in other clusters. In the context of tax gap analysis, clustering techniques were used to determine whether large corporations could be organized into relatively distinct groups on the basis of certain key variables to estimate the potential level of non-compliance within each cluster. In contrast to the extreme value method, cluster analysis can overestimate the tax gap. Therefore, the CIT reporting gap from cluster analysis is used as an upper-bound estimate.

Sources: Brazil (2024) and Canada (2024).

Value added tax gap

The VAT gap is typically related to tax non-compliance in VAT that can include various fraud activities (for example, carousel schema) and overclaiming VAT refunds in various sectors. This tax gap component is generally the first estimate that a jurisdiction examines due to its well-established top-down methodology.

Almost all jurisdictions with a tax gap programme estimate the VAT gap. Of those:

- Around two thirds estimate the reporting gap and 59% estimate the payment gap. Also, the registration gap (estimated by 19%) and filing gap (estimated by 30%) are more common for this tax type than for others.

- 74% estimate the gross tax gap and 44% estimate the net tax gap.
- 89% use top-down approaches and 33% use bottom-up approaches. Some jurisdictions developed bottom-up methodologies in addition to their top-down approaches. Only a few jurisdictions use only bottom-up approaches to estimate their VAT gaps. The main data sources for bottom-up approaches are random and risk-based audit data (see Figure 11.9.).

For more information, the European Commission (European Commission, 2023[2]) and the IMF (Hutton, 2017[1]) published details on main methodologies used to estimate VAT gaps.

Figure 11.9. Overview of VAT gap estimation

Number of jurisdictions that conduct the relevant analysis or apply the relevant methods

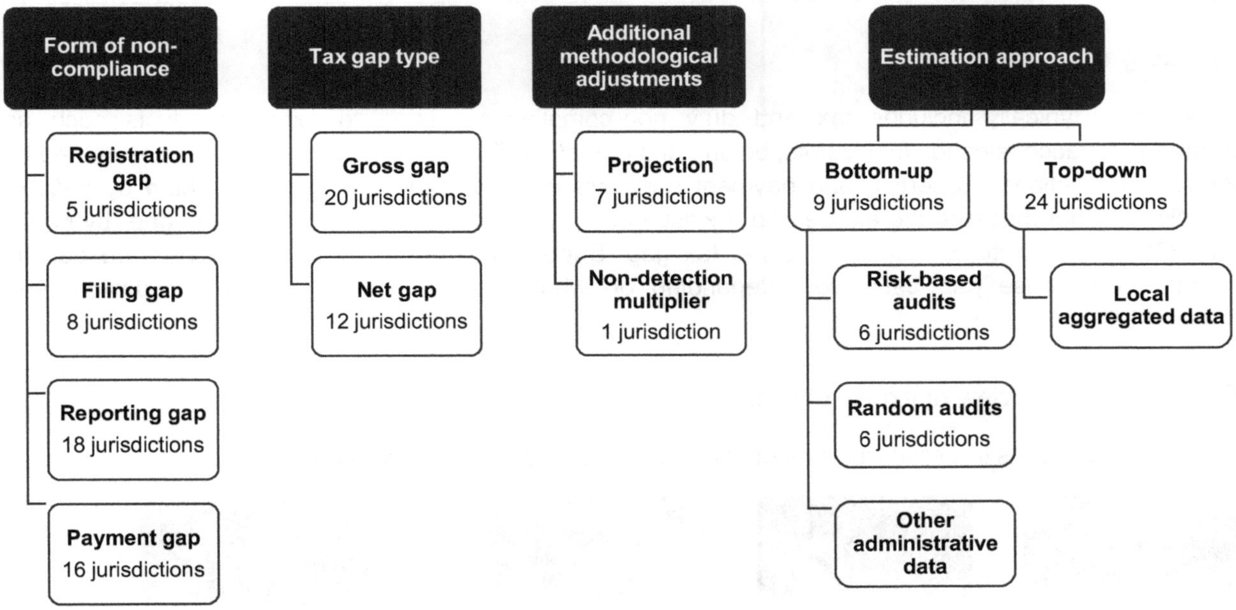

Note: 27 jurisdictions conduct VAT gap estimations.
Source: Annex Table 11.A.9 and Annex Table 11.A.10.

Box 11.7. Italy – VAT frauds and tax gap estimation

The Italian Revenue Agency has implemented two different bottom-up approaches for the estimation of the VAT gap overall and of the portion due to Missing Trader Intra Community (MTIC) fraud, by using data from risk-based audits.

- ***VAT gap***: the methodology combines traditional parametric inference methods, modern machine learning techniques and nearest neighbour imputation procedures. To address the selection bias due to the non-random selection of audited taxpayers, while preserving the distribution of data, the model relies on the conditional independence assumption building up a three steps procedure. Firstly, the Italian Revenue Agency estimates the selection probabilities on a target population through a logistic model and the units are then grouped into classes of "approximately constant selection probability". The second step includes prediction of individual VAT gap values by bagging of regression trees, within each stratum. The third step applies the nearest neighbour imputation method based on predictive means to match non-audited taxpayers with audited taxpayers.

- ***VAT gap due to MTIC fraud***: The main challenges faced in the implementation of the approach is the possible double counting related to the estimation of the gap for all actors involved in the fraud mechanism. To address this issue, we focus on Missing Trader (MT) as a main actor of the fraud. For the identification of the MT we adopt the risk criteria suggested by an internal survey. The model is based on a two-step procedure. The first step involves the estimation, through a logistic model, of the probability of being a MT. The second step computes the MTIC fraud gap multiplying the (estimated) probability of being a MT and the evaded tax.

Source: Italy (2024).

Excise gap

Excise gap typically includes tax and duty non-compliance related to excise products such as cigarettes/tobacco, alcohol, fuel, spirits, betting and gambling. This component is rare and is estimated by 29% of jurisdictions. Reporting and payment gaps are common, and are each estimated by 63% of jurisdictions that measure the excise gap. Excise gap is typically reported as a gross tax gap (by 63%), and 38% of jurisdictions estimate the net tax gap. Bottom-up and top-down approaches are equally common for excise gap estimation, depending on what data is available in the jurisdiction (see Figure 11.10.).

Figure 11.10. Overview of excise gap estimation

Number of jurisdictions that conduct the relevant analysis or apply the relevant methods

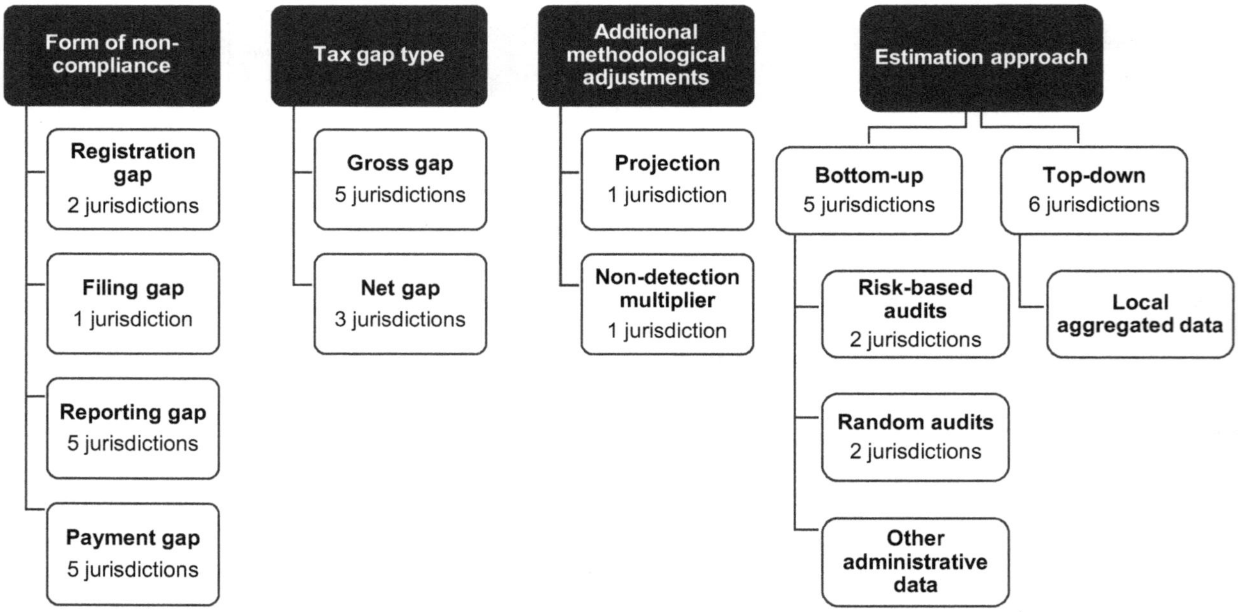

Note: 8 jurisdictions conduct excise gap estimations.
Source: Annex Table 11.A.11 and Annex Table 11.A.12.

Box 11.8. Sweden – Excise gap for various excise products

Sweden currently imposes around 15 different excise taxes, with the most significant in terms of revenue being energy taxes, carbon tax and taxes on alcohol and tobacco. The Swedish Tax Agency (STA) has conducted tax gap assessments specifically for alcohol and tobacco, congestion charges, and some energy taxes related to a tax rebate scheme. Due to the varied designs and target populations of these excise taxes, there is no general approach for assessing the overall tax gap in this area, especially since certain errors in excise taxes that give rise to tax gaps are near impossible to capture. Therefore, each excise tax must be evaluated individually.

The tax gap for alcohol and tobacco mainly arises from illegal production and imports, which are difficult to detect using internal data. The STA therefore relies on an external survey for its tax gap assessment, conducted by another government agency that specialises in alcohol and tobacco use in the Swedish population. Congestion charges are another particular area. It is assessed by identifying registration plates that have been intentionally or unintentionally concealed from traffic cameras. Energy taxes, on the other hand, are assessed using traditional random audits.

Source: Sweden (2024).

Other tax gap components

Other tax gaps generally contain non-compliance related to other types of taxes that exist in the jurisdiction's tax system that may differ from others. Some examples include payroll, regional taxes, social security contributions, and inheritance taxes. Slightly more than one third of jurisdictions (36%) estimate other tax gap components. Jurisdictions usually estimate both payment gap (70%) and reporting gap (90%). Around 70% of jurisdictions estimate the gross tax gap and half estimate the net tax gap. Bottom-up approaches are more common (used by 70%) than top-down methodologies (used by 40%) mostly due to availability of random audits (see Figure 11.11.).

Figure 11.11. Overview of other tax gap estimations

Number of jurisdictions that conduct the relevant analysis or apply the relevant methods

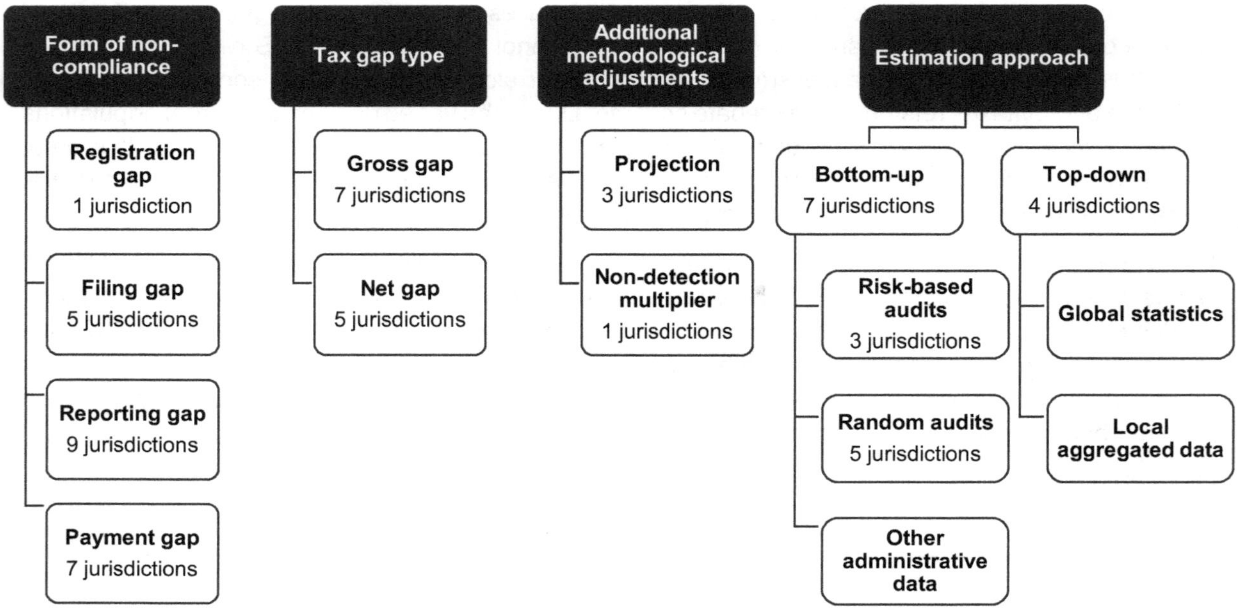

Note: 10 jurisdictions conduct other tax gap estimations.
Source: Annex Table 11.A.13 and Annex Table 11.A.14.

Box 11.9. Latvia – Social security contributions (SSC) tax gap for undeclared wages

The tax gap for undeclared wages is estimated by a bottom-up approach using mainly tax return data. In Latvia, all employers are requested to submit monthly tax returns on wages that includes following data: detailed data on employees, hours worked during taxation period (month), renumeration and taxes withheld (SSC and PIT). A profession of an employee is also reported to the tax authority when employment relations are established.

Given that the wage depends on the following main parameters: 1) the employment industry; 2) territorial location of an employer; 3) profession of an employee and length of a working day, the Latvian Tax Administration's approach is based on comparison of an actual wages with an average wage for each profession type in particular industry and region (further – "average wage"). For profession types recognised to have extra high risks of undeclared wages the "average wage" is set based on research of publicly available job advertisements.

As employee's decision on choice of a particular job can be affected by non-fiscal factors (for example, location or a social "package" provided by employer), for the purpose of tax gap estimates, an assumption is made: an employee has received undeclared wages if their actual wage is less than 70% of an "average wage". The difference between an "average wage" and actual wage is used to estimate the amount of an undeclared wage for each employee and employer. After an undeclared wage is estimated the effective SSC rate is applied for calculation of the SSC gap (same procedure is consequently applied for PIT gap estimation).

The main advantage of this method is possibility to personalise the tax gap for an employee and an employer and to analyse the phenomenon from different perspectives, for example, to identify risky industries, to define a demographic profile of an employee receiving undeclared wages.

Source: Latvia (2024).

Tax gap use

Jurisdictions have various reasons to estimate tax gaps including supporting data-driven decision making. The main applications mentioned by jurisdictions are as follows:

- Satisfying legislative requirements
- Providing transparency to the public and parliament
- Monitoring emerging trends and checking the health of the tax system
- Identifying areas in the tax system and administration that may need improvements
- Informing compliance areas on risks of non-compliance and the underlying behavioural drivers
- Driving additional compliance research
- Providing information to policy makers and enabling data-driven decisions
- Facilitating organisational investments and planning
- Measuring long-term performance of a tax administration or alongside other indicators

Although tax gap estimates can provide a lot of useful insights for tax administrations, they might not be a good basis for explicit performance targets due to a number of limitations (OECD, 2017[3]). Nevertheless, some jurisdictions do use tax gap estimates to understand overall performance of the tax system.

Tax gaps can be used not only by tax administrations but by other parties as well such as the public, politicians, other government departments, academics and other organisations. Their tax gap use could vary from the use of the tax gap estimates by the tax administration. For example, in Sweden, beyond the tax administration use, tax gap estimates are used to raise the quality of national accounts statistics.

Box 11.10. Australia – Tax gap use

The Australian Taxation Office (ATO) recognises that estimates of tax gap alone are not always a good measure of specific agency performance given that the tax gap measures whole of system performance, which is also impacted by factors outside of the agency's control.

The ATO recognises these limitations in using tax gap as a performance measure, and particularly that it is not the best indicator of short-term performance. It is also hard to set targets without considering the historical context of tax gap. For this reason, Australia uses longer-term tax gap trend analysis to assess agency performance and finds that it is a useful indicator of the medium-term performance, particularly in the context of ATO's stewardship role of the tax and super systems.

Sometimes tax gaps will go up or down through no fault of, or unrelated to the actions of the agency. For this reason, the ATO's performance assessment includes meaningful qualitative context so that the audience can clearly understand the extent to which the ATO has contributed to the improvement or sustainment of the tax gap over the medium term.

Changes of tax gap performance are indicators of the overall health of the system including the agency and so, in the ATO, tax gap estimates form part of the strategy development and resource planning decisions.

Source: Australia (2024).

Impact of the COVID-19 Pandemic on tax gap estimations

The COVID-19 pandemic was an unprecedented event that affected the whole world. Many jurisdictions implemented different measures to contain the pandemic and to address the economic impact as a result of, for example, lockdowns and other precautionary measures taken.

The pandemic also had an impact on tax administrations as many governments took action to support individuals and businesses by extending tax payment terms or suspending the collection of outstanding tax debt. (CIAT/IOTA/OECD, 2020[9])

Many jurisdictions have already noticed an impact of the pandemic on their tax gap estimates and some are already adjusting their methodologies accordingly. However, the full impact on the tax gap will need to be examined in the future.

Box 11.11. Australia – Impacts of the COVID-19 pandemic on tax gap measurement

The economic impacts of the interactions between the COVID-19 pandemic and economic stimulus measures evolved over time and lasted over a number of years. These economic disruptions would have had a direct impact on taxpayers' financial situations and compliance behaviours, and hence tax collections.

For tax gap measurement, the COVID-19 pandemic presented both challenges and opportunities. The biggest challenges to measuring tax gap related to understanding the COVID-19 impacts on data. The ATO noticed significant changes in national account statistics and other external data with large changes that were difficult to validate as no other information existed on similar-sized economic shocks. The COVID-19 pandemic saw consumption patterns change leading to a significant reduction in the GST / VAT tax gap.

The ATO also had to contend with challenges with internally-generated data. Gap estimates that rely on operational audit data were impacted as the number of audits across some market segments declined as the ATO shifted its focus to supporting taxpayers. While the ATO was still able to generate estimates, the reliability rating of some of these "provisional" estimates was reduced to reflect a smaller sample size used to generate the estimate. Australia also changed the method for the medium business tax gap estimate to a combination of a logistic and Poisson Pseudo Maximum Likelihood regression model. This change was necessary as the assumptions underpinning the existing Extreme Value Method were no longer valid due to a reduction in compliance cases and coverage.

In terms of opportunities, the COVID-19 pandemic provides the ATO with an opportunity to apply tax gap thinking to economic stimulus measures for generating "payment" gap estimates for payment programs designed to support businesses and individuals.

Source: Australia (2024).

Tax gap estimation is not an easy exercise and it usually requires a lot of experience and diverse expertise. For further information on tax administration's work on tax gap estimation see Table 11.6. which contains a selection of links to a number of tax gap reports.

Table 11.6. Links to selected tax gap reports and websites published by tax administrations

Jurisdiction	Report	Links (accessed on 22 August 2024)
Australia	Australian tax gaps – overview	https://www.ato.gov.au/about-ato/research-and-statistics/in-detail/tax-gap/australian-tax-gaps-overview
Brazil	Corporate Income Tax Gap report from 2015 to 2019 (English version)	https://www.gov.br/receitafederal/pt-br/centrais-de-conteudo/publicacoes/estudos/tax-gap/tax-gap-dos-tributos-irpj-csll/cit-tax-gap-report-2015-to-2019-english-version.pdf/view
Canada	Overall federal tax gap report: Estimates and key findings for non-compliance, tax years 2014-2018	https://www.canada.ca/en/revenue-agency/corporate/about-canada-revenue-agency-cra/tax-canada-a-conceptual-study/tax-gap-brief-overview/overall-federal-tax-gap-report.html
Italy	Report on the unobserved economy and tax and social security evasion - year 2023 (Italian version)	https://www.finanze.gov.it/export/sites/finanze/.galleries/Documenti/Varie/Relazione-evasione-fiscale-e-contributiva-2023_26set-finale.pdf
Sweden	Tax Gap Report 2020 (English version)	https://www.skatteverket.se/download/18.96cca41179bad4b1aa8c0b/1632316511065/Tax%20gap%20report%202020.pdf
United Kingdom	Measuring tax gaps 2024 edition: tax gap estimates for 2022 to 2023	https://www.gov.uk/government/statistics/measuring-tax-gaps
United States	Tax Gap Projections for Tax Years 2020 & 2021	https://www.irs.gov/pub/irs-pdf/p5869.pdf

Notes

[1] All data in this chapter is based on the 2023 survey responses (updated as of July 2024) from the members of the OECD Forum on Tax Administration's Community of Interest (COI) on Tax Gap, an informal network of tax gap analysts. All percentages are calculated based on the data from the 28 jurisdictions that replied to the survey and estimate a tax gap. Jurisdictions with tax gap programmes that did not reply to the survey are out of scope for this chapter.

The data in this chapter may differ from the International Survey on Revenue Administration (ISORA) results since the two surveys were conducted during different timeframes and the questions were worded slightly differently. For example, the COI survey asked whether a tax administration estimates the tax gap for the different tax types, while ISORA asked whether the tax administration or any other government agency produces periodic estimates of the tax gap for the different tax types.

[2] Although the Netherlands Tax Administration estimates the total gap for each entity, it is still possible to establish the estimation of the tax gap of a specific tax revenue based on these random audits. However, it is a strategic decision to focus on the total tax gap of each entity.

References

Barra, P., E. Hutton and P. Prokof'yeva (2023), *Corporate Income Tax Gap Estimation by using Bottom-Up Techniques in Selected Countries: Revenue Administration Gap Analysis Program*, International Monetary Fund, Washington, DC, https://doi.org/10.5089/9798400246265.005. [5]

CIAT/IOTA/OECD (2020), *"Tax administration responses to COVID-19: Measures taken to support taxpayers", OECD Policy Responses to Coronavirus (COVID-19)*, OECD Publishing, Paris, https://doi.org/10.1787/adc84188-en. [9]

Council of the European Union (2006), "Council Directive 2006/112/EC of 28 November 2006 on the common system of value added tax", *Official Journal of the European Union* OJ L 347, https://data.europa.eu/eli/dir/2006/112/2024-01-01. [10]

European Commission (2023), *VAT gap in the EU – 2023 report*, Publications Office of the European Union, https://doi.org/10.2778/911698. [2]

Fiscalis TGPG (2018), *The Concept of Tax Gaps Report II: Corporate Income Tax Gap Estimation Methodologies by FISCALIS Tax Gap Project Group (FPG/041)*, European Commission, Brussels, https://taxation-customs.ec.europa.eu/system/files/2018-07/tgpg-report-on-cit-gap-methodology_en.pdf (accessed on 10 September 2024). [6]

HMRC (2020), *Non-detection multipliers for measuring tax gaps*, HMRC, http://www.gov.uk/government/publications/non-detection-multipliers-for-measuring-tax-gaps/non-detection-multipliers-for-measuring-tax-gaps (accessed on 10 September 2024). [7]

Hutton, E. (2017), *The Revenue Administration-Gap Analysis Program: Model and Methodology for Value-Added Tax Gap Estimation*, International Monetary Fund, Washington, DC, https://doi.org/10.5089/9781475583618.005. [1]

OECD (2017), *"The measurement of tax gaps", in Tax Administration 2017: Comparative Information on OECD and Other Advanced and Emerging Economies*, OECD Publishing, Paris, https://doi.org/10.1787/tax_admin-2017-19-en. [3]

Swedish Tax Agency (2023), *Using the Delphi method to determine a non-detection multiplier for the tax gap assessment*, Swedish Tax Agency, Malmö, https://skatteverket.se/download/18.7da1d2e118be03f8e4f45d8/1703064480910/Using%20the%20Delphi%20method%20to%20determine%20a%20non-detection%20multiplier%20for%20the%20tax%20gap%20assessment.pdf (accessed on 10 September 2024). [8]

Thackray, M., S. Jennings and M. Knudsen (2021), *The Revenue Administration Gap Analysis Program: An Analytical Framework for Personal Income Tax Gap Estimation*, International Monetary Fund, Washington, DC, https://doi.org/10.5089/9781513577173.005. [4]

Annex 11.A. Data Tables

Annex 11.A. contains a set of fourteen tables that hold the data provided by members of the OECD Forum on Tax Administration's Community of Interest on Tax Gap, an informal network of tax gap analysts, in response to a survey on tax gap estimations conducted in 2023:

- Annex Table 11.A.1. General overview of tax gap estimation
- Annex Table 11.A.2. Tax gap estimation components
- Annex Table 11.A.3. Tax gap approaches, data and methodological adjustments
- Annex Table 11.A.4. Number of bottom-up methodologies by data sources
- Annex Table 11.A.5. PIT gap measurement: Type of gap estimation conducted
- Annex Table 11.A.6. PIT gap measurement: Approaches and methods used
- Annex Table 11.A.7. CIT gap measurement: Type of gap estimation conducted
- Annex Table 11.A.8. CIT gap measurement: Approaches and methods used
- Annex Table 11.A.9. VAT gap measurement: Type of gap estimation conducted
- Annex Table 11.A.10. VAT gap measurement: Approaches and methods used
- Annex Table 11.A.11. Excise gap measurement: Type of gap estimation conducted
- Annex Table 11.A.12. Excise gap measurement: Approaches and methods used
- Annex Table 11.A.13. Other gap measurement: Type of gap estimation conducted
- Annex Table 11.A.14. Other gap measurement: Approaches and methods used

Annex Table 11.A.1. General overview of tax gap estimation

Jurisdiction	Estimating tax gap	Publishing overall tax gap	Legal requirement to publish	Publication frequency	Third-party support
Australia	Yes	Yes	No	Annually	Yes
Belgium	Yes	No	No		Yes
Brazil	Yes	Yes	No	Irregularly	Yes
Canada	Yes	Yes	No	Every three years	Yes
Chile	Yes	No	No		Yes
Colombia	Yes	No	No		No
Denmark	Yes	No	No		Yes
European Commission	Yes	No	No		Yes
Finland	Yes	No	No		No
France	Yes	No	No		Yes
Greece	Yes	No	No		No
Hungary	Yes	No	No		Yes
Iceland	Yes	No	No		Yes
Indonesia	Yes	No	No		Yes
Israel	Yes	No	No		No
Italy	Yes	Yes	Yes	Annually	No
Latvia	Yes	No	No		No
Lithuania	Yes	No	No		Yes
Netherlands	Yes	Yes	Yes	Every two years	No
Portugal	Yes	No	No		No
Romania	Yes	No	No		Yes
Singapore	Yes	No	No		No
Slovakia	Yes	No	No		No
Spain	Yes	No	No		No
Sweden	Yes	Yes	Yes	Every four years	Yes
Switzerland	Yes	No	No		No
United Kingdom	Yes	Yes	No	Annually	No
United States	Yes	Yes	No	Every three years (with annual projections)	Yes
Total "Yes"	**28**	**8**	**3**		**15**

Source: FTA 2023 survey on tax gap estimations.

Annex Table 11.A.2. Tax gap estimation components

Jurisdiction	Policy gap	Registration or filing gap	Reporting gap	Payment gap	Gross tax gap	Net tax gap
Australia	No	Yes	Yes	Yes	Yes	Yes
Belgium	Yes	No	No	No	Yes	No
Brazil	Yes	No	Yes	Yes	Yes	Yes
Canada	No	No	Yes	Yes	Yes	Yes
Chile	No	Yes	Yes	Yes	Yes	No
Colombia	No	No	Yes	Yes	Yes	No
Denmark	No	Yes	Yes	Yes	Yes	No
European Commission	Yes	Yes	Yes	Yes	No	Yes
Finland	No	Yes	No	No	No	Yes
France	No	No	Yes	Yes	Yes	Yes
Greece	Yes	No	Yes	No	Yes	No
Hungary	Yes	No	Yes	Yes	Yes	No
Iceland	No	Yes	Yes	No	Yes	Yes
Indonesia	Yes	No	Yes	Yes	Yes	Yes
Israel	No	No	No	Yes	No	Yes
Italy	No	Yes	Yes	Yes	Yes	No
Latvia	No	Yes	Yes	Yes	Yes	Yes
Lithuania	No	No	No	No	Yes	No
Netherlands	No	Yes	Yes	Yes	No	No
Portugal	No	No	No	No	Yes	No
Romania	Yes	No	Yes	Yes	Yes	No
Singapore	No	No	No	No	Yes	No
Slovakia	No	No	Yes	Yes	Yes	Yes
Spain	No	No	No	No	Yes	No
Sweden	No	No	Yes	No	Yes	Yes
Switzerland	Yes	No	Yes	No	No	No
United Kingdom	No	No	Yes	Yes	Yes	Yes
United States	No	Yes	Yes	Yes	Yes	Yes
Total "Yes"	**8**	**10**	**21**	**18**	**23**	**14**

Source: FTA 2023 survey on tax gap estimations.

Annex Table 11.A.3. Tax gap approaches, data and methodological adjustments

Jurisdiction	Projection for at least one tax gap component	Non-detection multiplier	Bottom-up approach	Top-down approach	Random audit for at least one tax gap component
Australia	Yes	Yes	Yes	Yes	Yes
Belgium	No	Yes	No	Yes	No
Brazil	Yes	No	Yes	Yes	No
Canada	Yes	No	Yes	Yes	Yes
Chile	Yes	No	No	Yes	No
Colombia	No	No	No	Yes	No
Denmark	No	No	Yes	Yes	Yes
European Commission	Yes	No	No	Yes	No
Finland	No	No	Yes	Yes	Yes
France	No	No	Yes	No	Yes
Greece	No	No	No	Yes	No
Hungary	Yes	No	Yes	Yes	Yes
Iceland	No	No	No	Yes	No
Indonesia	No	No	Yes	Yes	No
Israel	No	No	No	Yes	No
Italy	Yes	Yes	Yes	Yes	No
Latvia	No	No	Yes	Yes	No
Lithuania	Yes	No	Yes	Yes	No
Netherlands	No	No	Yes	Yes	Yes
Portugal	No	No	No	Yes	No
Romania	No	No	No	Yes	No
Singapore	No	No	No	Yes	No
Slovakia	No	No	No	Yes	No
Spain	No	No	No	Yes	No
Sweden	No	Yes	Yes	Yes	Yes
Switzerland	No	No	Yes	No	Yes
United Kingdom	Yes	Yes	Yes	Yes	Yes
United States	Yes	Yes	Yes	No	Yes
Total "Yes"	**10**	**6**	**16**	**25**	**11**

Source: FTA 2023 survey on tax gap estimations.

Annex Table 11.A.4. Number of bottom-up methodologies by data sources

Jurisdiction	Random audits	Risk-based audits	Total
Australia	6	11	17
Canada	1	2	3
Denmark	13	1	14
Finland	1	1	2
France	1	2	3
Hungary	1	1	2
Indonesia	0	6	6
Italy	0	4	4
Netherlands	6	0	6
Sweden	4	1	5
Switzerland	1	0	1
United Kingdom	6	9	15
United States	4	2	6
Total	**44**	**40**	**84**
Average	**3.4**	**3.1**	**6.5**

Note: The table only contains data from jurisdictions that use bottom-up approaches.
Source: FTA 2023 survey on tax gap estimations.

Annex Table 11.A.5. PIT gap measurement: Type of gap estimation conducted

Jurisdiction	PIT gap estimation	Registration gap	Filing gap	Reporting gap	Payment gap	Gross tax gap	Net tax gap
Australia	Yes	No	No	Yes	Yes	Yes	Yes
Brazil	Yes	No	No	Yes	No	No	Yes
Canada	Yes	No	No	Yes	Yes	Yes	Yes
Colombia	Yes	No	No	Yes	Yes	Yes	No
Denmark	Yes	Yes	Yes	Yes	Yes	Yes	No
Greece	Yes	No	No	Yes	No	No	No
Indonesia	Yes	No	No	Yes	Yes	Yes	Yes
Italy	Yes	No	Yes	Yes	Yes	Yes	No
Latvia	Yes	No	Yes	Yes	Yes	Yes	Yes
Lithuania	Yes	No	No	No	No	Yes	No
Netherlands	Yes	No	Yes	Yes	Yes	No	No
Romania	Yes	No	No	Yes	Yes	Yes	No
Spain	Yes	No	No	No	No	Yes	No
Sweden	Yes	No	No	Yes	No	Yes	Yes
United Kingdom	Yes	No	No	Yes	Yes	Yes	Yes
United States	Yes	No	Yes	Yes	Yes	Yes	Yes
Total "Yes"	**16**	**1**	**5**	**14**	**11**	**13**	**8**

Note: The table only contains data from jurisdictions that conduct PIT gap measurement.
Source: FTA 2023 survey on tax gap estimations.

Annex Table 11.A.6. PIT gap measurement: Approaches and methods used

Jurisdiction	No. of bottom-up approaches	No. of top-down approaches	No. of methods on risk-based data	No. of methods on random audit data	Projections	Non-detection multiplier
Australia	4	0	2	2	Yes	Yes
Brazil	1	0	0	0	No	No
Canada	0	2	0	0	No	No
Colombia	0	1	0	0	No	No
Denmark	5	2	0	5	No	No
Greece	0	1	0	0	No	No
Indonesia	5	1	2	0	No	No
Italy	0	3	0	0	Yes	No
Latvia	1	0	0	0	No	No
Lithuania	1	0	0	0	No	No
Netherlands	3	0	0	3	No	No
Romania	0	1	0	0	No	No
Spain	0	1	0	0	No	No
Sweden	2	1	0	2	No	No
United Kingdom	6	0	2	4	Yes	Yes
United States	4	0	0	2	Yes	Yes
Total sum or "Yes"	**32**	**13**	**6**	**18**	**4**	**3**

Note: The table only contains data from jurisdictions that conduct PIT gap measurement.
Source: FTA 2023 survey on tax gap estimations.

Annex Table 11.A.7. CIT gap measurement: Type of gap estimation conducted

Jurisdiction	CIT gap estimation	Registration gap	Filing gap	Reporting gap	Payment gap	Gross tax gap	Net tax gap
Australia	Yes	No	No	Yes	Yes	Yes	Yes
Brazil	Yes	No	No	Yes	Yes	Yes	Yes
Canada	Yes	No	No	Yes	Yes	Yes	Yes
Chile	Yes	Yes	Yes	Yes	Yes	Yes	No
Colombia	Yes	No	No	Yes	Yes	Yes	No
Denmark	Yes	No	Yes	Yes	Yes	Yes	No
France	Yes	No	No	Yes	Yes	Yes	Yes
Indonesia	Yes	No	No	Yes	Yes	Yes	Yes
Italy	Yes	No	Yes	Yes	Yes	Yes	No
Romania	Yes	No	No	Yes	Yes	Yes	No
Slovakia	Yes	No	No	Yes	No	No	Yes
Sweden	Yes	No	No	Yes	No	Yes	Yes
United Kingdom	Yes	No	No	Yes	Yes	Yes	Yes
United States	Yes	No	No	Yes	Yes	Yes	Yes
Total "Yes"	**14**	**1**	**3**	**14**	**12**	**13**	**9**

Note: The table only contains data from jurisdictions that conduct CIT gap measurement.
Source: FTA 2023 survey on tax gap estimations.

Annex Table 11.A.8. CIT gap measurement: Approaches and methods used

Jurisdiction	No. of bottom-up approaches	No. of top-down approaches	No. of methods on risk-based data	No. of methods on random audit data	Projections	Non-detection multiplier
Australia	4	0	3	1	Yes	Yes
Brazil	1	1	0	0	No	No
Canada	3	0	2	1	Yes	No
Chile	0	1	0	0	No	No
Colombia	0	1	0	0	No	No
Denmark	3	0	1	2	No	No
France	1	0	1	0	No	No
Indonesia	5	1	2	0	No	No
Italy	0	1	0	0	Yes	No
Romania	0	1	0	0	No	No
Slovakia	0	1	0	0	No	No
Sweden	2	0	1	1	No	Yes
United Kingdom	3	0	2	1	Yes	Yes
United States	4	0	2	0	Yes	No
Total sum or "Yes"	**26**	**7**	**14**	**6**	**5**	**3**

Note: The table only contains data from jurisdictions that conduct CIT gap measurement.
Source: FTA 2023 survey on tax gap estimations.

Annex Table 11.A.9. VAT gap measurement: Type of gap estimation conducted

Jurisdiction	VAT gap estimation	Registration gap	Filing gap	Reporting gap	Payment gap	Gross tax gap	Net tax gap
Australia	Yes	No	No	Yes	Yes	Yes	Yes
Belgium	Yes	No	No	No	No	Yes	No
Brazil	Yes	No	No	Yes	No	No	Yes
Canada	Yes	No	No	Yes	Yes	Yes	Yes
Chile	Yes	Yes	Yes	Yes	Yes	Yes	No
Colombia	Yes	No	No	No	Yes	Yes	No
Denmark	Yes	Yes	Yes	Yes	Yes	Yes	No
European Commission	Yes	Yes	Yes	Yes	Yes	No	Yes
Finland	Yes	No	Yes	No	No	No	Yes
France	Yes	No	No	Yes	Yes	Yes	Yes
Greece	Yes	No	No	No	No	Yes	No
Hungary	Yes	No	No	Yes	Yes	Yes	No
Iceland	Yes	Yes	Yes	Yes	No	Yes	Yes
Indonesia	Yes	No	No	Yes	Yes	Yes	Yes
Israel	Yes	No	No	No	Yes	No	Yes
Italy	Yes	No	Yes	Yes	Yes	Yes	No
Latvia	Yes	Yes	Yes	Yes	Yes	Yes	Yes
Lithuania	Yes	No	No	No	No	Yes	No
Netherlands	Yes	No	Yes	Yes	Yes	No	No
Portugal	Yes	No	No	No	No	Yes	No
Romania	Yes	No	No	Yes	Yes	Yes	No
Singapore	Yes	No	No	No	No	Yes	No
Slovakia	Yes	No	No	Yes	Yes	Yes	Yes
Spain	Yes	No	No	No	No	No	No
Sweden	Yes	No	No	Yes	No	Yes	No
Switzerland	Yes	No	No	Yes	No	No	No
United Kingdom	Yes	No	No	Yes	Yes	Yes	Yes
Total "Yes"	**27**	**5**	**8**	**18**	**16**	**20**	**12**

Note: The table only contains data from jurisdictions that conduct VAT gap measurement.
Source: FTA 2023 survey on tax gap estimations.

Annex Table 11.A.10. VAT gap measurement: Approaches and methods used

Jurisdiction	No. of bottom-up approaches	No. of top-down approaches	No. of methods on risk-based data	No. of methods on random audit data	Projections	Non-detection multiplier
Australia	1	1	1	1	Yes	No
Belgium	0	2	0	0	No	Yes
Brazil	0	1	0	0	Yes	No
Canada	0	1	0	0	No	No
Chile	0	1	0	0	Yes	No
Colombia	0	1	0	0	No	No
Denmark	3	1	0	3	No	No
European Commission	0	1	0	0	Yes	No
Finland	1	1	1	1	No	No
France	2	0	1	1	No	No
Greece	0	1	0	0	No	No
Hungary	2	3	1	1	Yes	No
Iceland	0	1	0	0	No	No
Indonesia	5	1	2	0	No	No
Israel	0	1	0	0	No	No
Italy	2	1	2	0	Yes	No
Latvia	0	1	0	0	No	No
Lithuania	1	2	0	0	Yes	No
Netherlands	0	1	0	0	No	No
Portugal	0	1	0	0	No	No
Romania	0	2	0	0	No	No
Singapore	0	1	0	0	No	No
Slovakia	0	2	0	0	No	No
Spain	0	0	0	0	No	No
Sweden	0	2	0	0	No	No
Switzerland	1	0	0	1	No	No
United Kingdom	0	1	0	0	No	No
Total sum or "Yes"	**18**	**31**	**8**	**8**	**7**	**1**

Note: The table only contains data from jurisdictions that conduct VAT gap measurement.
Source: FTA 2023 survey on tax gap estimations.

Annex Table 11.A.11. Excise gap measurement: Type of gap estimation conducted

Jurisdiction	Excise gap estimation	Registration gap	Filing gap	Reporting gap	Payment gap	Gross tax gap	Net tax gap
Australia	Yes	Yes	No	Yes	Yes	Yes	Yes
Canada	Yes	No	No	Yes	Yes	Yes	Yes
Denmark	Yes	Yes	Yes	Yes	Yes	Yes	No
Greece	Yes	No	No	No	No	Yes	No
Italy	Yes	No	No	No	No	No	No
Sweden	Yes	No	No	Yes	No	Yes	No
United Kingdom	Yes	No	No	Yes	Yes	No	Yes
United States	Yes	No	No	No	Yes	No	No
Total "Yes"	**8**	**2**	**1**	**5**	**5**	**5**	**3**

Note: The table only contains data from jurisdictions that conduct Excise gap measurement.
Source: FTA 2023 survey on tax gap estimations.

Annex Table 11.A.12. Excise gap measurement: Approaches and methods used

Jurisdiction	No. of bottom-up approaches	No. of top-down approaches	No. of methods on risk-based data	No. of methods on random audit data	Projections	Non-detection multiplier
Australia	2	1	1	0	No	Yes
Canada	0	1	0	0	No	No
Denmark	3	1	0	2	No	No
Greece	0	1	0	0	No	No
Italy	0	0	0	0	No	No
Sweden	1	1	0	0	No	No
United Kingdom	2	4	2	1	Yes	No
United States	1	0	0	0	No	No
Total sum or "Yes"	**9**	**9**	**3**	**3**	**1**	**1**

Note: The table only contains data from jurisdictions that conduct Excise gap measurement.
Source: FTA 2023 survey on tax gap estimations.

Annex Table 11.A.13. Other gap measurement: Type of gap estimation conducted

Jurisdiction	Other gaps estimation	Registration gap	Filing gap	Reporting gap	Payment gap	Gross tax gap	Net tax gap
Australia	Yes	No	No	Yes	Yes	Yes	Yes
Brazil	Yes	No	No	Yes	No	No	No
Denmark	Yes	Yes	Yes	Yes	No	Yes	No
Italy	Yes	No	Yes	Yes	Yes	Yes	No
Latvia	Yes	No	Yes	Yes	Yes	Yes	Yes
Netherlands	Yes	No	Yes	Yes	Yes	No	No
Romania	Yes	No	No	No	Yes	Yes	No
Sweden	Yes	No	No	Yes	No	Yes	Yes
United Kingdom	Yes	No	No	Yes	Yes	No	Yes
United States	Yes	No	Yes	Yes	Yes	Yes	Yes
Total "Yes"	**10**	**1**	**5**	**9**	**7**	**7**	**5**

Note: The table only contains data from jurisdictions that conduct other gap measurement.
Source: FTA 2023 survey on tax gap estimations.

Annex Table 11.A.14. Other gap measurement: Approaches and methods used

Jurisdiction	No. of bottom-up approaches	No. of top-down approaches	No. of methods on risk-based data	No. of methods on random audit data	Projections	Non-detection multiplier
Australia	4	4	4	2	Yes	No
Brazil	0	1	0	0	No	No
Denmark	1	0	0	1	No	No
Italy	2	2	2	0	No	Yes
Latvia	1	0	0	0	No	No
Netherlands	3	0	0	3	No	No
Romania	0	1	0	0	No	No
Sweden	1	0	0	1	No	No
United Kingdom	0	0	3	0	Yes	No
United States	8	0	0	2	Yes	No
Total sum or "Yes"	**20**	**8**	**9**	**9**	**3**	**1**

Note: The table only contains data from jurisdictions that conduct other gap measurement.
Source: FTA 2023 survey on tax gap estimations.

Annex A. Overview of the ISORA data tables

Annex A contains links to the ISORA tables that hold the annual and periodic ISORA data for fiscal years 2018 to 2022, and that are published on the RA-FIT data portal (https://data.rafit.org/).

The online tables show the data for the more than 175 jurisdictions that have completed at least one of the last four rounds of ISORA which were launched between September 2020 and September 2023. They are grouped into:

- ***Annual Tables*** (see Table A A.1.) which contain:
  - Thirteen sets of tables containing the raw ISORA survey data. Those are the tables starting with "A".
  - Six sets of tables with indicators derived from the data submitted via the ISORA survey (tables starting with "D"). The formulae and data points used for calculating the indicators are shown below each of these tables.
- ***Periodic Tables*** (see Table A A.2.) which hold the data from the periodic part of the 2023 ISORA survey. Those tables start with "B" and they are grouped in seven table sets.

Using the ISORA data in those tables, the Tax Administration 2024 publication examines various aspects of tax systems and their administration in 58 OECD and non-OECD jurisdictions. (See Annex B for the list of tax administrations covered by this publication.)

Table A A.1. Overview of the ISORA data tables: Annual tables

Table grouping	Table name	Link
Revenue types collected	Table A.0 Participation of tax administrations in ISORA	https://data.rafit.org/regular.aspx?key=74180893
	Table A.1 Revenue types for which the administration has responsibility: Income tax and taxes on goods and services	
	Table A.2 Revenue types for which the administration has responsibility: Other taxes	
	Table A.3 Revenue types for which the administration has responsibility: Other taxes (continued), SSC and non-tax revenue	
	Table A.4 Employer withholding taxes and combined tax and customs administrations	
Revenue collection	Table A.5 Net revenue collected by the tax administration: Total	https://data.rafit.org/regular.aspx?key=74180904
	Table A.6 Net revenue collected by the tax administration by tax type: Personal income tax	
	Table A.7 Net revenue collected by the tax administration by tax type: Corporate income tax	
	Table A.8 Net revenue collected by the tax administration by tax type: Value added taxes	
	Table A.9 Net revenue collected by the tax administration by tax type: Excises (domestic)	
	Table A.10 Net revenue collected by the tax administration by tax type: Other taxes	
	Table A.11 Net revenue collected by the tax administration: Social security contributions	

Table grouping	Table name	Link
	Table A.12 Net revenue collected by the tax administration: Non-tax revenues	
	Table A.13 Composition of value added taxes collected by the tax administration: Gross domestic	
	Table A.14 Composition of value added taxes collected by the tax administration: Gross import, even where collected by customs	
	Table A.15 Composition of value added tax collected by the tax administration: Refunds	
Expenditure and FTE resources	Table A.16 Tax administration expenditures: Operating and salary expenditure	https://data.rafit.org/regular.aspx?key=74180905
	Table A.17 Tax administration ICT expenditure and percentage of FTEs working on headquarter functions	
	Table A.17A FTEs for joint tax and customs administrations	
	Table A.17B Expenditures for joint tax and customs administrations	
	Table A.18 Total FTEs of the tax administration and FTEs of the tax administration by function: Registration and services	
	Table A.19 Number of FTEs by function: Audit and debt collection	
	Table A.20 Number of FTEs by function: Disputes and HR	
	Table A.21 Number of FTEs by function: ICT and all other functions	
Staff metrics	Table A.22 Staff metrics: Staff strength levels at start of FY and departures	https://data.rafit.org/regular.aspx?key=74180906
	Table A.23 Staff metrics: Staff strength levels at end of FY and recruitments	
	Table A.24 Staff metrics: Gender information	
	Table A.25 Staff metrics: Gender distribution – Female	
	Table A.26 Staff metrics: Gender distribution – Male	
	Table A.27 Staff metrics: Gender distribution - Other gender	
	Table A.28 Staff metrics: Academic qualifications	
	Table A.29 Staff metrics: Age distribution below 35 years	
	Table A.30 Staff metrics: Age distribution 35 to 54 years	
	Table A.31 Staff metrics: Age distribution 55 years and above	
	Table A.32 Staff metrics: Length of service below 10 years	
	Table A.33 Staff metrics: Length of service 10 years and above	
Segmentation	Table A.34 Large taxpayer office / program: Existence and revenue collected	https://data.rafit.org/regular.aspx?key=74180907
	Table A.35 Large taxpayer office / program: Functions - Registration, return and payment processing, and services	
	Table A.36 Large taxpayer office / program: Functions - Audit, debt collection, dispute resolution	
	Table A.37 Large taxpayer office / program: Staff	
	Table A.38 Large taxpayer office / program: Taxpayers	
	Table A.39 Large taxpayer office / program: Audits	
	Table A.40 High net wealth individuals (HNWIs) office / program: Existence and revenue collected	
PIT and employer withholding: Registration and filing	Table A.42 Number of taxpayers by tax type: Personal income tax	https://data.rafit.org/regular.aspx?key=74180908
	Table A.43 Number of taxpayers by tax type: Employers that withhold tax from employees	
	Table A.50 Return filing: Expected and received returns - Personal income tax	
	Table A.51 Return filing: Returns received on time - Personal income tax	
	Table A.52 Return receipt channels: Paper and electronic, not prefilled - Personal income tax	
	Table A.53 Return receipt channels: Electronic returns, prefilled - Personal income tax	

Table grouping	Table name	Link
	Table A.54 Return filing: Expected and received returns - Employers that withhold tax from employees	
	Table A.55 Return filing: Returns received on time - Employers that withhold tax from employees	
	Table A.56 Return receipt channels: Paper and electronic, not prefilled - Employers that withhold tax from employees	
	Table A.57 Return receipt channels: Electronic returns, prefilled - Employers that withhold tax from employees	
	Table A.58 Personal income tax withholding: Requirements and total withholdings	
CIT, VAT, Excise: Registration and filing	Table A.41 Number of taxpayers by tax type: Corporate income tax	https://data.rafit.org/regular.aspx?key=74180909
	Table A.44 Number of taxpayers by tax type: Value added tax	
	Table A.45 Number of taxpayers by tax type: Excise	
	Table A.46 Return filing: Expected and received returns - Corporate income tax	
	Table A.47 Return filing: Returns received on time - Corporate income tax	
	Table A.48 Return receipt channels: Paper and electronic, not prefilled - Corporate income tax	
	Table A.49 Return receipt channels: Electronic returns, prefilled - Corporate income tax	
	Table A.59 Return filing: Expected and received returns - Value added tax	
	Table A.60 Return filing: Returns received on time - Value added tax	
	Table A.61 Return receipt channels: Paper and electronic, not prefilled - Value added tax	
	Table A.62 Return receipt channels: Electronic returns, prefilled - Value added tax	
Payments and VAT refunds	Table A.63 Payments due and received: Corporate income tax	https://data.rafit.org/regular.aspx?key=74180910
	Table A.64 Payments received on time: Corporate income tax	
	Table A.65 Payments due and received: Personal income tax	
	Table A.66 Payments received on time: Personal income tax	
	Table A.67 Payments due and received: Employers that withhold tax from employees	
	Table A.68 Payments received on time: Employers that withhold tax from employees	
	Table A.69 Payments due and received: Value added tax	
	Table A.70 Payments received on time: Value added tax	
	Table A.71 Electronic payments	
	Table A.72 Treatment of most approved VAT refunds	
	Table A.73 Value of all VAT 'credits'	
Arrears	Table A.74 Closing stock of arrears: Total and non-collectable	https://data.rafit.org/regular.aspx?key=74180911
	Table A.75 Closing stock of arrears relating to state owned enterprises: Total and non-collectable	
	Table A.76 Closing stock of arrears by tax type: Corporate income tax	
	Table A.77 Closing stock of arrears by tax type: Personal income tax	
	Table A.78 Closing stock of arrears by tax type: Tax withheld by employers from employees	
	Table A.79 Closing stock of arrears by tax type: Value added tax	
Audit	Table A.80 Verification / audit activity: All audits (excluding electronic compliance checks)	https://data.rafit.org/regular.aspx?key=74180894
	Table A.81 Verification / audit activity: Value of additional assessments raised - All audits (excluding electronic compliance checks)	
	Table A.82 Verification / audit activity: Value of additional assessments raised - Corporate income tax	

Table grouping	Table name	Link
	Table A.83 Verification / audit activity: Value of additional assessments raised - Personal income tax	
	Table A.84 Verification / audit activity: Value of additional assessments raised - Tax withheld by employers from employees	
	Table A.85 Verification / audit activity: Value of additional assessments raised - Value added tax	
	Table A.86 Verification / audit activity: Electronic compliance checks	
Criminal investigation and dispute resolution	Table A.87 Tax crime investigations: Role of the administration	https://data.rafit.org/regular.aspx?key=74180895
	Table A.88 Tax crime investigations: Number of cases	
	Table A.89 Dispute resolution: Review mechanisms	
	Table A.90 Dispute resolution: Review procedure	
	Table A.91 Dispute resolution: Number of cases - Tax cases under internal procedures	
	Table A.92 Dispute resolution: Number of cases - Tax cases under independent review by external bodies	
	Table A.93 Dispute resolution: Number of cases - Tax cases under independent review by a higher appellate court	
Stakeholder interactions: Registration channels, contacts and pre-filling	Table A.94 Registration channels: Online, Telephone, Email	https://data.rafit.org/regular.aspx?key=74180896
	Table A.95 Registration channels: Mail / post, In-person, other	
	Table A.96 Incoming service contacts: Track keeping and number of contacts by channel - Online and digital assistance	
	Table A.97 Incoming service contacts: Number of contacts by channel - Telephone call and e-mail	
	Table A.98 Incoming service contacts: Number of contacts by channel - Mail / post and in-person	
	Table A.99 Pre-fill of PIT returns: Income information - Personal information, and wage and salary	
	Table A.100 Pre-fill of PIT returns: Income information - Pension, interest, and dividends	
	Table A.101 Pre-fill of PIT returns: Income information - Capital gains / losses, and other income	
	Table A.102 Pre-fill of PIT returns: Expense information - Donations, school and university fees, and childcare expenses	
	Table A.103 Pre-fill of PIT returns: Expense information - Insurance premiums, health and medical expenses, and retirement contributions	
	Table A.104 Pre-fill of PIT returns: Expense information - Interest, and other expenses	
Stakeholder interactions: Compliance and innovation	Table A.105 Compliance approaches: Electronic invoicing	https://data.rafit.org/regular.aspx?key=74180897
	Table A.106 Compliance approaches: Devices that register transactions	
	Table A.107 Cooperative compliance approaches	
	Table A.108 Innovative technologies: Implementation and usage - Blockchain, artificial intelligence, and cloud computing	
	Table A.109 Innovative technologies: Implementation and usage - Data science, robotic process automation, and APIs	
	Table A.110 Innovative technologies: Implementation and usage - Whole-of-government identification, digital authentication technology, and virtual assistants	
Derived indicators: Revenue and Resources	Table E.1 External variables for derived indicators: Gross domestic product and total government revenue	https://data.rafit.org/regular.aspx?key=74180898
	Table E.2 External variables for derived indicators: Total population and labour force	
	Table D.1 Revenue related ratios: Revenue to total government revenue and GDP	
	Table D.2 Revenue related ratios: Tax to GDP and non-tax revenue to total revenue	
	Table D.3 Tax structure and SSC proportions: PIT, CIT and VAT	

Table grouping	Table name	Link
	Table D.4 Tax structure and SSC proportions: Excises, Other taxes and SSC	
	Table D.5 Resource ratios: Full-time equivalent (FTE)	
	Table D.6 Resource ratios: Cost	
Derived indicators: Staff	Table D.7 Staff allocation by location and function: Registration, services, processing, and audit and verification	https://data.rafit.org/regular.aspx?key=74180899
	Table D.8 Staff allocation by function: Debt collection, dispute management, and HR management	
	Table D.9 Staff allocation by function: ICT support and all other functions	
	Table D.10 Staff dynamics	
	Table D.11 Academic qualifications	
	Table D.12 Staff age distribution: Staff below 45 years	
	Table D.13 Staff age distribution: Staff 45 years and above	
	Table D.14 Length of service: Less than 10 years	
	Table D.15 Length of service: 10 years or more	
	Table D.16 Gender distribution	
Derived indicators: Segmentation, registration and filing	Table D.17 Large taxpayer office / program ratios: Full-time equivalents (FTEs)	https://data.rafit.org/regular.aspx?key=74180900
	Table D.18 Large taxpayer office / program ratios: Corporate taxpayers, additional assessments raised, and net revenue administered	
	Table D.19 Registration of personal income taxpayers	
	Table D.20 Percentage inactive taxpayers on registers: CIT, PIT and PAYE	
	Table D.21 Percentage inactive taxpayers on registers: VAT and Excise	
	Table D.22 Rate of returns received on-time: CIT	
	Table D.23 Rate of returns received on-time: PIT	
	Table D.24 Rate of returns received on-time: PAYE	
	Table D.25 Rate of returns received on-time: VAT	
Derived indicators: Filing channels	Table D.26 Electronic filing: CIT and PIT	https://data.rafit.org/regular.aspx?key=74180901
	Table D.27 Electronic filing: PAYE and VAT	
	Table D.28 Proportion of returns by channel: CIT - Paper and electronic, not prefilled	
	Table D.29 Proportion of returns by channel: CIT - Electronic, prefilled	
	Table D.30 Proportion of returns by channel: PIT - Paper and electronic, not prefilled	
	Table D.31 Proportion of returns by channel: PIT - Electronic, prefilled	
	Table D.32 Proportion of returns by channel: PAYE - Paper and electronic, not prefilled	
	Table D.33 Proportion of returns by channel: PAYE - Electronic, prefilled	
	Table D.34 Proportion of returns by channel: VAT - Paper and electronic, not prefilled	
	Table D.35 Proportion of returns by channel: VAT - Electronic, prefilled	
Derived indicators: Payment and arrears	Table D.36 Rate of payments received on-time: CIT	https://data.rafit.org/regular.aspx?key=74180902
	Table D.37 Rate of payments received on-time: PIT	
	Table D.38 Rate of payments received on-time: PAYE	
	Table D.39 Rate of payments received on-time: VAT	
	Table D.40 Electronic payment proportions and third party withholding	
	Table D.41 Arrears ratios: Closing stock and collectable arrears	
	Table D.42 Arrears ratios: Year-on-year change	
	Table D.43 Arrears ratios relating to state owned enterprises: Closing stock and collectable arrears	
	Table D.44 Arrears in relation to collection by tax type: CIT and PIT	

Table grouping	Table name	Link
	Table D.45 Arrears in relation to collection by tax type: PAYE and VAT	
Derived indicators: Audit and disputes	Table D.46 Audit ratios: Hit rate and additional assessments raised	https://data.rafit.org/regular.aspx?key=74180903
	Table D.47 Audit ratios: Additional assessments raised by tax type - CIT and PIT	
	Table D.48 Audit ratios: Additional assessments raised by tax type - PAYE and VAT	
	Table D.49 Administrative review cases and litigation	

Source: CIAT, IOTA, IMF, OECD, International Survey on Revenue Administration, https://data.rafit.org/?sk=e1ed4b20-815e-4e76-bc6d-9032fc89f4f4&sId=1716492452268 (accessed on 10 September 2024).

Table A A.2. Overview of the ISORA data tables: Periodic tables

Table grouping	Table name	Link
Institutional arrangements, governance and management practices	Table B.1 Institutional framework and management autonomy	https://data.rafit.org/regular.aspx?key=74180913
	Table B.2 Roles in addition to revenue collection	
	Table B.3 Selected governance practices: Audit, code of conduct and integrity	
	Table B.4 Selected governance practices: Plans, reports and standards; and organizational chart	
	Table B.5 Structural reforms: Implementation and nature	
	Table B.6 Structural reforms: Main drivers	
Human resource management	Table B.7 Human resource authority	https://data.rafit.org/regular.aspx?key=74180914
	Table B.8 Remuneration and performance management	
	Table B.9 HR management approach: Staff surveys	
	Table B.10 HR management approach: Strategy / multi-year work force plan and training strategy	
	Table B.11 HR management approach: Support for new staff and staffing plan	
	Table B.12 HR management approach: staffing plan and flexible working arrangements	
	Table B.13 HR management approach: Leadership development, time reporting, diversity policy	
	Table B.14 Capability needs assessment	
	Table B.15 Specialist skills	
Segmentation	Table B.16 Large taxpayer office / program: Main criteria	https://data.rafit.org/regular.aspx?key=74180915
	Table B.17 High net wealth individuals (HNWIs) office / program: Main criteria	
	Table B.18 High net wealth individuals (HNWIs) office / program: Functions, staff and taxpayers	
	Table B.19 Small taxpayers	
Compliance risk management	Table B.20 Compliance risk management: Strategy	https://data.rafit.org/regular.aspx?key=74180916
	Table B.21 Compliance risk management: Gender-disaggregated data	
	Table B.22 Compliance risk management: Characterization of challenges related to international tax issues	
	Table B.23 Compliance risk management: Staff related to international tax issues	
	Table B.24 Compliance risk management: Tax gap	
	Table B.25 Compliance risk management: Compliance intervention framework	
	Table B.26 Compliance risk management: Interventions before return filing	
	Table B.27 Compliance risk management: Interventions after return filing, and measurement of intervention effectiveness	

Table grouping	Table name	Link
	Table B.28 Compliance risk management: Post-filing enforcement actions	
	Table B.29 Compliance risk management: Enforcement effectiveness indicators	
Tax operations: Registration, filing, payment, arrears	Table B.30 Taxpayer gender recorded; and mandatory electronic filing and payment	https://data.rafit.org/regular.aspx?key=74180917
	Table B.49 Withholding at source	
	Table B.50 Reporting of payment details	
	Table B.31 Tax arrears collection powers and their usage - Part 1	
	Table B.32 Tax arrears collection powers and their usage - Part 2	
	Table B.33 Tax arrears collection powers and their usage - Part 3	
	Table B.34 Tax arrears collection powers and their usage - Part 4	
Tax operations: Audit, verification, third-party data	Table B.35 Voluntary disclosures; and verification / audit activity: Automated compliance checks	https://data.rafit.org/regular.aspx?key=74180918
	Table B.36 Verification / audit activity: Random audits	
	Table B.37 Verification / audit activity: Selection processes / criteria	
	Table B.38 Administrative sanctions for taxpayer non-disclosure: Application and selected features	
	Table B.51 Third-party data	
Taxpayer service	Table B.39 Service channels: Statistics about service channel usage	https://data.rafit.org/regular.aspx?key=74180919
	Table B.40 Service channels: Features of the service approach	
	Table B.41 Service channels: Online services - Part 1	
	Table B.42 Service channels: Online services - Part 2	
	Table B.43 Taxpayer rights: Documentation	
	Table B.44 Taxpayer rights: Complaints mechanisms	
	Table B.45 Satisfaction surveys	
	Table B.46 Gender-based analysis of taxpayer satisfaction, and service and assistance strategy	
	Table B.47 Taxpayer education	
	Table B.48 Rulings on the application of tax laws	
	Table B.52 Taxpayer compliance burden	

Source: CIAT, IOTA, IMF, OECD, International Survey on Revenue Administration, https://data.rafit.org/?sk=e1ed4b20-815e-4e76-bc6d-9032fc89f4f4&sid=1716492468609 (accessed on 10 September 2024).

Annex B. Participating tax administrations

Table A B.1. Overview of tax administrations included in this report

Jurisdiction	Tax administration	Website address	Currency code
Argentina	Federal Administration of Public Revenues	www.afip.gob.ar	ARS
Australia	Australian Taxation Office	www.ato.gov.au	AUD
Austria	Federal Ministry of Finance	www.bmf.gv.at	EUR
Belgium	Federal Public Service Finance	https://finances.belgium.be	EUR
Brazil	Federal Revenue Service of Brazil	www.rfb.gov.br	BRL
Bulgaria	National Revenue Agency	https://nap.bg/	BGN
Canada	Canada Revenue Agency	www.cra-arc.gc.ca	CAD
Chile	Servicio de Impuestos Internos	www.sii.cl	CLP
China (People's Republic of)	State Taxation Administration	www.chinatax.gov.cn	CNY
Colombia	National Tax and Customs Administration	www.dian.gov.co	COP
Costa Rica	Directorate of Taxation, Ministry of Finance	www.hacienda.go.cr	CRC
Croatia	Tax Administration, Ministry of Finance	www.porezna-uprava.hr	HRK
Cyprus	Cyprus Tax Department	www.mof.gov.cy/tax	EUR
Czechia	Financial Administration of the Czech Republic	www.financnisprava.cz	CZK
Denmark	Danish Tax Administration	www.skatteforvaltningen.dk	DKK
Estonia	Estonian Tax and Customs Board	www.emta.ee	EUR
Finland	Finnish Tax Administration	www.vero.fi	EUR
France	Direction Générale des Finances Publiques (General Directorate of Public Finances)	www.impots.gouv.fr	EUR
Georgia	Georgia Revenue Service	www.rs.ge	GEL
Germany	Federal Ministry of Finance, Federal Central Tax Office, and the State Tax Authorities	www.bundesfinanzministerium.de	EUR
Greece	Independent Authority for Public Revenue	www.aade.gr	EUR
Hong Kong (China)	Inland Revenue Department	www.ird.gov.hk	HKD
Hungary	National Tax and Customs Administration	https://nav.gov.hu	HUF
Iceland	Iceland Revenue and Customs	www.skatturinn.is	ISK
India	Income Tax Department Central Board of Indirect Taxes & Customs	www.incometaxindia.gov.in www.cbic.gov.in	INR
Indonesia	Directorate General of Taxes	www.pajak.go.id	IDR
Ireland	Office of the Revenue Commissioners	www.revenue.ie	EUR

Jurisdiction	Tax administration	Website address	Currency code
Israel	Israel Tax Authority	www.taxes.gov.il	ILS
Italy	Revenue Agency	www.agenziaentrate.gov.it	EUR
Japan	National Tax Agency	www.nta.go.jp	JPY
Kenya	Kenya Revenue Authority	www.kra.go.ke	KES
Korea	National Tax Service	www.nts.go.kr	KRW
Latvia	State Revenue Service	www.vid.gov.lv	EUR
Lithuania	State Tax Inspectorate under the Ministry of Finance	www.vmi.lt	EUR
Luxembourg	Administration des contributions directes (Direct Tax Administration) Administration de l'enregistrement, des domaines et de la TVA (Indirect Tax Administration)	www.impotsdirects.public.lu https://aed.gouvernement.lu/	EUR
Malaysia	Inland Revenue Board of Malaysia	www.hasil.gov.my	MYR
Malta	Office of the Commissioner for Revenue	https://cfr.gov.mt	EUR
Mexico	Tax Administration Service	www.sat.gob.mx	MXN
Morocco	General Administration of Taxes	www.tax.gov.ma	MAD
Netherlands	Netherlands Tax Administration	www.belastingdienst.nl	EUR
New Zealand	Inland Revenue Department – Te Tari Taake	www.ird.govt.nz	NZD
Norway	Norwegian Tax Administration	www.skatteetaten.no	NOK
Peru	Superintendencia Nacional de Administración Tributaria (SUNAT)	www.sunat.gob.pe	PEN
Poland	National Revenue Administration	www.podatki.gov.pl	PLN
Portugal	Portuguese Tax and Customs Authority	www.portaldasfinancas.gov.pt	EUR
Romania	National Agency for Fiscal Administration	www.anaf.ro	RON
Saudi Arabia	Zakat, Tax and Customs Authority	https://zatca.gov.sa	SAR
Singapore	Inland Revenue Authority of Singapore	www.iras.gov.sg	SGD
Slovak Republic	Financial Administration of the Slovak Republic	www.financnasprava.sk	EUR
Slovenia	Financial Administration of the Republic of Slovenia	www.fu.gov.si	EUR
South Africa	South African Revenue Service	www.sars.gov.za	ZAR
Spain	Spanish Tax Agency (AEAT)	https://sede.agenciatributaria.gob.es/	EUR
Sweden	Swedish Tax Agency	www.skatteverket.se	SEK
Switzerland	Federal Tax Administration	www.estv.admin.ch	CHF
Thailand	The Revenue Department	www.rd.go.th	THB
Türkiye	Turkish Revenue Administration	www.gib.gov.tr	TRY
United Kingdom	HM Revenue & Customs	www.hmrc.gov.uk	GBP
United States	Internal Revenue Service	www.irs.gov	USD

www.ingramcontent.com/pod-product-compliance
Lightning Source LLC
Chambersburg PA
CBHW061209240926
51846CB00006B/1156
* 9 7 8 9 2 6 4 9 0 0 8 8 2 *